Italy: Politics and Policy

Italy: Politics and Policy

edited by

**Robert Leonardi and
Raffaella Y. Nanetti**

Dartmouth

Aldershot • Brookfield USA • Singapore • Sydney

Published by
Dartmouth Publishing Company Limited
Gower House
Croft Road
Aldershot
Hants GU11 3HR
England

Dartmouth Publishing Company
Old Post Road
Brookfield
Vermont 05036
USA

British Library Cataloguing in Publication Data
Italy : politics and policy.
   1.Italy - Politics and government - 1976-
   I.Leonardi, Robert II.Nanetti, Raffaella Y., 1943-
   945'.0929

ISBN 1 85521 764 3

Printed and bound in Great Britain by Ipswich Book Co. Ltd., Ipswich, Suffolk

contents

list of contributors

Giuliano Amato an ex-Prime Minister of Italy and currently the President of the Anti-trust Commission, is professor of Constitutional Law at the University of Rome 'La Sapienza'. Amongst his publications are *Europa Conviene?* with M L Salvadori (Bari-Rome, 1988), *Due Anni Al Tesoro,* (Bologna, 1990) and *Forme di Stato e Forme di Governo,* (Bologna, 1991).

Vittorio Bufacchi is lecturer in Political Theory in the Department of Government at the University of Manchester. He has co-edited with Richard Bellamy and Dario Castiglione *Democracy and Culture in the Union of Europe* (Lothian, London, 1995) and is now writing a book with Simon Burgess on *Italian Politics Since 1989* for Macmillan.

Mark Donovan is Lecturer in European Politics, School of European Studies, Cardiff University of Wales. His main area of research is west European party systems and especially party politics in Italy. His most recent and forthcoming publications include: *Parties, Elections and the Transformation of Italian Politics* (Hurst 1996) with Phil Daniels and 'The Politics of Electoral Reform in Italy' in *International Political Science Review,* January 1995.

Marcello Fedele is professor of Sociology of Administration at the University of Rome 'La Sapienza' and Visiting Scholar at the European Institute, London School of Economics and Political Science. Amongst his publications are *Classi e partiti negli anni '70,* (Rome, 1979), *La deriva del potere. Saggio sul sistema politco americano,* (Bari 1982), *Le forme politiche del regionalismo* (Milano, 1988) and *Democrazia Referendaria. L'Italia dal primato dei partiti al trionfo dell'opinione pubblica* (Rome, 1994).

Laurence Gray is professor of political science at John Cabot University and Director of International Studies. He is also senior lecturer at Saint. Mary's College Rome Program. His research interests comprise East Asian and West European politics and is currently undertaking a study of the centre-right and centre-left coalition blocs in Italy. His most recent publications include *The Consolidation of Democracy in the Philippines* (University of Louvain, 1994)

William Howard is a recent graduate of John Cabot University and is currently pursuing graduate work in International Relations at Syracuse University. His research is on voter alignment and new party affiliations in Italy.

Robert Leonardi is Director of the Economic and Social Cohesion Laboratory of the European Institute, London School of Economics. He has worked extensively on the Italian political parties and institutions and regional development. His most recent publication is *Convergence, Cohesion and Integration in the European Union* (Macmillan, London, 1995).

Raffaella Y Nanetti is Director of the Urban Planning Program at the University of Illinois at Chicago. Most recently, she has worked on the evaluation of regional development in Objective 1 regions in Italy and the other Mediterranean countries. Her most recent publication is *Regional Development in a Modern European Economy. The Case of Tuscany,* edited with R Leonardi (Pinter, London, 1994).

Loretta Napoleoni is a PhD candidate at the London School of Economics and Political Science working on the impact of the terrorist emergency upon the judiciary. Her publications include 'Impatto del Big Bang Sulla Struttura Del Mercato Finanziario Internazionale', *Queste Istituzioni,* n.IV, 1988; 'The Monetary Policy of the National Bank of Hungary Towards the Full Convertibility of the Florint', National Bank of Hungary, Spring, 1983 and 'Fisiologia dello Riconversione Industriale', in Valerio Selan (ed), *La Riconversione Industriale in Italia* (Università degli Studi di Roma, Rome, 1979).

Martin Rhodes is Lecturer in Government at the University of Manchester and Jean Monnet Fellow at the European University Institute in Florence. Currently, his main field of research is in comparative European industrial relations, labour markets and social policy. His most recent publications include 'Regional Development and Employment in Europe's Southern and Western Peripheries', in M Rhodes (ed.), *The Regions and the New Europe,* (Manchester University Press, Manchester, 1995) and '"Subversive Liberalism": Market Integration, Globalisation and the European Welfare State', *Journal of European Public Policy,* Vol. 2, no. 2, 1995.

Marco Tarchi is a researcher in Political Science at the Faculty of Political Science at the University of Florence. Amongst his recent publications are *La 'rivoluzione legale'. Identità collettive e crollo della democrazia in Italia e Germania,* (Bologna, 1993), *Cinquant'anni di nostalgia. La destra italiana dopo il fascismo,* (Milan, 1995), and *Esuli in Patria. I fascisti nell'Italia repubblicana* (Milan, 1995).

Giuliano Urbani a parliamentarian and ex-Minister of Reform of the Public Administration, is professor of Political Science at the University Bocconi of Milan. His publications include *La teroria del sistema politico: prospettive,* (Bologna, 1989), *Dentro la politica,* (Milan, 1992) and *L'Italia del buongoverno* (Milan, 1994) with E Carnazza.

Carolyn M. Warner is Assistant Professor of Political Science at Arizona State University. She is currently preparing a manuscript on the role of political party strategies and institutions on the construction of the French and Italian Christian Democratic Parties, 1944-1958 and is also working on a monograph on how party leaders control the electoral and political costs of their policies. Professor Warner has co-authored 'Structure and Irony in History', *Political Theory,* Vol. 20, no. 1, 1992, with Professor David D Laitin.

preface

With the publication of Italy: Politics and Policy, Volume 1, the Economic and Social Cohesion Laboratory - a research unit specializing in European economic and social affairs - operating with the European Institute of the London School of Economics has initiated, in collaboration with the Polity research group led by Marcello Fedele of "La Sapienza" University in Rome, this series on Italy as part of a wider range of publications dealing with economic and political developments in the European Union. The focus of the series is not only on political and economic developments in Italy taken from an internal perspective. What is important for the initiators of the series is the course of current events in Italy - i.e., the political as well as economic decisions - in light of the country's external relations and increasing integration into the European Union and preparations for European Monetary Union. The reasons for this focus are evident in the role the Maastricht criteria for EMU have played in determining the structure of the national budget. The financial bills covering the period from 1993 to 1996 have had a significant impact on the nature of economic and social policy. The attempt to reduce the budget deficit has required cuts in the funding of the health system, pensions, social policies, administrative reform, regional development, and privatization. It is possible to argue that when the exigencies of European integration came into conflict with the policies perpetuating the political fortunes of the governing parties of the First Republic (corruption, unbridled government spending, and the use of public resources for private ends), the latter had to give way. Thus, the Italian case is not only of interest to those concerned with political events and policy trends in one country; instead, it is of interest to a wider audience attempting to understand how individual nation-states are preparing their internal political and economic systems for further steps in European integration. In other words, Italy represents a case study of how countries are changing their internal policies to meet the needs of operating as influential actors in decision-making taking place in European-level institutions. Without such changes, countries run the risk of being relegated to the economic and political periphery of Europe, no longer capable of influencing in a positive manner the course of European events. This is particularly important to Italy given its role as a founding member of the ECSC in 1951 and the EEC in 1958. European integration has operated as the lodestar in Italian affairs for over 40 years, and no government can afford from, an economic and political perspective, to disengage from the process. Therefore, the course of Italian events from 1994 onwards is of great interest, not only in tracing how Italian politics have adapted to the collapse of the First Republic, but they are also indicative of changes that are taking place in other political systems in southern Europe, which share with Italy a number of socioeconomic and political characteristics. The future of Italian affairs is probably full of unexpected twists and turns of political events, as was the case in 1994 which is the focus of this volume. For the same reasons, we are committed to following the course of future events and trying to explain them to the wider audience of students of Italian politics, but also to engage those operating in the Italian economy and political system in a constructive dialogue. The series also aims to present an insider's view of the political system by commissioning individual pieces from the direct protagonists in Italian political and economic affairs. In this manner, the series will provide a view of Italian politics and policy from outside "observers" as well as inside "practitioners". We believe that, in this way, two traditional pitfalls of Italian politics can be avoided. On the one hand, the link between practitioners and observers can help to avoid the, at times, "carefree" use of political concepts and practices that are prevalent elsewhere, in the internal debate on institutional and political reform. On the other, the series will try to stimulate the outside observer to come into closer contact with practitioners in order to hone their ability to analyze the personalities operating in the system and the events that have changed the course of Italian politics. We hope that with this volume we are able to kick-off a detailed analysis of the changes necessary in the Italian system in preparation for EMU and the future course of European integration. In the past, these changes have transformed Italy from a semi-peripheral country in the immediate post-war period to the West's fifth industrial power. It would not be surprising to the authors if the future course of Italian affairs were to change the nature of the Italian political system from one of an imperfect democracy to a system where the alternation between progressive and conservative coalitions becomes an accepted part of electoral outcomes and government policies. What is at stake here, is not only how well Italy is governed, but whether Italy is able to take its rightful place in the community of European democratic regimes.

Robert Leonardi and Raffaella Y. Nanetti

chronology

Important political events in Italy - 1994

Anna Maresso

January

1. The Christian Democrat referendum leader, Mario Segni, strongly criticises the Ciampi government's economic measures as ineffectual in achieving the stipulated goal of economic recovery.

Widespread consumer and pharmaceutical industry confusion ensues as new regulations on the classification, pricing and distribution of pharmaceuticals come into effect.

2. Fininvest magnate Silvio Berlusconi proposes a policy of less taxes as a platform to unite centrist-minded parties.

3. Mario Segni formally announces the name and symbol of his new political movement, Patto per l'Italia.

4. In the Cusani investigation, Ferruzzi manager, Marcello Portesi, claims that in 1992 the Lega's then treasurer solicited and received 200 million lire from the company.

5. Called before the Cusani investigation, Umberto Bossi denies all knowledge of the payment by Ferruzzi. He is backed up by Alessandro Pattelli, the Lega ex-official at the centre of the accusations.

6. Under interrogation for the SISDE payments affair, the ex-director of the Italian secret service alleges that the Interior Ministry received regular monthly payments. Implicated in the accusations are Interior Minister Mancino, President Scalfaro, ex-Prime Minister Amato and the Chief of Police, Parisi, all of whom are said to have been involved in a cover-up.

Emilio Fede, director of Fininvest-owned TG4 creates a storm by demanding the resignation of Indro Montanelli, editor of *Il Giornale,* which is also owned by Fininvest, for the newspaper's alleged anti-Berlusconi bias.

8. The Interior Minister rejects the resignation of Police Chief Parisi, who offers to relinquish his post after he is informed that he is to be formally investigated in connection with the SISDE affair.

9. Bossi announces that the Lega has shelved its plans for federalism in favour of promoting greater regionalism as part of a larger strategy of forging centre-right alliances.

Montanelli resigns from *Il Giornale,* citing irreconcilable differences with Berlusconi and announces plans to found his own newspaper, *La Voce.*

10. Pope John Paul II sends a letter to all Italian bishops exhorting them to promote the 'political unity of Catholics'.

12. Prime Minister Ciampi opens the debate on the no-confidence motion introduced by Radical Party leader Marco Pannella.

The constitutional court gives the go-ahead for three referendums concerning union representation.

13. The no-confidence motion before the chamber is changed to a vote of confidence in the government, but citing deep divisions within parliament, the prime minister tenders his resignation, opening the way for President Scalfaro to dissolve parliament and announce a date for national elections.

14. The Jewish community strongly objects to the proposed date of March 27 for the national elections as this is the day of Passover.

16. President Scalfaro dissolves parliament but rejects Ciampi's resignation, thus enlisting him as the head of a caretaker government with full powers.

With the formal declaration of 27 March as election day, Marco Pannella begins a hunger strike on behalf of the Jewish community.

17. The Lega's Roberto Maroni confirms that there will be no electoral alliance with the Christian Democrats and that he has discussed candidacy lists with Silvio Berlusconi.

To resolve the clash of election day with the Jewish Passover, the government issues a decree to extend voting over two days.

18. The old Christian Democrat party is split as Mino Martinazzoli launches the Partito Popolare Italiano (Italian Popular Party), whilst the 'neo-centrists' form the Centro Cristiano Democratico (Christian Democratic Centre) under Pier Ferdinando Casini, Clemente Mastella and Francesco D'Onofrio.

19. TGl reveals that a 'mole' (spy) in the Quirinale has uncovered threats made to President Scalfaro and his daughter.

Achille Occhetto invites the newly-formed Popular Party to align itself with the Progressives.

21. The Minister of the Interior tenders his resignation after learning that he will be investigated over the SISDE affair, but caretaker Prime Minister Ciampi rejects his offer and reaffirms the government's support.

Popular Party leader, Mino Martinazolli rejects the Lega as a possible alliance partner, thus placing the liberal-democratic alliance proposed by Mario Segni in jeopardy.

22. Rifondazione Comunista elects Fausto Bertinotti as general secretary and votes to enter an alliance with the PDS.

'Alleanza Nazionale' is adopted as the electoral banner under which the neo-fascist Movimento Sociale Italiano (MSI) will present its candidates.

Giorgio La Malfa is re-elected general secretary of the Italian Republican Party (PRI).

23. Silvio Berlusconi declares that he will personally enter the electoral arena should the existing centrist forces find themselves incapable of formalising an alliance.

24. Umberto Bossi and Mario Segni reach an accord, agreeing on the principle of directly electing the prime minister and reaffirming that Italy is indivisible.

25. Martinazzoli declares that the Popular Party will never enter an alliance with the Lega, prompting the Lega to warn Segni that their co-operation will end if he harbours any alliance with Martinazzoli.

26. Berlusconi declares himself an electoral candidate and abandons all his duties at Fininvest to lead the Polo della Libertà (Liberty Pole).

Two days after signing his accord with the Lega, Mario Segni retracts his signature and chooses to side with the Popular Party.

27. A political storm erupts over parties soliciting many of the 'clean hands' magistrates to join their election candidate lists. Magistrate Tiziana Parenti causes controversy by joining the Berlusconi camp whilst Antonio di Pietro refuses offers from Mario Segni and Leoluca Orlando.

Alarming figures show that unemployment has reached 19 per cent in the South, more than twice as high as in the North.

28. At the MSI party congress, Gianfranco Fini declares his preparedness to open up to Berlusconi and parties of the centre.

The Alleanza Democratica network is formed.

29. Following statements by several mafia *pentiti*, 12 magistrates in Messina are put under investigation for corruption, extortion and abuse of official office.

30. With only a slim majority, the Republican Party decides to align with the Popular Party and Mario Segni's Pact for Italy, whilst its leader, La Malfa, decides not to stand as an electoral candidate.

31. Umberto Bossi tells Berlusconi that he will not deal with fascists and vetoes any idea of an electoral pact with Alleanza Nazionale/MSI.

February

1. The Progressive alliance is formed with eight left-of-centre parties.

2. In the Cusani 'clean hands' investigation, allegations are made that PDS leader Achille Occhetto received one billion lire for helping to reduce the tax liability of Enimont.

3. Strong divisions over policies and candidate lists within the Progressive Alliance partners results in the Greens, Alleanza Democratica and the Cristiano Sociali leaving the group.

4. The Lega's congress opens in Bologna with the party confirming its intention to enter an accord with Silvio Berlusconi and to reject Alleanza Nazionale/MSI and the Popular Party.

5. At its assembly, Segni's Pact for Italy rejects the parties of the left, the Lega and the Berlusconi camp as possible alliance partners.

The Greens decide at their convention to rejoin the Progressive Alliance.

6. Forza Italia opens its convention in Rome, launching a 'liberal-democratic war against the left' and declaring its receptiveness to Alleanza Nazionale/MSI, but not to Mario Segni, or the Popular Party.

7. The state broadcaster, RAI, decides to immediately implement new rules governing equal television air-time for party election campaigns.

9. The public prosecutor's office in Rome opens an inquiry into the Banco di

Napoli and requests that ex-socialist vice-secretary Di Donato be arrested.

The executive of the Republican Party agrees to back Mario Segni as a candidate for prime minister.

10. Umberto Bossi and Silvio Berlusconi conclude an electoral pact, agreeing on common candidate lists for the senate as a first step.

Alleanza Democratica returns to the Progressive alliance.

11. Silvio Berlusconi's brother, Paolo, is arrested and admits to having paid a 'commission' for the sale of three buildings to Cariplo.

13. Chief of the 'clean hands' pool of magistrates, Francesco Saverio Borrelli, confirms that investigations will continue during the election period.

Two Italian volunteers are kidnapped by bandits in Somalia.

14. Silvio Berlusconi becomes a candidate for the constituency of Rome.

15. The PDS presents its party programme for the 1994 elections.

A PDS member, Morandina, confesses that he received 200 million lire from Fiat as a 'consultation fee'.

16. Massimo D'Alema of the PDS is questioned after Socialist ex-prime minister Bettino Craxi accuses the party of having received kick-backs.

17. Interest rates fall by half a percentage point.

18. Poggiolini reveals that, during a ten-year period, the pharmaceutical industry paid 15 thousand billion lire in kick-backs to the health ministry.

19. Bettino Craxi announces that he will not stand as a candidate in the elections.

21. On the final day for submitting candidate lists, statistics show a rise in the proportion of women standing in the elections.

22. Berlusconi proposes that magistrate Antonio Di Pietro would make a suitable justice minister in a government formed by Forza Italia.

23. After a fiery debate, the chamber of deputies votes 249 to 175 not to authorize the arrest of socialist Di Donato, thus granting him a *de facto* amnesty in connection with the Banco di Napoli investigation.

24. PDS leader, Achille Occhetto visits the City of London to reassure the financial community of the left's sound policy platforms.

Silvio Berlusconi declares that a government led by him would create one million jobs in its first year.

25. The government reissues the so-called *salva Rai* decree, with the *cassa depositi e prestiti* earmarking 330 billion lire for bailing-out the financially troubled state broadcaster.

26. Italy and the other G7 partners conclude their summit in Frankfurt by declaring an end to the world recession and pinpointing unemployment as the primary economic obstacle to tackle.

27. The Freedom Alliance is beset by polemics as Umberto Bossi attacks Berlusconi and warns him not to betray the North.

28. Achille Occhetto reaffirms the PDS's commitment to remain within NATO, despite the contrary position of its alliance partner, Rifondazione Comunista.

March

1. President Scalfaro creates a controversy by proposing that public and private schools be given equal financial treatment.

"Black Tuesday" for the Italian lira as it falls drastically against the deutschmark, precipitating heavy selling of government bonds.

2. The European Union cuts Italy's milk production quota by 350 tonnes.

3. Silvio Berlusconi precipitates a debate on taxation by proposing a single rate of 30 per cent.

4. The United Nations Security Council announces its desire to include Italian soldiers in the contingents sent to Bosnia, despite the opposition of General Secretary Boutros-Ghali.

5. Umberto Bossi brands Forza Italia as a reincarnation of the old Christian Democratic Party and instructs local branches of the Lega not to aid Silvio Berlusconi.

6. Berlusconi attempts to minimize Forza Italia's tensions with the Lega by publicly stating that the two parties will overcome their differences.

7. Ten arrests for corruption are made in Naples, including two judges accused of working for the camorra.

8. At the Cusani kick-backs trial, the court rejects a request by magistrate Di

Pietro and Cusani's lawyer Spazzali to question Achille Occhetto and Massimo D'Alema, arguing that their testimonies are irrelevant.

9. Magistrates request the arrest of six Fininvest executives, prompting Berlusconi to claim that the finance police are making a political attack.

10. Mario Segni supporters protest outside Palazzo Chigi complaining that RAI has completely marginalised them during the election campaign.

11. Silvio Berlusconi declares war on 'clean hands' pool chief Borrelli and submits a legal petition to President Scalfaro against the Milan magistrates investigating Publitalia, the Berlusconi advertising agency which is spearheading his electoral campaign.

13. The Lega's polemics against its alliance partner Forza Italia continue with Bossi declaring that he will not accept Berlusconi as prime minister.

Italy attends the G7 summit on unemployment in Detroit.

14. Three journalists named by magistrates for allegedly receiving money from the Ferruzzi company are investigated.

16. Polls conducted by Forza Italia show that they have an electoral lead over the other parties.

17. A truce is declared between Berlusconi and Borrelli with the withdrawal of the latter's petition against the director and other managers of Publitalia.

Gianfranco Fini gives Alleanza Nazionale/MSI backing for Berlusconi to become prime minister.

18. Interior Minister Mancino accuses Berlusconi of having the electoral backing of the mafia.

19. Near Caserta, an anti-camorra parish priest, Don Diana, is assassinated after testifying against local politicians and criminal bosses.

20. Two RAI journalists are killed in Somalia as Italian troops prepare to leave Mogadishu.

21. A shortfall of 16 thousand billion lire is discovered in the public accounts.

23. PDS general secretary Achille Occhetto and Forza Italia leader Silvio Berlusconi participate in a televised electoral debate.

PDS MP Luciano Violante resigns as head of the parliamentary committee on the mafia after making controversial comments regarding Publitalia, Silvio

Berlusconi's advertising agency.

24. The magistrate of Palmi (Calabria), Grazia Omboni, orders a controversial raid on the offices of Forza Italia to seize lists of electoral candidates and club presidents.

25. The electoral campaigning period officially ends.

26. A mafia plan to assassinate MP Luciano Violante is discovered.

27. The first day of the national elections sees voter turn-out down by ten per cent.

28. On the second day of the elections, there are early indications of strong support for Berlusconi's Freedom Alliance.

Record levels of trading occur at the stock exchange.

29. The election results are confirmed with Forza Italia, the Lega and Alleanza Nazionale winning an absolute majority in the chamber of deputies and a relative majority in the senate.

30. Silvio Berlusconi meets with Umberto Bossi to discuss the formation of a government, whilst Gianfranco Fini announces that he will not seek a ministerial post in order to guarantee the creation of a centre-right government.

Mino Martinazzoli resigns as leader of the Popular Party.

31. The stock market index rises by 4.3 per cent, with record trading levels continuing and the lira rising rapidly.

April

1. Although Umberto Bossi is absent, Silvio Berlusconi meets with Lega officials to discuss the issue of federalism.

2. Umberto Bossi reaffirms his objection to Berlusconi becoming prime minister.

The PDS begins to discuss the issue of its leadership, with Massimo D'Alema and Walter Veltroni being the two major contenders for the position of general secretary.

4. Umberto Bossi continues to promote the formation of a parliamentary government and broaches a dialogue with the left, causing Berlusconi to appeal to the Lega's MPs to honour their alliance pledge and the popular mandate.

7. In Rome, Umberto Bossi and Gianfranco Fini meet to discuss federalism and the possibility of a presidential system of government.

8. The Lega declares that the implementation of anti-trust legislation is a precondition for Berlusconi if he wishes to become prime minister.

At his last formal press conference, caretaker prime minister Ciampi speaks of economic upturn and recovery.

10. President Scalfaro rules out the option of dissolving both chambers of parliament should Berlusconi's attempt to form a government not succeed.

11. The first meeting between all three partners of the centre-right coalition takes place to discuss nominations for the speakers of both chambers of parliament.

12. The caretaker government endorses 32 decrees to simplify the civil service.

13. Mancino and Beniamino Andreatta, having been elected parliamentary leaders of the PPI, announce their intention to resign from their ministerial posts in the current caretaker government.

14. The centre-right coalition's nomination of Carlo Scognamiglio as speaker of the senate and Irene Pivetti as speaker of the chamber of deputies causes controversy as the latter has been accused of anti-semitism.

The PDS, Greens, Rete, Alleanza Democratica and the Cristiano Sociali announce their unified parliamentary group.

15. The 12th Italian legislature is inaugurated.

16. The Lega's Irene Pivetti is elected as the youngest-ever speaker of the chamber of deputies, whilst Carlo Scognamiglio narrowly defeats the veteran Spadolini for the speaker's position in the senate.

The Ciampi government formally resigns.

17. Mario Segni's supporters are divided over whether to respond favourably to Berlusconi's invitation to enter into a governing pact with Forza Italia.

18. In contradiction of party leader Umberto Bossi, the Lega's Roberto Maroni announces that he is prepared to negotiate with the Popular Party regarding their possible entry into a governing alliance.

Silvio Berlusconi publicly suggests that 'clean hands' magistrate Antonio Di Pietro should be given the justice portfolio in a Berlusconi cabinet.

19. The Progressive's plan for a unified parliamentary group is temporarily dismantled due to internal differences. It is reconstituted as a 'federal grouping'.

20. Gianfranco Fini and the Lega reject a proposal to give Marco Pannella the foreign affairs ministry, whilst Di Pietro announces that he has never been approached by Berlusconi nor offered a ministerial post.

Sergio Berlinguer is elected the leader of the Progressive's new parliamentary 'federal grouping'.

21. Bossi boycotts the inclusion of Parisi and Dini in a centre-right government, making it a precondition for the Lega to remain in the coalition.

Speaker of the chamber of deputies, Irene Pivetti causes controversy by declaring that Mussolini did a great deal for women during his years in power.

22. President Scalfaro's decision to endorse July elections for the new *consiglio superiore della magistratura* (CSM), using the existing rules instead of formulating new procedures advocated by speaker Pivetti, generates heated debate within the government.

23. President Scalfaro consults party leaders prior to designating one of them to form a government.

The Lega stakes a claim on key cabinet posts, especially targeting the Interior ministry for Roberto Maroni.

25. Celebrations occur all over Italy to mark the anniversary of the Liberation.

26. Ex-PSI Prime Minister Giuliano Amato abandons Segni's Pact for Italy group.

27. The Lega's Roberto Maroni proposes the idea of a three-person committee to manage Silvio Berlusconi's Fininvest holdings, in order to guarantee against a conflict of interest between his business and governmental responsibilities.

28. Silvio Berlusconi is formally instructed by President Scalfaro to form a government, whilst a panel of 'three wise men' will undertake a study into options for anti-trust legislation applicable to Berlusconi's business holdings.

29. Silvio Berlusconi, Umberto Bossi and Gianfranco Fini attend a summit to discuss the allocation of ministries amongst their parties and their government

programme.

Cusani is jailed for eight years and appeals against the verdict.

30. 'Clean hands' chief magistrate Francesco Borrelli announces that none of the judges in the pool, including Antonio Di Pietro, will accept ministerial posts.

May

1. May Day celebrations take place throughout Italy.

2. Prime Minister Berlusconi undertakes his first consultations with trade union leaders and heads of industry.

The Milan public prosecutor's office issues a request for the arrest of Mario Dell'Utri, the managing director of Berlusconi's advertising company, Publitalia.

3. The Berlusconi Government reissues the *salva RAI* decree to keep the state broadcaster solvent.

4. A motion by the socialists in the European parliament declaring that there should not be any fascist ministers in the new Italian government provokes outrage in Italy, with President Scalfaro admonishing the Brussels parliamentarians for their presumptuous interference in Italian domestic affairs.

5. New revelations are made by Broccoletti in the SISDE inquiry, accusing President Scalfaro of also having received payments when he was interior minister.

6. The Lega declares that it would be prepared to forego the interior ministry on the condition that the portfolio be given to an outsider or "third man". The name of magistrate Antonio Di Pietro is again raised.

7. Di Pietro again publicly refuses to join the new government in any capacity, prompting Roberto Maroni of the Lega to re-stake his claim to the post.

9. Berlusconi's cabinet list is finalised.

10. The Berlusconi government is presented to the public; eight ministers are from Forza Italia, five from the Lega, including Roberto Maroni as interior minister, five from Alleanza Nazionale, two from the Unione del Centro, two from the Centro Cristiano Democratico and three "technocrats".

11. The Berlusconi government is sworn-in by President Scalfaro.

12. Ex-Health Minister Francesco De Lorenzo is arrested for allegedly taking bribes.

13. US President Bill Clinton sends his best wishes to Silvio Berlusconi on the inauguration of his new government.

14. The Miglio affair erupts, with the Lega's chief ideologue resigning from the party and refusing to support a forthcoming parliamentary motion of confidence in the new government.

15. Berlusconi appeals to the parties of the centre to support a vote of confidence in his government.

16. In the senate Berlusconi presents his government's goals of increasing employment, accelerating privatization, reducing taxes and guaranteeing the independence of the investigating magistrates.

From abroad, ex-Prime Minister Bettino Craxi sends a medical certificate stating that his ill health prevents him from returning to Italy to hand in his passport to the Italian authorities.

18. The senate narrowly passes a confidence motion in the Berlusconi government with 159 votes in favour, 153 votes against and two absentees. Four Popular Party senators who abstained from the vote are suspended by their party leaders.

19. Speaker of the chamber, Irene Pivetti makes the controversial announcement that she does not intend to confer any chairs of parliamentary committees to members of the opposition.

Telecom Italia is created from the merger of SIP, Italcable, ISITEL, Telespazio and SIZIM, making it the sixth largest conglomeration in the world.

20. With 366 votes in favor and 245 votes against, the Berlusconi government wins its crucial vote of confidence from the chamber of deputies.

21. The public prosecutor's office in Palermo requests that the trial of ex-Christian Democrat Prime Minister Giulio Andreotti for alleged complicity with mafia bosses be postponed.

Former Prime Minister Giovanni Goria dies.

23. Defence Minister Antonio Martino undertakes his first foreign trip, travelling to Washington to meet President Clinton and to promote the Berlusconi government's plans for a more high profile Italian foreign

policy role.

24. In the Enimont 'clean hands' inquiry, magistrate Ghitti commits 32 people to trial, amongst whom are Craxi, Forlani, La Malfa and De Michelis.

25. Tensions with France unfold as President Mitterrand accuses Berlusconi of harbouring fascists in his government and threatening a French boycott of any interaction with Alleanza Nazionale ministers.

26. Justice Minister Alfredo Biondi authorises an inquiry into Calabrian magistrates and the prosecutor, Boemi, as a result of allegations made by mafia boss Totò Riina during his trial.

27. The government issues its first economic decree, which includes provisions for the simplification of insurance provisions and a change to privatization rules.

28. Despite international wariness of Italy's new ministerial line-up, President Clinton reiterates his support for the Berlusconi government, stating that it will be judged by its achievements.

June

1. Relations with Israel become strained over the latter's disapproval of neo-fascist ministers being included in the government.

After Bank of Italy's alarming assessment of the Italian economic situation, the government announces its intention to investigate possible reform of the social security system.

2. US President Clinton meets with President Scalfaro, Prime Minister Berlusconi and the Pope on the first day of his visit to Italy.

Alleanza Nazionale's leader, Gianfranco Fini, makes the controversial statement that up until 1938, fascism was a good thing.

4. The Taradash-RAI affair erupts as Marco Taradash, the chairman of the parliamentary watchdog committee on the media, submits a dossier of allegedly incriminating evidence against the former executives of RAI to the Rome public prosecutor and presses criminal charges.

5. The Israeli vice-minister of foreign affairs again attacks the neo-fascist ministers in the Italian government and states that the speaker of the chamber, Irene Pivetti, is anti-semitic.

6. The Government proposes new legal measures, including provisions that

would impact on informers, in the 'clean hands' investigations.

7. Prime Minister Berlusconi provokes allegations of intimidating the state broadcaster when he publicly attacks RAI for its allegedly hostile editorial line against his government, claiming that such a stance is unprecedented in other European democracies and that RAI should actively support the elected coalition.

8. Government measures to stimulate the economy are contained in its first "employment package" which includes measures for tax breaks for employers hiring more workers, investment incentives and the removal of some minor taxes.

9. Berlusconi declares that the results of European parliamentary elections will be a referendum on his leadership and the strength of his coalition.

10. The constitutional court rules that INPS, the department of social security, must pay all beneficiaries whom it had previously been underpaying, the shortfalls in their entitlements. The government estimates that this will cost 16 thousand billion lire.

11. The result of the European elections confirm Berlusconi's support base, with 4.8 million votes posted for Forza Italia.

12. The final results for Italian MEPs in the European elections give an absolute majority to the government coalition parties, with Forza Italia securing just over 30 per cent of the vote, Alleanza Nazionale holding steady and losses incurred by the Lega.

13. PDS general secretary Achille Occhetto resigns after the party's defeats at the national and European elections.

14. High profile mafia boss Maniero escapes from prison in Padova, sparking a political row over breaches of security and who should be held responsible.

15. The Dalai Lama visits Rome and arranges to meet with Prime Minister Berlusconi.

17. Minister for Institutional Reform, Francesco Speroni, threatens to resign when his project for regional electoral reform is blocked by cabinet.

18. Treasury officials finalize the government's "anti-deficit" package which will require spending cuts in order to recoup 6 thousand billion lire in 1994 and 30-40 thousand billion 1995.

19. Umberto Bossi announces that the Lega will not participate in a "unified party" (*partito unico*) arrangement with Berlusconi and Fini, but will pursue a more independent line within the coalition.

20. 'Black Monday' for the Italian stock market with falls of 4.2 per cent.

21. Italy records an inflation level of 3.7 per cent, the lowest in 25 years.

23. Minister for parliamentary relations, Giuliano Ferrara, is appointed the government's official spokesman.

24. At the Corfu European Council summit, Italy joins its European Union partners in agreeing to the accession of Austria, Finland, Norway and Sweden to the Union pending referendums in each country.

25. After the UK veto of Belgian Prime Minister Dehaene to succeed Jacques Delors as the new president of the European Commission, Italian ex-Prime Minister Giuliano Amato is proposed as a possible candidate.

26. In local government elections parties of the left win office in many cities.

27. A survey of PDS local branches demonstrates their overwhelming support for Walter Veltroni to succeed Achille Occhetto as leader of the party.

29. The *salva RAI* decree is reissued a second time by the government as the sixty-day tenure of the previous decree expires.

30. The entire management body of RAI, including the general manager, resign, prompting changes to the government's decree that effectively consign governing powers to the parliamentary speakers.

July

1. The PDS National Council elects Massimo D'Alema as the new leader of the party with 249 votes against 173 for Walter Veltroni.

2. Controversy erupts as the prime minister's office issues a memo stating that it reserves the right to decide on appointments within the Bank of Italy.

4. The public prosecutor of Rome requests the arrest of Bettino Craxi on charges of having accepted bribes in connection with the building of Rome's subway.

5. In Milan, six high-ranking officers of the finance police, some of whom had been working on the 'clean hands' investigations, are arrested for alleged corruption.

Forza Italia announces that it is opposed to the proposed decree reforming the corruption trial procedures put forward by justice minister Biondi the previous month.

6. Administrative affairs minister Giuliano Urbani contradicts the heads of Forza Italia, stating that the movement supports the proposal to have an electoral system with a French-style, double round of voting.

At the European Parliament, Forza Italia forms a party grouping on its own.

7. The chamber of deputies approves the government's privatization decree with the bipartisan support of the Progressives.

8. Berlusconi opens the G7 summit in Naples.

9. Speaker of the chamber Pivetti refuels the RAI controversy by claiming that she is being pressured over the new management appointments by the prime minister, who informed her that the RAI's executives ought to be accountable to the government.

A bomb is discovered in the Milan stock exchange.

10. The G7 summit concludes in Naples.

11. The speakers of both houses of parliament announce the five new members of the RAI's executive board.

12. Interior minister Roberto Maroni discloses that SISDE had spied on President Scalfaro along with 21 other politicians.

Minister Maroni announces a reform of SISDE with replacements occurring within the executive ranks of the secret service. Head of the carabinieri, General Maino, and head of the army, General Siracusa, are appointed to direct the organization.

13. The government approves a decree (the Biondi decree) on pre-trial detention, curtailing magistrates' powers of arrest and detainment of suspects before trial on charges involving violence, drugs and the mafia, which would also apply to corruption cases with the result that many of the suspects in the 'clean-hands' investigations would be released.

Letizia Morati is confirmed as the new president of the RAI.

14. The Biondi decree sparks violent controversy in parliament and within the judiciary where four of the 'clean hands' pool request to be transferred to other duties in protest over the government's action.

15. The Lega and Alleanza Nazionale propose amendments to the Biondi decree which would exempt corruption and extortion suspects from the   new rules.

16. Interior minister Roberto Maroni offers to resign after claiming that Forza Italia cabinet colleagues lied to him regarding the terms of the Biondi decree. Lega leader, Umberto Bossi demands that the government withdraw the decree.

17. Italy is defeated by Brazil in a penalty shoot-out in the final of the World Cup Soccer tournament in Los Angeles.

18. Prime Minister Berlusconi backs down and withdraws the Biondi decree, announcing that it was never the government's intention to absolve corruption suspects.

Camorra boss Zaza dies of a heart attack.

19. Magistrates request that ex-minister for the interior Mancino be brought to trial for alleged links to the mafia.

20. The *Consiglio Superiore della Magistratura* publicly condemns the Biondi decree prompting further government accusations of magisterial interference in the executive's affairs.

21. Tensions within the coalition over the rescinded Biondi decree worsen as Forza Italia and Lega MPs trade insults and a fracas ensues in the chamber of deputies. The decree is formally blocked by parliament.

22. Berlusconi, Bossi and Fini meet to finalize the government's economic strategy before gaining cabinet approval for austerity budget measures.

23. Twenty-three arrests are made in Milan in connection with the 'clean hands' investigations, including businessmen, members of the finance police and Fininvest executives.

25. A private meeting at the prime minister's house including Berlusconi, his Forza Italia colleagues, minister Cesare Previti and chamber of deputies undersecretary, Gianni Letta and Paolo Berlusconi's lawyers provokes an outcry from the opposition which alleges that the meeting represents unacceptable collusion between the government and Berlusconi's personal business interests.

26. Prime Minister Berlusconi strongly attacks the 'clean hands' pool of magistrates, telling them that if they wish to practise politics they should first obtain an electoral mandate from the people.

A warrant for the arrest of Paolo Berlusconi is issued by magistrates.

27. Prime Minister Berlusconi denies that there is a crisis in his government and rejects Fini's call for a cabinet reshuffle.

28. Paolo Berlusconi refuses to give himself up for arrest, instigating a manhunt by the police.

29. Silvio Berlusconi presents his proposal for a five-member committee to implement the separation of his Fininvest interests from his prime ministerial duties.

At the Popular Party Congress, Rocco Buttiglione is elected as the new leader of the party.

30. Lega leader Umberto Bossi presents an alternative plan for separating the prime minister from his direct control of Fininvest.

31. Marco Pannella sets up the 'Movement for Civil Struggle, the Environment and Reforming the Reformers'.

August

1. In the senate, the Lega's negative vote contributes to the Government's economic programme being defeated three times in committee.

2. In response to calls for his government's resignation Berlusconi defends himself in parliament, stating that he will separate himself from his business interests, but that he will not accept the expropriation of his company holdings.

3. The *consiglio d'amministrazione* blocks approximately 100 RAI appointments amid allegations that Berlusconi is pressuring the state broadcaster to reduce its advertising and audience share, effectively reducing its revenues.

4. Veteran leader of the Italian Republican Party, Giovanni Spadolini, dies.

The senate approves the government's anti-deficit economic measures.

5. Leaving from Italian bases, NATO airplanes bomb Serbian targets in Bosnia.

6. Government advertisements publicising its achievements in the areas of employment, health, drug enforcement, justice and the environment are broadcast on RAI channels and are strongly denounced as propaganda by the opposition.

7. Popular Party leader Rocco Buttiglione and PDS general secretary Massimo D'Alema meet, but do not reach agreement on the possible formation of a shadow government.

8. The parliamentary media watchdog authority suspends the 'government spots' on the RAI channels, sparking a further debate between government members, the media and the opposition parties.

9. The Alleanza Nazionale minister for the environment, Altero Matteoli, fuels tension within the coalition by making public statements against abortion.

10. The president's office announces that from October, the Quirinale will be open to the public every Sunday.

11. The dramatic fall of the lira prompts the Bank of Italy to raise interest rates by half a per cent, causing a storm within the coalition with Forza Italia accusing Umberto Bossi of precipitating a currency crisis whenever he makes destabilising statements.

The minister for employment, Mastella, creates controversy by blaming the fall of the lira on 'the New York Jewish lobby'.

12. As the lira and stock market prices continue to dive, Prime Minister Berlusconi attempts to reassure markets by denying claims that the coalition is in crisis.

13. An anonymous telephone call tips off police that there are two bombs planted in front of La Standa department store in Florence.

Emergency services are put on the alert as forest fires rage over most of southern Italy.

14. From Milan, Berlusconi warns that the fall of his government could precipitate public disorder and reassures citizens that he and Umberto Bossi agree on matters ninety per cent of the time.

16. The *Independente* newspaper publishes unflattering comments allegedly made by Berlusconi about the media, businessmen Gianni Agnelli and De Benedetti, Umberto Bossi and magistrate Di Pietro. The prime minister later appears on television to correct the misinterpretations.

17. Environment minister Matteoli proposes that island prisons be dismantled.

19. As the lira again loses ground, the governor of the Bank of Italy is attacked by Alleanza Nazionale, with AN transport minister Publio Fiori calling

for the governor's resignation for alleged abuse of office.

20. The PDS announces that it does not support the idea of establishing an 'institutional government' to replace the current Berlusconi coalition.

21. The Lega clashes with its coalition partners over proposed pension cuts in the austerity budget measures.

22. From the European Forum meeting in Austria, President Scalfaro makes a statement reassuring the public that the autonomy of the Bank of Italy will be safeguarded.

Eight Italian tourists die in an airline disaster in Morocco.

24. A breakdown at the ENEL electricity plant in Latina and a power line fire at Valmontone result in a three-hour blackout throughout southern Italy from southern Lazio to Calabria, leaving households, businesses, hospitals and railways without electricity between 11.20am and 2.30pm.

25. Head of police Vincenzo Parisi resigns his post more than a year before his scheduled retirement in November 1995 and is to be replaced by police superintendent of Rome, Ferdinando Masone.

26. At cabinet, ministers modify a decree on education to abolish resit exams from 1995, approve the renewal of the *salva RAI* decree for a third time and endorse a 10 thousand billion lire loan to IRI to cover its debt repayments.

Cabinet blocks minister Biondi's proposals for solving overcrowding in jails by allowing the release of prisoners who have been sentenced to between three and a half and eight years and still have only one year of their sentences to serve.

27. Minister Biondi angrily threatens to resign if his prison reforms are not reconsidered and endorsed by the government.

28. The Naples court decides that ex-DC health minister De Lorenzo, who is being investigated in a major bribery case, will remain in detention pending his trial on the grounds that he may be capable of tampering with the evidence.

30. Cabinet approves pension reforms which form an integral part of the budget, including a crackdown on false claims and streamlining responsibility for the management and administration of invalid pensions into one agency.

31. Both the office of the president and that of the prime minister deny claims by Umberto Bossi that Berlusconi asked President Scalfaro for new elections in order to avoid anti-trust legislation.

September

1. The government is divided over the position Italy should take on abortion during the forthcoming World Population Conference in Cairo, with Berlusconi refusing minister Guidi's resignation as head of the Italian delegation after his anti-abortion stance is questioned.

2. Whilst still divided on the issue, the government rejects Chancellor Kohl's proposal for a two-speed Europe.

3. From a conference in Cernobbio, Antonio Di Pietro suggests a new approach to the corruption investigations which would amount to a semi-amnesty for those involved. The scheme would involve a three-month period being put aside for offences to be confessed and offenders named, profits from such dealings would then be handed over and in return, the accused would be dealt with more lightly by the courts.

5. Antonio Di Pietro's proposals receive a controversial response, dividing both the pool of magistrates and the coalition parties.

Lega MPs Franco Rocchetta, Vittorio Aliprandi and Marilena Marin are expelled from the party by Bossi on the grounds that they attempted to damage it.

6. Gianfranco Fini and deputy-Prime Minister Roberto Maroni give reassurances that government spokesman Giuliano Ferrara is speaking in a personal capacity and not on behalf of the government when he denounces the Di Pietro proposals and demands that the president intervene against the magistrates who sponsored these proposals.

7. The government launches its campaign against tax evasion, targeting dentists and property managers in particular.

8. Treasury Minister Lamberto Dini intervenes to stem public alarm over proposed pension cuts by giving reassurances that existing rights will not be affected.

In Bari, 400 illegal Albanian refugees are taken into custody by officials.

9. Cabinet approves legislation which allows women to join the armed forces as volunteers.

10. In Milan, a protest march in support of Leoncavallo, a local community centre, results in violent clashes between protesters and police, prompting interior minister Maroni to announce severe new measures to counteract

urban violence.

12. Alleanza Nazionale presents its own economic strategy which rejects indiscriminate budget cuts.

13. A meeting between Prime Minister Berlusconi and union leaders to discuss pension reform leads to hopes that a proposed general strike will be averted.

14. No concrete results emerge from a meeting between Berlusconi and Popular Party leader Buttiglione in which the prime minister proposes that the PPI join his coalition.

15. Workers threaten to strike as the anti-trust commission gives industry minister Gnutti the go-ahead for privatising ENEL.

16. The government sets up a committee of ministers Tatarella, Speroni, Urbani, Fisichella and D'Onofrio to investigate the problem of electoral reform.

17. The government names the new executives of RAI, prompting an angry reaction from Umberto Bossi who accuses Berlusconi of having nominated candidates personally close to him, or to Forza Italia.

18. Massimo D'Alema closes the *Festa dell'Unità* by reiterating the PDS's commitment to fostering its ties with other progressive parties.

19. In response to the RAI executive appointments, journalists call for a strike and the *consiglio d'amministrazione* announces its plans to discuss the matter with the speakers of parliament.

20. ISTAT presents figures that three out of four Italians own their own homes.

21. Party colleagues of Forza Italia parliamentary leader, Vittorio Dotti do not approve his strategy for the formation of an alliance with the Popular Party.

Defence minister Cesare Previti is designated the coordinator of the Forza Italia movement.

22. With a growth rate of 5.3 per cent, industrial production accelerates during the month of September.

23. The Lega, the PDS and the Popular Party present a parliamentary agenda item (order of the day) to suspend the RAI appointments and reorganisation of the broadcaster until an editorial watch-dog committee is put into place.

24. Despite internal opposition from veteran fascists, Gianfranco Fini announces the imminent end of the MSI, confident that the party's congress will sanction the evolution of the party into the neo-fascist Alleanza Nazionale.

27. Berlusconi announces the acceleration of the government's privatisation programme with treasurer Dini presenting the scheduled calendar for the privatization of major public trading enterprises.

28. After an all-night meeting, cabinet gives its approval to the budget bill.

29. The 'three wise men' submit their report on how to resolve the prime minister's conflict of business and governmental interests.

Chamber of deputies speaker, Irene Pivetti tells Berlusconi that his government is issuing too many emergency decrees instead of conducting government business via legislative bills that are fully debated in parliament.

30. Controversy erupts over the "blind trust" proposal put forward by the "three wise men", with parliament calling upon the government to release the document for debate in the house.

October

1. At the last minute President Scalfaro requests and obtains modifications to the budget bill before parliament with the result that the social security reforms will be separated from the budget.

2. The President's official residence is open to the public for the first time.

3. In Milan, ex-Forza Italia and Lega supporters form "Italia Libera".

4. Berlusconi attacks the 'clean-hands' magistrates, accusing them of employing inquisitorial methods and misusing the justice system for distorted ends.

The parliamentary watch-dog committee on the media rejects the RAI's new editorial plan, prompting the Lega to vote with the opposition in protest.

5. In a defiant counter-attack on Berlusconi, head of the 'clean hands' pool, Francesco Borrelli gives an interview in which he states that the Telepiu investigation poses the risk that the highest political echelons will be compromised and that those who fear the consequences are seeking to discredit the Pool.

6. In response to Borrelli's comments, cabinet unanimously approves a petition against him and submits it to President Scalfaro, who is the formal head

of the *Consiglio Superiore della Magistratura.*

The government does not command a majority on the *condono edilizio* (illegal building amnesty) decree in the senate, which would grant an amnesty to building speculators who built illegally on the condition that they pay fines aimed at reducing the spending deficit.

7. The government's petition against Borrelli is formally submitted to the *Consiglio Superiore della Magistratura* which must make a judgement and decide on any disciplinary action.

8. The main recommendations of the "three wise men" report are released publicly with the authors recommending that either Silvio Berlusconi resign from his Fininvest group or that an autonomous manager be nominated. However, the report falls short of obliging the prime minister to sell his holdings.

10. Prime Minister Berlusconi makes a polemical speech in parliament claiming that the legislature is a waste of time and that in blocking his government at every turn, parliament 'will not let him work'.

11. Jas Gawronski is appointed the new spokesman for the prime minister's office.

12. The Lega releases a draft alternative blueprint for anti-trust legislation which would divest Fininvest of two of its television networks, but the document lacks the signature of Lega leader, Umberto Bossi.

13. Silvio Berlusconi and foreign affairs minister Antonio Martino visit Moscow as guests of President Boris Yeltsin to discuss economic matters.

14. A general strike, involving three million people takes place in major Italian cities in protest over the government's proposed budget.

Prime Minister Berlusconi and President Yeltsin sign the first-ever friendship and co-operation treaty between Italy and Russia.

15. In response to the general strike and to union leaders' plans for a national meeting the following week, Berlusconi reiterates that the government's economic strategy will not be changed.

17. With a unanimous vote, the *Consiglio Superiore della Magistratura* rejects the government's petition against head magistrate Borrelli, arguing that his comments were a defence against the attacks made on the independence of the 'clean hands' pool.

18. Bank of Italy president Fazio defends the central bank's autonomy and designates Desario as the new general manager, despite the government having nominated an external candidate.

Justice minister Biondi makes arrangements for an inquiry into the 'clean hands' magistrates on the grounds that 10 cases contain errors and that the team is targeting Fininvest whilst ignoring bribery allegations against left-wing suspects.

19. The coalition decides that pensions will be revalued according to the rate of inflation.

20. A brawl erupts in parliament over the government's RAI executive appointments when Alleanza Nazionale deputies take exception to Greens MP Mauro Paissan, when he accuses the coalition of being corrupt and trying to tear the state broadcaster apart.

Italy enters the United Nations Security Council for the next two years.

21. The treasurer, Lamberto Dini, rejects the proposed modifications to pension reform put forward by unionists and the Lega.

22. In Bari, the consumption of raw fish is prohibited as two cases of cholera are discovered.

23. A major airport strike will continue for seven days.

24. The carabinieri begin an investigation into left-wing co-operatives in Sicily, requesting the names of all Sicilian managers and administrative documents since 1980.

25. Alleanza Nazionale deputies involved in the parliamentary brawl with Paissan are suspended by the speaker of the chamber, Irene Pivetti.

26. Divisions within the Lega occur after the finalisation of the budget with minister Maroni opposing party leader Umberto Bossi's suggestion that the Lega should exit the coalition in favour of an 'institutional' government.

28. The government nominates economist Mario Monti and Radical Emma Bonini as the Italian commissioners of the European Commission.

November

1. Bank of Italy announces that between the months of April and August there was a 27 billion lire flight of capital from Italy.

2. The *consiglio d'amministrazione* unanimously agrees on the new package of appointments for the RAI's management, with the list including many nominees close to Forza Italia and Alleanza Nazionale.

Two men are arrested in Calabria after the shooting of seven-year-old American boy Nicholas Green in his parents' car on the Salerno-Reggio Calabria freeway.

3. Amid false rumours that Silvio Berlusconi will resign as prime minister, the lira falls to an historic low of 1031.70 against the deutschmark.

4. A warrant for the arrest of ex-DC public works minister Giovanni Prandini is issued in connection with alleged bribery payments made for road building by ANAS.

5. With Alleanza Nazionale and the Centro Cristiano Democratico abstaining from the vote, cabinet decides in favour of Lega minister Speroni's plans for a two-round voting system in regional elections.

6. Minister Giuliano Ferrara publishes an open letter to Prime Minister Berlusconi exhorting him to engage all parties in finding a resolution to institutional reform.

The Lega presents its blueprint for Italy to be divided into nine regions.

7. Catastrophic flooding in north-eastern Italy prompts the government to declare a state of emergency.

9. After just 95 days as director-general of RAI, cabinet appoints Gianni Billia as the new president of INPS, reopening the vacancy for RAI's number one position.

10. The speakers of both houses announce that ex-prime minister Giuliano Amato has been appointed the new head of the watchdog authority on market competition, otherwise known as the 'anti-trust commission'.

11. Union leaders warn Berlusconi that they will rally their members for a general strike should parliament override PDS and Lega amendments to the budget bill and support a vote of confidence in the government's budget measures.

12. One million people protest in Rome against the government's budget and its proposed pension cuts.

13. National day of mourning for the victims of the floods which devastated

north-eastern Italy.

14. The Government wins a motion-of-confidence vote on its *condono edilizio* decree.

15. In Naples, violent exchanges occur between police and 4000 students protesting against reforms to secondary schooling.

16. Lega leader Umberto Bossi holds talks with unions and agrees to press the coalition partners to remove controversial pension provisions from the budget bill but the proposal is rejected by cabinet.

17. Unions declare a further national strike day for 2 December.

18. The heads of regional governments demand the dismissal of Roberto Maroni as head of the extraordinary Commission for Flood Damaged Areas, arguing that they have been effectively kept out of decision-making and implementation of measures through the Minister's direct conferral of powers to local mayors.

19. Parliament is suspended for ten minutes in order to restore order after Alleanza Nazionale and Lega deputies clash over Budget Bill amendments.

20. Tensions between Forza Italia and the Lega are exacerbated as Roberto Maroni is required to clarify remarks he made to Il Messagero that Silvio Berlusconi and certain elements within the government are not unhappy with the creation of social unrest in Italy.

21. In the run-up to local elections, exit polls show a loss of support for Forza Italia and the Lega whilst Alleanza Nazionale and the Progressives experience appreciable gains.

22. Whilst hosting a United Nations conference on organised crime, Silvio Berlusconi learns that he is to be the first serving Italian prime minister to be formally investigated on corruption relating to bribery payments allegedly made to the finance police to reduce the tax liability of three Fininvest companies.

Prime Minister Berlusconi appears on television to deny the corruption allegations against him and to confirm that he will not be resigning the premiership.

23. Justice minister Alfredo Biondi sends inspectors to the office of public prosecutions in Rome to investigate claims that 'clean hands' judges, led by Gerado D'Ambrosio, are covering up allegations against the PCI/PDS.

24. Former Catania crime boss Giuseppe Pulvirenti discloses to judges that the

mafia had plans to assassinate well-known journalist Maurizio Costanzo.

25. Francesco Cossiga retracts the preface he wrote for a controversial book on the Italian constitution written by Antonio Di Pietro.

26. Budget minister Giancarlo Pagliarini announces that the government is planning to introduce new taxes in the new year after the budget bill is passed.

29. The supreme court decides that the so-called *fiamme gialle* investigation into bribery payments received by the finance police, including alleged payments by Silvio Berlusconi, will be transferred from the jurisdiction of the Milan pool to that of the Brescia magistrates.

30. The Lega discloses its proposals for anti-trust legislation which would prohibit anyone owning more than one private television station and thus force Prime Minister Berlusconi to sell two of his three stations.

December

1. A fire on board the Achille Lauro sinks the ship off the coast of Africa with all except two of the passengers and crew on board being saved.

2. An accord is reached between the government and unions over pension reform, thus averting the planned general strike.

3. Students protest against the government in 14 major Italian cities.

4. Forza Italia and Alleanza Nazionale supporters hold rallies in Milan, Naples, Genova and Palermo in support of Prime Minister Berlusconi.

Bettino Craxi is sentenced in absentia to five and a half years imprisonment for corruption.

5. Parties of the centre-left defeat coalition forces in four out of six mayoral elections, with the biggest upset in the city of Brescia where the Lega minister Vito Gnutti is defeated by the Popular Party's founder, Mino Martinazzoli.

6. Magistrate Antonio Di Pietro requests that Umberto Bossi be given a jail term for having accepted unlawful party funding.

7. High-profile 'clean-hands' magistrate, Antonio Di Pietro resigns.

8. The constitutional court issues a judgement on the 1990 'Mammì law' which sanctions the co-existence of private and public television channels, stating that it must be rewritten due to its general incoherence and because it allows

Fininvest to maintain a dominant position by owning three channels.

9. The senate budget committee approves the *condono edilizio* decree as amended by Forza Italia and Alleanza Nazionale, postponing its enforcement date to the end of the year.

10. Speaker of the chamber Irene Pivetti criticizes the government on the issue of unemployment, charging that Berlusconi's claim that his government would create one million jobs was merely an electoral ploy.

11. Achille Occhetto and ex-administrative secretary Stefanini are questioned by magistrates over alleged illicit party funding by the 'red' co-operative, 'Unieco' of Reggio Emilia.

13. Magistrate Arnaldo Valente, the supreme court judge responsible for transferring the so-called *fiamme gialle* investigation from the Milan clean hands pool to Brescia, resigns.

14. Prime Minister Berlusconi is questioned for seven and a half hours by investigating magistrates, including Borrelli, and later appears on television to confirm that he has no intention of resigning.

Eleven judicial inspectors from the ministry of justice hand in their letters of resignation, triggering an offer of resignation from the ministry's head, Ugo Dinacci.

15. Crisis unfolds in the government as parliament approves a motion put forward by the Lega's speaker of the chamber, Irene Pivetti, to establish a special commission to reform the television sector.

Lega leader Umberto Bossi meets with the leadership of the PDS and the Popular Party, fuelling speculation that the Berlusconi coalition is set to crumble.

16. A documentary on World War II screened by the RAI creates controversy by claiming that Mussolini's mistress, Clara Petacci, was raped by left-wing partisans before her execution.

17. The 11 ministry of justice inspectors who had previously resigned, retract their resignations and return to work.

Prime Minister Berlusconi acts to reassure President Scalfaro of his government's support and esteem after distancing himself from attacks made against the president by government spokesman, Giuliano Ferrara.

18. The PDS announces that it will submit a no-confidence motion with the support of the Popular Party and the Lega in order to force the resignation of the Berlusconi government.

19. The chamber of deputies votes 232 to 166, with 31 abstentions to approve the deficit-cutting budget package designed to cut spending and reduce the public deficit.

20. Prime Minister Berlusconi appears on national television appealing for the public to rally in mass street marches to support his government as it is on the threshold of collapse following Umberto Bossi's threat to withdraw from the coalition.

Panic selling occurs on the Italian stock market and the deutschmark reaches an historic high of 1.050 against the lira.

21. Lega leader Umberto Bossi abandons the government coalition, leaving Prime Minister Berlusconi without a parliamentary majority.

In the SISDE investigation, ex-director Riccardo Malpica is sentenced to three-and-a-half years for abuse of office and Maurizio Broccoletti and Gerardo Di Pasquale are sentenced to nine-years imprisonment for having criminal associations.

22. Silvio Berlusconi resigns as prime minister and calls for fresh elections, claiming that the current parliament has lost its electoral legitimacy after Umberto Bossi's betrayal of the coalition.

23. Tensions rise within the Lega as Roberto Maroni and other dissidents express their opposition to Bossi's abandonment of the coalition and his alleged plans to negotiate an alliance with the Popular Party or the Progressives.

Silvio Berlusconi demands that he be put in charge of a caretaker government in the run-up to new elections.

24. Ugo Dinacci, head of the justice department and a close aid of minister Biondi, is arrested for alleged links to the mafia.

After consulting parliament and party leaders, President Scalfaro rejects the option of calling new elections.

27. President Scalfaro begins consultations with party leaders to form a new government.

28. The Lega announces its support for the creation of a transitional

'presidential' government where participating coalition parties are not held together by a political pact, whilst Forza Italia and Alleanza Nazionale repeat their calls for new elections.

29. Silvio Berlusconi again demands that he be placed in charge of a caretaker government pending fresh elections.

30. President Scalfaro refuses Berlusconi's request to lead a caretaker government and ends his first round of political consultations.

31. The clash between President Scalfaro and Berlusconi continues. Scalfaro announces a second round of consultations with party leaders.

one

Continuity and change in the Italian political system

Robert Leonardi and Raffaella Y. Nanetti

The Fall of the Berlusconi Government

The calling of the 26-27 March 1994 parliamentary elections was seen by many observers as the beginning of a new phase in Italian political development. The resignation of the Carlo Azeglio Ciampi government on 13 January 1994 and the dissolution of parliament three days later brought to an end the First Republic that had been characterized by an electoral system based on proportional representation and governmental coalitions organized around the two leading Christian Democratic and Socialist parties. With the formation of the Berlusconi government on 20 May and the swearing-in of the deputies and senators who constituted the 12th legislature of the Italian Republic, the expectation was that a new phase in Italian political development had begun (Fedele, 1994; Gilbert, 1995; Mignone, 1995). The new phase was optimistically labelled "the Second Republic" in reference to the new electoral law used to elect members of parliament, the political parties which contested the elections, the influx of a new cohort of freshman parliamentarians, and the innovative nature of the ruling government coalition constituted by new parties (Forza Italia and the CCD) and former opposition parties (Alleanza Nazionale, Lega Nord, and Lista Pannella) (Buonadonna and Ginex, 1994).

However, the political events of the following weeks and months were to demonstrate that the transition from the First to the Second Republic was more apparent than real. The quick ascendancy and the even quicker demise of the Berlusconi government showed that many of the characteristics of the First Republic had reemerged *tout court* in the actions and orientations of the ruling government coalition, the governing parties and the opposition. After only seven months in office, the Berlusconi government coalition collapsed on 22 December 1994, plunging the country into a virulent political crisis which required all of the tenacity and wisdom of the President of the Republic, Luigi Scalfaro, to resolve. The nomination of Lamberto Dini, former minister of the treasury in the previous Berlusconi government and ex-director general of the Bank of Italy, to head a government composed exclusively of technocrats and academics gave the executive branch some form of stability, however temporary. The Dini government gave itself four simple objectives: pass a new law for the regional elections; introduce long overdue reforms to Italy's pension system; pass a new budget law in order to reduce the annual deficit; and regulate access to the media during electoral campaigns. However, the Dini government could not resolve the fundamental political dilemma left by the collapse of the Berlusconi government. It did not possess the authority to create a stable political majority to solidly underpin governmental action and redefine executive/legislative relations within the new political framework that had been ushered in by the change in electoral rules. That problem could only be resolved by another round of national elections. Thus, the Dini government was resigned to live a precarious life within parliament.

The fall of Berlusconi demonstrated that the public policy deficiencies of the First Republic (inability to control the public deficit, privatize state-owned enterprises, stabilize the currency and re-launch public confidence in the economy) had not been resolved by the change of electoral law, rise of new political parties, or nomination of new governing elites. Rather, the policy shortcomings of the First Republic were aggravated by the persistence of a traditional approach to policy-making. Methods in the management of public policies based on party dominance and occupation of positions of power had not changed. Compromise between political groupings became increasingly difficult to forge and the very nature of the fundamental political rules governing the system were called into question.

To understand the origins and the outcomes of the 1994/1995 political and institutional crisis in Italy, we need to separate what has remained the same and what has changed within the political party system and governmental process leading up to and coming out of the March 1994 parliamentary elections. The analysis will first look at the two years preceding the election and then at the 10 months following it. It will show that significant changes occurred over the previous two years in relation to the "superstructure" of the defining elements of political competition such as the parties, the electoral rules and the political elites, while very little change took place in the "structure" of Italian government - ie the defining elements of government decision-making such as relations within the majority coalition, the role of institutions engaged in decision making and their approach to defining priorities and carrying out policies. More importantly, the analysis will show that in the months following the elections very little change was produced by the new government coalition in either the superstructure or structure of Italian politics.

What has Changed in the Italian Political System

The Political Parties

The Italian political system has changed profoundly since 1992. Prior to the March elections, the political party system underwent a series of upheavals, producing an entirely new alignment of political parties and burying forever the old ideological cleavages between left and right.[1]

Christian Democracy and the Italian Socialist Party, along with their former government allies (Social Democrats and Liberals), underwent a series of political convulsions producing political schisms, new parties and new political alignments in preparation for the 1994 parliamentary elections. The former Christian Democratic party split into four political formations: the Italian Popular Party (PPI), Pact for Italy (Patto Segni), Christian Democratic Centre (CCD), and Christian Social Movement (MCS). The first two of the ex-DC parties (PPI and Patto Segni) presented a common slate of candidates throughout the country while the CCD joined the rightist coalition in both the North and South. The MCS cast its lot with the progressive, left-wing alliance.

The Socialist Party underwent a number of schisms over time as it painfully and unsuccessfully tried to evolve away from the political programme and ruling group installed by Bettino Craxi during his domination of the party apparatus between 1976 and 1993. First, Giorgio Benvenuto (former head of the UIL trade union) tried to reform the party;[2] then the task was transferred to Ottaviano Del Turco (former deputy-leader of the CGIL trade union). But at every turn these attempts at reform were blocked by the party's silent majority which continued to hope that the PSI's conservative political orientations could be preserved. The belief was that Craxi would eventually return to lead the PSI and bring an end to his self-imposed political exile.[3] Despite various attempts by the Milan magistrates conducting the "clean hands" anti-corruption investigation to extradite Craxi, he remained in Tunisia.[4]

The former minor parties of the centre - Liberals, Social Democrats and Republicans - were also significantly affected by the anti-corruption campaign. The Liberal Party (PLI) was severely hit by the corruption scandals due to the prominent role played by Francesco De Lorenzo, former minister of health, who was heavily involved in the "price-rigging for profit" scheme uncovered in Italy's pharmaceutical industry. On the heels of bribes paid by the pharmaceutical industry to De Lorenzo and key public administrators (e.g. Duilio Poggiolini), the Ministry of Health raised the prices of pharmaceuticals subsidized by Italy's nationalized health system and thereby increased the profits of Italy's pharmaceutical companies and kick-backs available to the politicians and administrators controlling the Ministry of Health. The Liberal Party's national secretary, Renato Altissimo, was also involved in the kick-back scandal associated with the Enimont affair in which the Italian government gave permission to Raul Gardini to end the Enimont joint-venture between his Montedison corporation and ENI, the publicly-owned petrochemical giant, on the condition that Gardini pay the governing parties huge kick-backs.[5] The mortal blow dealt by the scandals to the fortunes of the PLI encouraged a number of Liberals to abandon the party and join Forza Italia, the party founded by Silvio Berlusconi on 24 November 1993. This was the case for ex-PLI members Raffaele Costa and Alfredo Biondi who constituted the Unione di Centro (Centrist Union) and were later rewarded with ministerial posts in the Berlusconi government.

In a parallel manner the former Italian Social Democratic Party (PSDI) was shamed out of existence. Carlo Vizzini, the party secretary, became involved in both the Enimont affair as well as in alleged collusion with the mafia in Sicily. A few of the former PSDI leaders (e.g. Enrico Ferri) tried to present themselves as independent candidates (under the banner of "Social Democracy") in what in the past had been "safe" electoral districts, but they were overwhelmed by the avalanche of votes for the new political parties. At a local level, the party split between those who gravitated left-ward to join the Progressives and those who went right toward Forza Italia. Nation-wide, Ferri's Social Democracy movement received 0.5 per cent of the vote *vis-à-vis* 2.7 per cent and 3.0 per cent of the vote in 1992 and 1987.

The Republican party (PRI) almost disappeared in 1994 due to the split in its ranks. Prior to the return of Giorgio La Malfa as PRI secretary after a brush with scandal connected to the Enimont affair, Giorgio Bogi had navigated the PRI into the moderate-progressive coalition formed under the banner of Alleanza Democratica. La Malfa instead joined the ex-PSI leader, Giuliano Amato, in backing Segni's independent and centrist oriented Patto per l'Italia (Pact for Italy) and in opposing the Progressive list. The severity of the split manifested within the PRI over the leadership's fundamental political orientations served to relegate the party to an insignificant role during the 1994 elections.

Change had also taken place in the non-governing parties. On the right, the Italian Social Movement (MSI) expanded itself into a broader right-wing movement organized under the banner of the MSI-National Alliance (Alleanza Nazionale). The partial local elections of 1993 showed that the MSI-AN had experienced significant expansion in the South on the heels of the collapse of the electoral fortunes of the previous moderate parties (DC, PSI, PSDI, PLI and PRI). Moderate voters rarely stayed anchored to the new catholic political formations. Instead, they moved right to support the MSI and the new right-wing alliance. Prior to the 1994 parliamentary elections, Alleanza Nazionale picked up significant support through the migration to the party of prominent members of the former DC right-wing, such as Publio Fiori and Gustavo Selva.[6]

The attempt by the left to redefine its political orientation added to the list of new national political formations. The transformation of the left had begun with the splintering in 1990 of the former Italian Communist Party (PCI) into two new political parties: the Democratic Party of the Left (PDS) and Communist Refoundation (RC). The two new left-wing parties were subsequently joined by other forces on the left (Orlando's Rete, the Greens, and the left-wing Catholic MCS) in the formation of the Progressive bloc which ran a common list of candidates in the chamber and senate.[7]

The new electoral rules

Since the beginning of the 1980s, Italian political commentators, academics and journalists had been engaged in an impassioned debate on how the rules of the game could be changed to bring about a more responsible political system. By the end of the 1980s two conclusions were generally accepted. First, in order to change the system of government dominated by the political parties, the electoral rules of proportional representation used since the beginning of the Italian Republic had to be abandoned. PR allowed the centrist parties, such as the DC and PSI, to occupy governmental power on an indefinite basis. The most viable alternative seemed to be the adoption of a first-past-the-post, single-member district system.

Second, it became clear during the course of the 1980s that substantial electoral reform could not be introduced through parliament. Parliament had stifled previous attempts such as, for example, during the deliberations of the Bozzi Commission in the mid-1980s. Given the obstructive tactics of the anti-reform bloc within parliament and the government, the proponents of electoral reform felt that change could only come through the mobilization of public opinion through referenda - i.e. by abolishing the old laws and forcing parliament to draft new laws in line with the public's majoritarian orientation. The referendum campaign led by Mario Segni succeeded in abolishing preference voting within the PR system in 1991 and then introducing single-member districts for senate elections (18 April 1993).

The latter referendum was particularly noteworthy given the overwhelming vote in favor of abolishing the old PR system: the positive votes represented an absolute majority of Italians voting and of those with the right to vote. Thus, the vote was a clear indication of voter sentiment to move away from proportional representation toward a more majoritarian system. The 1993 referendum result turned the tide against the anti-electoral reform faction within parliament and, especially, the DC-PSI-led government.[8] The avalanche of votes garnered by the single-member district proposal forced parliament to pass a law in August 1993 to change the basis of national elections. Given that the 1993 referendum had changed, on a *de facto* basis, the electoral rules for the senate but not for the chamber, parliament was forced to adopt new rules for the chamber. The final decision was to introduce a system of election for the chamber which was very similar to the one introduced by the referendum in the senate.

The new rules did away with proportional representation in the allocation of three-quarters of the electoral seats, but kept PR in the allocation of the remaining 25 per cent. The bulk of the seats were, thus, distributed on the basis of a one ballot first-past-the-post system in which the candidate receiving the plurality of the votes was awarded the seat (Bartolini and D'Alimonte, 1994).

During the debate on the new electoral law, a number of political formations led by PDS Secretary Achille Occhetto argued for the adoption of electoral rules used in the selection of city mayors based on a French-style, two-ballot majority system. The proposal was considered potentially damaging by those forces (especially the ex-DC and former governing parties) not willing to join either a left-wing or right-wing political bloc. The bulk of the DC hoped to retain its role as an identifiable centrist bloc open to dialogue with both left and right and thereby perpetuate its role as linchpin in the political system.

The Distribution of Votes and Seats in Parliament

The senators and deputies taking their seats in the 12th legislature were not significantly different from those who participated in previous legislatures from the point of view of numerous important characteristics. The average age, socioeconomic background and education of the parliamentarians in the 12th did not significantly change from what existed in the 11th legislature. What was instead significantly different in the composition of parliament in the two legislatures was the MPs' political backgrounds.[9] As is illustrated in Table 1, 66 per cent of the deputies and 56 per cent of the senators elected in 1994 had no previous experience in parliament. The least politically experienced parliamentarians were those elected by Forza Italia, while those with the greatest experience were members of the opposition bloc representing the Greens and the PDS. Forza Italia MPs with previous legislative experience were linked to Marco Pannella (Emma Bonino, Marco Taradash, Giuseppe Calderisi and Sergio Staziani), or came out of the ex-Liberal Party, such as Raffaele Costa and Alfredo Biondi. A higher than average number of freshman MPs in the chamber and senate were to be found in the bulk of the other ruling parties (Lega, Alleanza Nazionale, and Centro Cristiano Democratico) and in a number of the small opposition parties such as the Rete, Patto Segni and PSI.

The electoral vote showed that the right-wing forces gathered around the Polo della Libertà (Liberty Pole) in the North (FI, Lega, CCD, Pannella) and the Polo di Buon Governo (Good Government Pole) in the South (FI, AN, CCD)[10] had gained a major victory (see Tables 2 and 3). With 46.4 per cent of the vote in the chamber of deputies and 42.7 per cent in the senate, these two geographic electoral alliances had soundly beaten the leftist list which did not go beyond one-third of the votes in either the chamber or senate. The ex-Christian Democrats grouped around the PPI and Patto Segni only received one-eighth of the popular vote. Forza Italia emerged from the 1994 parliamentary elections as Italy's largest party and Berlusconi as the undisputed prime minister-designate.

The right-wing coalition had clearly ridden the widespread anti-incumbency and anti-party sentiment in getting their candidates elected to parliament. However, this did not mean that they were ready to govern. Among the governing parties approximately 75 per cent of the MPs reported no previous experience in parliament or in national and regional politics. The MPs from the majority coalition were essentially political neophytes, empowered by the election results to rule the country.

The positive side of the elections was that MPs belonging to the majority were not wedded to previous policies and represented a significant turnover in the ruling political class. But the negative side of the change was that the new MPs had to supply themselves with all of the essential notions of how to operate successfully within a legislative arena: they had to internalize in short order the written, as well as unwritten, rules of the political game, learn how to operate within the institutions of government and parliament and come up with a government programme from scratch.

As was the case for all of the party platforms during the electoral campaign (but especially that of Forza Italia), there was a strong emphasis on general principles and objectives, but little on how specific policies were to be implemented in the short and medium-term. As a consequence, the new government had to improvise a governmental programme and sift out the various (and at times contradictory) objectives expressed by the victorious parties during the electoral campaign.

The lack of familiarity with parliamentary procedure and norms quickly manifested itself in the selection of heads of the two chambers, parliamentary committees and government ministers. In choosing the heads of the standing committees, the majority turned to a number of representatives with particular policy axes to grind (Gustavo Selva, Vittorio Sgarbi, Tiziana Maiolo, Marco Taradash, Mirko Tremaglia, Tiziana Parenti).[11] All of these appointments within parliament and the selection of ministers in the new Berlusconi government delivered a clear political message - that the majority expected to govern according to its own perspective and priorities and break with the tradition of the past in which the government sought to extend its influence in parliament by making periodic use of the ideas and political support of opposition MPs.

Continuity within change: the Berlusconi Government between Partyocracy and Parliamentary Democracy

In a paper presented prior to the 1994 parliamentary elections, Mauro Calise (1994) set out to distinguish the structural differences separating three sets of democratic political regimes - presidential, parliamentary and partyocracy[12] - to illustrate the reasons why the Italian political system was going through a total collapse. In his analysis, Calise points to the structural defects of Italian government and decision-making which made it impossible to shift government priorities and programmes away from those centreed on the primacy of party-dominance and patronage orientation which led the system down the road to *Tangentopoli* (or "kick-back city").

Calise attributes three major characteristics to the pre-1994 partyocratic approach to government:

1. the head of government is selected on the basis of extra-electoral criteria;

2. both the executive and legislative branches are dependent upon party organization for their electoral support, as well as for the recruitment of the leadership cohort;

3. collegial leadership in the government and parliament.

We will add to these three characteristics five additional features which distinguish Italy's version of partyocratic parliamentary regime:

4. the stability of the government depends on the stability of the party organization/s. If governing parties are destabilized by internal or external conflicts, the ramifications will be felt by the entire governmental coalition and institutions;

5. the introduction of an unrestricted, winner-takes-all system;

6. the move from responsible to responsive government, where government responds to increasing demands no matter how senseless they might be;

7. the disregard for the limits of the law to a point where legality is determined by winners and losers in the ballot box;

8. the continued effort to centralize decision-making in the hands of national executives and party elites.

If we use these eight criteria to evaluate the politics of the post-March 1994 period, it is clear how much continuity there really was between the pre and post-1994 election governments. To begin with, the very designation of Berlusconi as prime minister was the result of a completely extra-parliamentary and post-election operation (Statera, 1994). Prior to the March elections, the members of his coalition could not even agree on who belonged to the electoral alliance (*Polo della Libertà*) and what the commitments were to govern together. Umberto Bossi had fired up his party's convention in Bologna at the beginning of February 1994 by stating that the Lega would never enter a coalition with "the fascists" of Alleanza Nazionale and kept repeating his position during and after the election campaign. All that Berlusconi was able to do prior to the election was to stitch together a *tactical* electoral alliance in different parts of the country in the hope that electoral victory would induce a change of opinion in the Lega. The tactic proved to be a winner, but it took Berlusconi another month to convince Bossi that he had to swallow his pride and agree to govern with the MSI-AN.[13]

As had been the case after previous elections, the setting-up of the Berlusconi government had to be mediated among the parties for a considerable amount of time before agreement was reached. After the election, according to Italian political tradition, the President of the Republic asks the leader of the relative majority party (in this case, Forza Italia) to form a government, but he should also be careful that the designated leader is certain to put together a governing majority. This requires that the parties agree on a common candidate for prime minister, be willing to become part of a governing cabinet and provide the necessary support in parliament. Agreement was reached among the right-wing parties on 28 April and Berlusconi was then asked by the President of the Republic to form a government. The following day the prime minister-designate met with Bossi and Fini to divide up the ministerial posts.

Throughout the seven-month tenure of the Berlusconi government relations between the party leaders were highlighted by a traditional collegial running of government and parliament by the majority political parties. As in previous governments, this was realized through the holding of periodic summits to iron-out differences among the parties and decide how to proceed with important issues in both the parliamentary and government arenas. The Berlusconi government was finally brought down when these summits could no longer paper over the deep policy differences which had isolated the Lega from the rest of the coalition. Once again, an Italian government fell without waiting for a formal vote of no-confidence in parliament. Berlusconi resigned because he had lost the confidence of one of his coalition partners and did not want to wait for a vote of no-confidence from one of the two chambers in parliament.

The other characteristic of partyocracy that continued unabated in the Berlusconi period was the role played by the party organizations in choosing candidates for leadership posts in parliament as well as in government. The designation of Carlo Scognamiglio as president of the senate, and Irene

Pivetti as president of the chamber of deputies, represented an initial demonstration of political power by the new coalition; it was also a reflection of the winner-take-all ethic adhered to by the victors. The unwillingness to maintain a clear separation between the allocation of posts in the legislative branch and those in the executive, indeed represented a break from the past, but, paradoxically, it also represented a greater triumph of partyocracy over the institutionalization of parliament within the Italian political system.

Ever since 1976, the presidency of the chamber of deputies had been assigned to the chief opposition party, PCI, as had been the case for the presidencies of the inter-parliamentary special committees, such as the one on the mafia and the regions. The ability to distribute these posts above and beyond considerations of majority/minority splits was a concession to the legislature's institutional autonomy, as well as to the prospects of cooperation between the opposition and the majority in arriving at consensual agreements on key legislation and stipulation of the rules of the game (Leonardi, Nanetti, Pasquino, 1978; Manzella, 1977).

Consensual agreements reached their peak during the 1976-79 "historic compromise" period. However, the amount of consensus interlinking the government and parliament was whittled down in subsequent years. Starting in 1983, the majority systematically sought to reduce the opposition's influence in the choice of policies and to shore-up the majority's internal cohesion in parliament while progressively isolating the opposition. [14]

After the 1994 elections the Berlusconi government continued this trend to the point of finally breaking off any contact with the opposition. The governing coalition demanded full control over positions of influence in parliament and negated any role by the opposition in the decision-making process. Typical of the government's rejection of a working relationship with the opposition in parliament was Berlusconi's 10 October polemical speech in the chamber of deputies against the legislature and legislative procedures as a waste of time and an impediment to the realization of the government's political agenda.

Having rejected any common ground between the government and the opposition in the distribution of parliamentary posts and in the forging of a parliamentary agenda, the government faced an increasingly difficult time in finding support in parliament for its legislative programme. As with previous governments, the Berlusconi government did not have a clear majority in parliament. In the senate the coalition was several votes shy of a majority, but it was able to get Carlo Scognamiglio elected president of the senate and receive a vote of confidence for the government through defections from the opposition parties and support from a majority of the 10 appointed life-time senators.

Rather than trying to find compromise solutions to government legislative proposals in order to broaden its support, the Berlusconi government embarked on a strategy of trying to detach individual MPs from the opposition parliamentary party groups or entice whole party groups to join the government coalition. From the beginning, Berlusconi and his allies tried to convince Segni's Patto per l'Italia and the PPI to join the government coalition en masse. When this failed, Forza Italia was successful in convincing individual MPs to abandon the PPI and Segni groups. The tactic achieved various levels of success throughout the period under consideration.[15]

The use of this tactic was heightened and directed toward the Lega once this party demonstrated its displeasure at the lack of interest on the part of the other government coalition parties toward regional electoral reform, pension reform and anti-trust legislation. When Bossi refused to moderate his dissent, the attack was directed toward undermining his leadership within his own party and, when that failed, to promote a schism in the party. Thus, the dual strategy of, on the one hand, reinforcing the government's voting bloc in parliament and, on the other hand, strengthening Berlusconi's position within the coalition through individual defections and the promotion of party splits, led to an overall destabilization of the governing parties and, subsequently, the coalition. The government fell more as a result of its own internal conflicts than of the opposition's determined efforts.[16] The attempt to weaken Bossi within his own party led to his necessary withdrawal from the coalition. Bossi had to take his party out of the coalition, or face its complete absorption into Forza Italia. Survival of the Lega as an independent political entity meant that it had to be withdrawn from the coalition.

Berlusconi, on the other hand, interpreted Bossi's withdrawal of support as a betrayal of the commitment made to the voters to govern together and prevent the left from coming to power. What was missing in the Berlusconi analysis of his own demise was a critical view of what went wrong within the coalition. He had not understood that operating within a partyocratic regime, his tenure in office was guaranteed only so long as he could keep his allies happy and working together. Success within his coalition was not dependent upon the amount of power he could personally accumulate, or on his increased leverage over his political allies, but on the cohesiveness of his coalition.[17]

We have already mentioned the penchant of the Berlusconi coalition to treat state-derived patronage as a winner-takes-all system. As had been the case before with Craxi and the DC, the spoils of government were conceived of as being for the taking by the victorious parties. This orientation was immediately realized with the "occupation" of the RAI, the state-owned broadcasting corporation. All of the strategic positions within the corporation were allocated to Berlusconi's Fininvest associates, family friends, or ideologically-aligned individuals. Illustrative of this approach were the actions of one Forza Italia RAI appointee, who toured the corridors of RAI's Saxa Rubra headquarters immediately after the election wrapped in a Forza Italia flag and shouting that the "communists" would be thrown out once the Berlusconi government was formed. Political reliability before professional competence became the hallmark of public appointees to positions of power within the public sector.

Such a criterion had long been tolerated (and implemented) in the designation of governmental appointees to public corporations and agencies in years past. However, it had been excluded in the recruitment and promotion of personnel within institutions which were, by law and tradition, separated from the practise, such as the top echelons in the Bank of Italy. In finding a replacement for Lamberto Dini, the Berlusconi government (and especially proponents of the MSI-Alleanza Nazionale) tried to implement the same winner-takes-all rule. The result was an immediate and negative reaction from the financial markets which began to doubt the trustworthiness of the ruling coalition in financial matters.[18] The desire to occupy all of the available positions of power was pushed to the point of putting on hold any further privatization of state-controlled enterprises, despite the fact that privatization had been on the top of the Liberty Pole's election platform.

During the 1994 electoral campaign, Berlusconi gave considerable voice to responsive politics by suggesting that a future government controlled by the right could provide individual, as well as group, economic benefits without tax increases. He advocated a flat 30 per cent tax rate and a balanced budget, and he promised to create a million new jobs within the first year of government without raising new taxes. At a local level, special programmes were promised to meet longstanding local aspirations tied to the realization of large public works projects. In Sicily, Forza Italia promised public funds to build the Messina Straits bridge connecting Sicily with the mainland, while in Calabria it promised the completion of the Gioia Tauro harbor and coal-burning power plant.

Once the campaign was over, these promises were quietly dropped, but the hopes they generated among important interest groups proved to be politically effective. Contrary to the economic programmes of centrist and rightist parties in other parts of Europe, Berlusconi's political message was an optimistic one, that prosperity was just around the corner and the period of economic sacrifice implemented by the Amato and Ciampi governments was over.

The conduct of the national electoral campaign created a significant amount of tension between the parties and the judiciary during the 1993-94 period. The unfolding of the Cusani trial for the Enimont scandal highlighted the involvement of the previous political leadership (e.g. Forlani, Craxi, Cirino Pomicino) in the exchange of influence over public policy for bribes. The usual defence articulated by the accused was that: they were oblivious to what their subordinates were doing; they were victims of a political conspiracy of which the magistrates were the tools; and every other party in the system was engaged in the same practices.

A similar approach was used when charges of financial impropriety started to lap at the doors of the Fininvest empire during and after the electoral campaign. The reaction of Berlusconi was that he was being persecuted by a judiciary trying to advance the interests of the left and hurt the electoral fortunes of his right-wing coalition. After the elections, the Berlusconi government began a concerted campaign to draw a *cordon sanitaire* around Fininvest to prevent the judges from investigating his company's involvement in corruption. This attempt eventually backfired when the government implemented the Biondi decree on preventive custody, immediately dubbed by the press "the safety net for thieves". The decree was issued on 13 July, and one week later it was withdrawn.

Equally disturbing was the cat-and-mouse game the prime minister's brother, Paolo Berlusconi, played with police and magistrates in June when a warrant was issued for his arrest, but he remained in hiding. Once Paolo Berlusconi turned himself in, he was released into protective custody in his brother's summer villa in Sardinia. These moves and later ones assumed by the justice minister ordering ministerial inspections of the Milan pool headed by Borrelli and the Palermo magistrates investigating the mafia, were illustrative of the increasingly instrumental use of the law and of the judicial system as a political tool in the struggle between government and opposition.

The final characteristic of partyocracy is the attempt by national party leaders to centralize power away from the periphery. In order to enhance their bargaining position, central elites need to have a free hand and not be tied down by the agreements, preferences and exigencies of those representing the party at a regional or local level. During 1994 this centralizing dynamic was evident in: the selection process engaged in by all the political party forces in choosing candidates to contest the parliamentary elections; the still-birth of federal reform of the Italian state which had represented such a large part of the Lega's political platform; and the centralization of power by national ministries away from regions (e.g. powers in agricultural policy) and localities (control over ports, beaches and health spas) (Volcic and Chiti, 1995).

In the progressive camp, the selection of candidates for the 1994 elections contained a strong central component for the purpose of maintaining "a balance" among candidates from all parties elected to parliament. It was in this manner that the PSI, Greens, AD, Rete, and representatives of other minor parties of the left succeeded in assuring their election to the senate and chamber of deputies. Interestingly, many of these minor progressive party leaders insisted on being presented in electoral districts in northern and central Italy where the PDS had its strongest voting base, rather than where these parties had historically gained their greatest number of seats and votes.

The right made its deals in two separate sections of the country, but in both cases the process was top-down. This was particularly easy for Forza Italia because, prior to the electoral campaign, it had no local party organizational structure. The party was constituted as a combination of local branches of Fininvest's Publitalia advertising agencies and Milan soccer clubs. Political content was supplied by information packs distributed by Forza Italia's central headquarters on the basis of an inductive process in which voters were asked in telephone surveys to list the country's most important problems and what they would like to see in an ideal political party platform. It was on this basis that Forza Italia's electoral programme was formulated.

Among the parties of the right, the Lega was the one most constrained by the wishes of its local leaders. The Lega was, to a great extent, a federal party composed of the Lega Lombarda in Lombardy and other locally based groups outside Lombardy such as the Liga Veneta and autonomously oriented movements in Piedmont, Friuli, Trentino and Liguria. The local branches of MSI-Alleanza Nazionale instead fell into step with the directives coming from Rome in the hopes that Fini would deliver the party from the political isolation it had endured for so long (Verzichielli, 1994).

The political forces representing the catholic centre also engaged in a considerable amount of centralized decision-making in the selection of candidates. In the case of the Patto Segni and PPI, the centralization of candidate selection was justified on the basis of preventing the insertion of local figures compromised by past scandals. This was the reason given for not accepting the candidacy of Ciriaco De Mita in Irpinia, but the net effect of the procedure was to emasculate the ability of the parties to choose candidates with local roots and support. Thus, the anti-corruption drive within the centrist parties was presented as the rationale for the centralization of decision-making in the selection of candidates for parliamentary seats. Centralization was not seen as the emasculation of local control and linkages with civil society which was one of the main objectives of the change in electoral rules in 1993.

● The fate of the 1994 electoral reform illustrates the point that the objectives of public policy can be significantly undermined by implementation. Part of the argument for the adoption of the first-past-the-post system was to encourage the selection of candidates with local recognition and roots in the community. Representation was supposed to become more personalized and direct, as was the case in the election of city mayors. Instead, the manner in which candidates were selected across the spectrum led to an even greater subordination of local candidates to national leaders. A number of representatives were selected with no ties to the local community and thus became even more subject to the discipline of national party leadership.

The reform of the Italian state along federal lines, advocated strongly by the Lega and pledged by the Berlusconi government, represents another one of those "grand reforms" which have periodically cropped up to animate the Italian political debate. These grand reforms generate a lot of newsprint and discussions on television talk shows, but produce very few concrete results. The proposal of federal reform produced in September by the Speroni Commission was not well received by the governing parties and led the government to completely abandon the idea of federalism. The government sought instead to increase the powers of the centre by reimposing control over the periphery.

The process of centralization continued until November when it was significantly weakened by the impact of the devastating floods which hit northern Italy (especially Piedmont, Lombardy and Liguria). Public outrage over delays in emergency aid and alleged failure to warn the local population forced the minister of the Interior, Roberto Maroni of the Lega, to sack two provincial prefects in the flood-ravaged areas and give powers to manage the reconstruction process to the regions and communes. The centralizers had to beat a quick retreat, but even this event did not lead to any significant shift in the government's policies toward federalism.

During the rest of the month of November and the first three weeks of December, the government had to beat back the criticism directed toward it by strikers protesting against its financial bill[19] and the growing pressure from the Milan pool of investigating judges. On 14 December, the judges questioned Berlusconi for seven hours concerning the alleged payment of bribes by Fininvest to the financial police. One week later, the government entered its death throes and Berlusconi formally resigned on 22 December, bringing an end to the first stage of the Second Republic.

Conclusions

What can be learned from the rise and fall of the Berlusconi government in relation to Italy's transition to the Second Republic? The politics of 1994 show that, to a large extent, the anticipated transition never took place; the actions of the Berlusconi government did not build upon the changes produced in the Italian political superstructure before the March 1994 elections. Rather, the politics of the right-wing coalition reflected the political principles, policy approaches, and management of patronage that had existed during the First Republic.

The fundamental objective of the Berlusconi government was to reestablish and preserve the policy status quo, which had been put in doubt by the reforms initiated by the Amato and Ciampi governments, while trying to stop, and even reverse, the broader systemic change sparked by the referendum campaigns, drive against corruption, struggle against the mafia, and debate on federalism.

The precise policy orientation of Forza Italia remained undefined for a long time, given the heterogeneous nature of the party and the contradictory positions voiced within its leadership framework. During the electoral campaign, Forza Italia seemed to be much closer in its political programme to Bossi than to Fini. However, once Silvio Berlusconi became prime minister, his public policy instincts and the need to preserve his economic empire drove him in the direction of favouring the alliance with Alleanza Nazionale and isolating Bossi within the coalition.

During the last six months of 1994, the label of Polo della Libertà was redefined to include Alleanza Nazionale and to encompass the entire governmental coalition. The expansion of the Polo to include Fini represented a significant political defeat for the Lega within the coalition; the tandem Berlusconi-Fini became the dominant pillar in the government and Umberto Bossi was cast into the role of necessary, but bothersome, ally.

Thus, the right-wing coalition that came to power in May 1994 was significantly divided internally, even more so than had been the case in the coalition governments presided over by the Christian Democratic Party in the past. The consequence of the rift between the Lega ("liberal") and Alleanza Nazionale ("corporatist") wings of the coalition was to reinforce the dominance of Forza Italia over the coalition. Once the contradiction between the structural reform programme championed by the Lega and the fundamental conservative orientation of the former fascists could no longer be papered over, the ambiguities within the Berlusconi coalition were to have a devastating impact on the government's internal stability and external credibility.

Rather than solving problems the Berlusconi government allowed them to fester and rather than seeking solutions to important political issues in parliament, the government sought to engage in confrontations with the opposition, the judiciary, the Bank of Italy, border nations[20] and international economic and financial interests. During its seven months in office, the Berlusconi government was able to transform itself from an instrument that might resolve Italy's political and economic problems, to the source of these problems. It is too early to tell whether a new period of reforms, this time in terms of governmental structural policies, will be initiated, but it is clear that the management of Italy's financial, economic, and social policies requires more than a temporary political fix.

Notes

1. The left-right dimension came back strongly during the electoral campaign due mainly to Berlusconi's reference to the progressive coalition and the PDS as "communists", anti-market, anti-democratic, and anti-reform.

2. Benvenuto went on to form the Rinascita Socialista movement which later went into Alleanza Democratica (AD).

3. The ex-Craxi group eventually broke off from Del Turco to form the Federazione Liberal Socialista and joined forces with Forza Italia.

4. Craxi established residence in what was formerly his summer home in Hammamet, Tunisia, and in 1994 his wife was granted Tunisian citizenship.

5. The Enimont affair was considered to be the "mother" of all kick-back scandals due to the huge sums, 153 billion lire or 96 million dollars, involved. During the span of three days between 21 and 24 July 1993, Gabriele Cagliari (ex-president of ENI) and Raul Gardini committed suicide.

6. The collapse of the DC in Lazio and Sicily led to a large migration of former members of the Andreotti faction to the AN-MSI lists.

7. In a number of electoral districts in Piedmont, Lazio, Sardinia, Sicily, and Basilicata, the Greens, Rete, PSI, and Sardinian Action Party tried to present independent lists separate from those proposed by the Progressive bloc. The result was the loss of crucial seats in the chamber of deputies and senate which gave the right a majority even though they received only 42.7 per cent in the senate and 46.4 per cent in the chamber of deputies elections.

8. A number of opposition parties were also against a change in the proportional system. Most notably, opposition came from Rifondazione Comunista, MSI, and Rete.

9. In the previous parliament (1992-94) freshman deputies constituted 43 per cent of the total, and in the 1987-1992 parliament, one out of four were new members (Verzichelli, 1994: 717).

10. The electoral strategy of Forza Italia in 1994 was constructed around two separate alliances, respectively called Liberty Pole which excluded the former fascist MSI in the North and Good Government Pole in the South which excluded the Lega.

11. Typical examples of the grinding of personal axes by the right-wing majority's appointees to the presidencies of parliamentary committees are Taradash's presentation of a dossier against the former RAI executives to the Rome Public Prosecutor and request to press for criminal charges after he was elected president of the RAI parliamentary committee and Maiolo's tour of Italian prisons to voice the complaints of detainees in high security facilities against the limitation of personal freedoms in the use of telephones and access to the media, a tour she initiated as the president of the chamber's standing committee on justice.

12. Calise defines particracy as a case "where a party holds monopolistic control over the governmental process" (Calise, 1994: 444). We prefer to use the term partyocracy to particracy (and will use it throughout this chapter) because we believe that partyocracy does not present a separate and district case from the two other systems. Rather, partyocracy represents a particular type of presidential or parliamentary regime.

13. Giorgio Galli (1995: 41) quotes Berlusconi as having stated that: "The forces that are today in government did not present themselves to the voters as a governing coalition. The agreement was only a technical one tied to the electoral rules; it was not direct and agreed upon by the parties".

14. Agreement between the government and opposition was theorized by Enrico Berlinguer, former PCI secretary, in 1974 as a response to the need for marxist and catholic subcultures to join

together in solving Italy's social and economic problems. Between 1976 and 1979 the PCI supported one-party Christian Democratic governments in parliament based on a programmatic accord, but it never became a part of the government coalition.

15. What Forza Italia could offer these MPs was: 1. agreement to insert them in its party lists during the next election, 2. visibility in the media and 3. access to state patronage given the winner-takes-all approach to the distribution of state resources. After the 1995 regional elections, Roberto Maroni reported that, had he left the Lega with a group of deputies, Berlusconi promised his group the presidencies of the regions of the North (Corriere della Sera, 24 April 1995).

16. Why Rocco Buttiglione (PPI secretary) joined the attempt to bring down the Berlusconi government in December 1994 and then, three months later, decided to become part of the Berlusconi alliance is still a mystery. When he made his later move, only a small fraction of the PPI MPs followed him into the alliance with Forza Italia and the formation of the CDU party.

17. During the period 1980-92 a similar mistake was made by Bettino Craxi within his own party. He destroyed the PSI by accumulating too much power and he also helped to destroy the five-party coalition by encouraging an accumulation of power to the point of rejecting any moral, legal, political or institutional limitation.

18. The independence of the Bank of Italy from the Ministry of the Treasury and government-influenced appointments was also one of the commitments underwritten by previous Italian governments as part of the country's participation in the European Monetary System.

19. The Berlusconi government proposed a drastic reduction of pensions without prior consultation with the trade unions. The reaction by the organized trade union movement and opposition parties forced the government to eventually amend its proposal.

20. The Berlusconi government interrupted negotiations with Slovenia over the normalization of contacts between the two governments until the Slovenes agreed to pay compensation for property lost by Italian residents during the Tito regime.

Table 1

Length of Service of Parliamentarians Serving in the Chamber and Senate, 12th Legislature

Chamber of Deputies

Party	First	Two	Three	>Three	Total	% First term
Forza Italia	103	5	1	3	112	92
Alleanza Nazionale	80	11	5	13	109	73
Lega Nord	72	37	2	0	111	65
Centro Cristiano Democratico	18	3	2	4	27	66
Partito Popolare Italiano	17	5	6	5	33	52
La Rete	5	1	1	0	7	71
Patto Segni	9	0	2	1	12	75
Partito Democratico Sinistra	53	29	15	7	104	52
Rifondazione Comunista	24	11	2	2	39	52
Partito Socialisto Italiano	9	2	0	1	12	75
Verdi	3	4	4	0	11	27
Independent Left	20	1	0	1	22	91
Progressivi (AD, MCS, Sin.D)	10	2	2	1	15	67
Others	8	6	2	0	16	50
Total	**431**	**117**	**44**	**38**	**630**	**68**

Senate*

Party	First	Two	Three	>Three	Total	% First term
Forza Italia	34	1	1	1	37	92
Alleanza Nazionale	33	7	3	7	50	66
Lega Nord	34	22	0	0	56	61
Centro Cristiano Democratico	8	1	1	2	12	67
Partito Popolare Italiano	14	10	4	2	30	47
La Rete	5	1	0	0	6	83
Partito Democratico Sinistra	16	25	12	1	54	30
Rifondazione Comunista	8	4	1	5	18	44
Partito Socialisto Italiano	7	2	2	2	13	54
Verdi	4	2	0	1	7	57
Independent Progressives	8	2	0	1	11	73
Progressivi (AD, MCS)	10	1	0	3	14	71
Others	1	4	0	2	7	14
Total	**182**	**82**	**24**	**27**	**315**	**58**

Source: Authors' calculations based on the *Annuario Parlamentare, Dodicesima Legislatura* (Rome: *La Navicella*, 1994).

* Life appointees have not been included in the calculation.

Table 2

1994 Italian Chamber of Deputies Election Results

Party	% PR Vote	PR Seats	Single Member Seats	Total Seats
Forza Italia	21.0			
FI		25	74	99
CCD		7	22	29
UDC			4	4
PLD			2	2
Pannella			6	6
AN	13.5	22	87	109
Lega Nord	8.4	10	107	117
Panella	3.5	0	0	0
Total Right	46.4	64	302	366
PDS	20.4	37	72	109
RC	6.0	12	27	39
Greens	2.7	0	11	11
PSI	2.2	0	14	14
Rete	1.9	0	6	6
AD	1.2	0	18	18
MCS			5	5
Rinascita Socialista			1	1
Ind. Left			10	10
Total Left	34.3	49	164	213
PPI	11.1	29	4	33
Patto Segni	4.7	13	0	13
Total Centre	15.7	42	4	46
SVP	0.6	0	3	3
Unione Valdotain			1	1
Lega Meridionale	0.2	0	1	1
PSDI	0.5	0	0	0
Lega Alpina Lombarda	0.4	0	0	0
Verdi-Verdi	0.1	0	0	0
Other Leagues	0.3	0	0	0
Autonomist Lists	0.1	0	0	0
Other Lists	1.5	0	0	0
Total Others	3.6	0	5	5
Total	**100.0**	**155**	**475**	**630**

Source: Bartolini and D'Alimento (1994: Appendix).

Table 3

1994 Italian Senate Election Results

Party	% Vote	PR Seats	Single Member Seats	Total Seats
Liberty Pole	19.9			
Good Government Pole	13.7			
Forza Italia	0.5	7	25	32
CCD		2	10	12
UDC			3	3
Pannella	2.3	1	1	2
AN	6.3	13	34	47
Lega Nord		5	55	60
Total Right	**42.7**	**28**	**128**	**156**
PDS		14	46	60
RC		4	14	18
Green		0	7	7
PSI		1	11	12
Rete		4	2	6
AD		3	7	10
MCS		0	4	4
Rinascita Socialista		0	1	1
Ind. Left		0	4	4
Total Left	**32.9**	**26**	**96**	**122**
PPI		27	3	30
Patto Segni		1	0	1
Total Centre	16.7	28	3	31
SVP	0.7	0	3	3
Union Valdotain	0.1	0	1	1
Lega Alpina Lombarda	0.7	1	0	1
Lista Magris	0.2	0	1	1
Pensioners	0.8	0	0	0
Sardinian Action Party	0.3	0	0	0
PSDI	0.2	0	0	0
Greens-Greens	0.2	0	0	0
Other Leagues	1.0	0	0	0
Autonomous Lists	0.5	0	0	0
Other Lists	3.1	0	0	0
Total Other	**7.8**	**1**	**5**	**6**
Total	**100.0**	**83**	**232**	**315**

Source: Bartolini and Alimonte (1994: p.636).

References

Bartolini, S. and D'Alimonte, R. (1994) "Plurality, Competition and Party Realignment in Italy: The 1994 Parliamentary Elections", mimeo. English version of "La competizione maggioritaria: Le origini elettorali del parlamento diviso", *Rivista Italiana di Scienza Politica,* XXIV, December, pp. 631-686.

Buonadonna, S. and Ginex, R. (1994) *Guida alla seconda repubblica,* Palermo, Arbor.

Calise, M. (1994) "The Italian Particracy: Beyond President and Parliament", *Political Science Quarterly,* Vol. 109, No. 3, Special Issue, pp. 441-460.

Fedele, M. (1994) *Democrazia referendaria,* Rome, Donizelli Editore.

Galli, G. (1995) *Diario politico 1994,* Milan, Kaos.

Gilbert, M. (1995) *The Italian Revolution,* Boulder, Westview Press

Leonardi, R. Nanetti, R. and Pasquino, G. (1978) "Institutionalization of Parliament and Parliamentarization of Parties in Italy", *Legislative Studies Quarterly,* Vol. 3, No. 1, February, pp. 161-186.

Manzella, A. (1977), *Il parlamento,* Bologna, Il Mulino.

Mignone, M.B. (1995), *Italy Today,* New York, Peter Lang.

Statera, G. (1994) *Il volto seduttivo del potere,* Rome, SEAM.

Verzichielli, L. (1994) "Gli eletti", *Rivista Italiana di Scienza Politica,* XXIV, December, pp. 715-739.

Volcic, D. and Chiti, V. (1995) *Intervista sul federalismo,* Florence, Giunti.

I. institutions

two

Competitive democracy and the new rules of the game

Giuliano Urbani

The Misadventures of Virtue: the Uncompleted Reform and its Effects

Responding to the referendum result of 18 April 1993, the parliament of the 11th legislature approved the reform which changed the Italian electoral system to a majoritarian one. This represented the most high-profile and far-reaching reform made to the Italian political system in the 1980s and 1990s. Predictably, the effects of the new rules have been of great relevance: a deep and accelerated 'realignment' of the forces in parliament; the greatest turnover of elected representatives in the republic's history; and politicians justifying their existence as an expression of 'civil society' as opposed to the 'political society', which had entered deep crisis.

The government created by popular vote in March 1994 was an expression of a coalition of parties which, in the spirit of the new rules, had aggregated around the 'Good Government' alliance (Forza Italia and the Lega Nord) and the 'Freedom Alliance' (Forza Italia and the National Alliance)[1] with the support of movements, groups and individual candidates (from the Christian Democrats centre to Pannella's "Reformists") who shared the electoral policies and platforms of the moderate electoral blocs.

Notwithstanding the scepticism of some observers and the preoccupations of others, one can argue that the electoral reform was largely a response to public demand for change. However, it would be wrong and dangerous to maintain that reform - and that reform in particular - had solved all the problems of a complex transitional phase. In fact, the growing difficulties that the Berlusconi government encountered up to its resignation in December 1994, demonstrated two fundamental factors. Firstly, the transition from the First to the Second Republic needed to be completed and perfected, taking into account the election result and the manner in which it was translated into parliamentary representation. Secondly, however incisive it may have been, the electoral reform represented only one segment - and certainly not a negligible one - of a wider reform of democratic institutions that could no longer be delayed. In political terms, parliamentary representation is configured as a sub-system of the wider and more complex institutional system, which needed to be synthesised and co-ordinated.

The need to empirically verify these institutional innovations, including those relating to the delicate matter of electoral reform, should not shock us. The exercise of democracy in so-called 'complex societies' requires a growing rate of flexibility and adaptation. Often courageous and far-sighted reforms meet unforeseen obstacles, or are met with cultural resistance that is not easily overcome. Italy's contemporary political history provides evidence of this. Notably, the extension of universal male suffrage and the introduction of proportional representation - which should have achieved the 'entrance of the masses into the state' after the First World War - are examples of how the results differed from the intended goal. In fact, the patent impossibility of constructing a coalition government represented a powerful incentive to divide the democratic framework, isolating its moderate components and radicalizing the latent conflicts between social movements, not all of whom wanted to integrate into the state and share the responsibilities of governing. Having reached this point, there was an indirect, but decisive, impulse for an authoritarian solution which was represented by the march on Rome and the beginning of fascist power.

Obviously, this historical reference is meaningful only for underlining how no reform, especially if it operates on only one of the many pieces that make up the mosaic of a highly structured political system, can be sheltered from unwanted effects. In our recent case, Italy's majoritarian electoral reform assumed a strategic function, localising and focusing on the nerve-centre of the institutional crisis. Some (Warner and Gambetta, 1994) have pinpointed a diversionary aim, in that by concentrating citizens' attention and political debate on the 'rules of the game', it would be possible to avoid a final showdown that would have resulted in a deeper and more structured change. Without indulging in a conspiracy theory and endorsing a demonic representation of the political and cultural forces that produced the electoral innovation on a wave of public pressure within a narrow time-frame, it is timely to critically question the level of change that the electoral reform was supposed to bring about.

From this perspective, it is undeniable that, for example, the parliamentary over-representation of a force like the Lega Nord - which was a minor partner in the majority coalition and electorally sited in a strategic, but territorially circumscribed area of the country - was one of the fruits made possible by a one-round majoritarian system with a proportional component. This is a system that constrains forces to form heterogeneous coalitions, operating in a contradictory cultural framework, in which intolerance for a 'consociational' democracy model is diffuse, but where the acquisition of rules for a 'competitive' democracy have not yet matured. Therefore, the electoral mechanism has ended up distorting the logic of functional coalition building aimed at creating 'good governments'. From this point of view, the inevitable construction of anomalous frameworks surely represents the antecedent of the relationship between the Lega and the other coalition partners. But the stresses produced by the electoral framework also caused disagreements and resentment within the internal relationships of the opposition forces. In many respects, the same difficulties experienced in producing a governing structure actually resurfaced as political problems that were not prevented or resolved because they were sacrificed to the immediate logic of constructing an alliance amongst very different partners. From here perhaps came many of the reservations and challenges to the Berlusconi government, even from quarters that were not prejudicially hostile.

From a pragmatic and secular perspective that does not confuse the technical instrument of the electoral system with ideological dogma, one needs to readdress the issue of having one round or two rounds of voting, in a rational manner, taking stock of the more general goals to which this choice must be subordinated. One should also be mindful of the fact that, without eroding the majoritarian component (after all, an electoral system can still be 70 or 80 per cent majoritarian), the eventual revision of the electoral rules was considered to be part of an institutional reform that still had not taken off. In the past few months, those who have experienced resistance to innovation from large sections of the civil service and those who have had to deal with a pile of problems and the urgency of implementing radical and courageous solutions within the bureaucracy, can specifically attest to this with conviction and vigour. Reform of the state needs a governing philosophy that brings governing responsibilities to the fore and makes them as distinct as possible. But, in keeping with a competitive spirit and a critical view of that consociational methodology which degenerated into the pure practice of dividing out power, we must avoid the surplus of conflict that impedes the correct functioning of the bureaucratic machine. In this sense, even the output derived from the operation of the electoral mechanism constitutes an *intentional* effect of the referendum strategy that risks being transformed into a *perverse* effect on the functioning of parliamentary democracy.

A Manageable State of Conflict

The distinction in political science between *consociational* democracy, *competitive* democracy and *conflictual* democracy, which is crucial to my argument, has already been introduced. When the very categories of scientific thought break into political debate, often burdening it with inappropriate interpretations, it is necessary to recuperate the comparative dimension in which concepts and typologies regain their meaning and importance. In fact, comparative politics represents not only a method through which hypotheses of a more or less abstract nature can be subjected to control and eventual generalisation, but also constitutes a growing field of study within political science as a whole.

Obviously, this type of analysis relates to our subject and draws on the historical character of all the political phenomena under discussion (and thus on the actions of political actors, their 'intention' etc). Political scientists should be aware of the limits within all conventional classification systems that represent a generalisation of specific cases which have some characteristics in common. The usefulness of typologies must always be judged by the aims of the empirical investigation and will grow if it is functional to that investigation. In this sense, it is only with difficulty that a scientific analysis of political systems can be separated from an examination of the need for the stability, efficiency and legitimacy that the democratic order must achieve in order to satisfy public expectations of the political class - especially in critical situations such as the one found in Italy in the past few years. This political class cannot be restricted to that found in formal representative institutions, harbouring its own interests and making it an expression of legitimacy that is inevitably oriented towards conserving the old status quo. In fact, in a dynamic of accelerated change, the role of a new elite, expressions of idealism, cultures and models of innovative social organization become essential. From this perspective, in our reflections on good government (Urbani and Carnazza, 1994) we sought to strictly combine the definition of a radically reformed political-institutional order with a commensurately radical alternation of political elites.

This brief digression on the character, limits and functional implications of scientific reflection when it is applied to the terribly urgent and concrete problems of institutional reorganization and political reform, allows us to deepen the distinction between the different types of democracy which, according to a well-known literature (Dahl, 1971; Lijphart, 1984), manifests itself primarily in mechanisms that are tied to the production of a government's parliamentary representation and creation. Between these two phases there is a connection that can aid the establishment of a virtuous cycle: if the level of social representation of political representatives is high (that is, if the political representation is legitimized and the turnover of elites is smooth), the government's actions will be more effective. In other words, the output of institutions of political representation will grow in concrete terms.

Some scholars have argued that when democracies are analyzed from a comparative perspective, their 'operative' output does not vary much, regardless of whether a majoritarian or consociational-consensual model is in force. But this is a purely academic and formal observation. In fact, the point is not to compare the abstract capabilities of two or more types of democracies in terms of the legitimacy of their political classes. Instead, one must understand which model is more appropriate to the conditions underlying the development of a specific political regime and of a specific historical and cultural conflict. Even though it is a well-worn truth, one can argue that a simple majoritarian paradigm (that is, where representatives are elected directly through the selection of a single candidate for each seat, without the backup of a proportional component and with an executive that is the direct expression and imperative of the majority in parliament) is more suited to a society that is culturally and 'structurally' homogeneous; that is, societies with a diffuse and shared 'civic culture' (Almond and Verba, 1963) and which are relatively stable due to a sufficient level of economic development (Lipset, 1963). Alternatively, so-called plural societies, in which marked differences in income distribution and access to resources persist, and where there are religious, ethnic-linguistic, ideological and other cleavages, seem to have to tone down the social effects of the political process through a recourse to 'consociational' rules.

Therefore, in mixed situations a problem arises quite dramatically where civil, social and economic development produce a dynamic of change that is rarely governed or directed from the political sphere, but which expresses an ideological-cultural identity and localised characteristics capable of conditioning the concrete functioning of political forces (and thus of democracy as well). The Italian case can legitimately be placed in this category, as demonstrated by the 12th Legislature, which was created after the electoral earthquake of March 1994. In this parliament there co-existed political forces that were the expression of a radical metamorphosis of electoral behaviour (the 'behavioural thaw' of political choices, as some social psychologists would say) and which were sited, despite everything, in cultures defined by traditional organizational localities or by territorially based identifications. One may observe that these characteristics are present in both the political and parliamentary arenas. On the side of the Polo, Forza Italia, in its original form a moderate party with marked personal leadership and the strong characteristics of a 'movement of opinion', coexisted with a more traditional actor, Alleanza Nazionale and with the Lega Nord, a movement that in many respects defies traditional classification. On the progressive opposition's side, the central role was played by a force whose ideological and organizational base was very old and substantially traditional - the PDS. Obviously, similar considerations are just as valid in relation to the tormented fragmentation of the Popular party (in all its manifestations) which became the organizational heir of the old DC.

It turned out that in Italy there was an absolute need to modernise the system of representation and give it rules more suited to an advanced western democracy that would be better able to raise the criteria defining the effective output of institutional services. This was evident in the wide support for the referendum campaigns to replace proportional representation. Let us not forget the 83 per cent vote in the April 1993 referendum in favour of abolishing the First Republic's almost pure system of proportional representation. At the same time, with the experiment underway, it would be wrong and counterproductive to ignore that Italy's history is profoundly different to that of Anglo-Saxon democracies, such as the United States and Great Britain. An exasperating example of the majoritarian logic, such as adopting a single- round system of voting without a proportional component, would take root with great difficulty in these times of rational political practices and given the organizational systems of parties. Even if we admitted that a two-party regime was a 'good' in itself (as some seemed to think - with the same naivety of those who promoted the electoral referendum that was propelled by a constitutional court ruling and sustained with great passion and a small amount of dogmatism by Marco Pannella), it would take at least 10 years before such a system planted itself in Italy's 'civic culture' and institutional order. Such a situation would give rise to conflicts and tensions that could compromise the most realistic and functional objective possible in the short-term - the very bipolarism of competitive democracy. In such a democracy, forces and movements, willing to undergo the necessary mediation between groups, but not to renounce their own identity, would congregate around the two principle electoral poles (centre-left and centre-right).

From this perspective, the introduction of a two-round system to elect parliamentarians in both chambers seems to be achievable and functional in terms of the concrete aim of political reform. Obviously, this is on the condition that it is accompanied by other important legislative measures that avoid the danger of falling into consociational mechanisms that would restore an unwarranted central role to parties and their bureaucracies. In other words, in accordance with the framework outlined below, governing instruments need to favour coherent and effective coalition dynamics between forces that have an incentive to value the reasons for maintaining solidarity and to control the centrifugal impulses presented by other coalition partners or their factions.

In confronting the theme of coalitions, we need to take stock of some apparently banal premises which, nevertheless, are dangerous to overlook in concrete political-legislative practice. Coalitions are produced when and if different interests and values warn against the threat of a common 'adversary' and if and when the costs of being in a coalition are not greater than the benefits to be gained from an alliance with different forces. Therefore, the theory of coalitions is a product of the political culture of pluralism and pragmatism, and as such responds to rationales that are not extemporaneous. In modern parliaments, coalitions are a systemic response to the lack of a party with an absolute majority. The forces converging in a government coalition will agree on a programme that will not require a drastic revision of the policies elaborated by each coalition partner.

In a situation where it is difficult to identify an organic political aggregation (for example, the hypothesis of a 'single party of the right' is unacceptable to those in the Freedom and Good Government alliances who support the preservation of cultural identity, moderate tradition and sensitivity to change of liberal-democratic thought) there is a forced need to support processes that do not prescribe coalitions amongst very different actors. Again, comparative politics teaches us that coalitions vary in their stability, duration, distribution of power and life expectancy. Moreover, from the political history of the First Republic, we know what roles and powers were distributed among coalition partners according to criteria that did not necessarily reflect their parliamentary weight. Without compromising the necessary flexibility toward electoral outcomes, the problem of clearly defining an alliance accord should be met in the most transparent manner possible, focusing on criteria for regulation, principles and procedures. The Italian case - even in a two-round scenario which would restore strategic space to a centre cleansed of attempts at consociationalism and interventionism - cannot assimilate itself into contexts that are too different and distant. For example, in Italy a 'pact of necessity' similar to that which tied the Australian Liberal Party with the agrarian National Party for decades is unthinkable, whereas federal Germany has experienced changes in coalitions where the permanent linchpin has been the electorally weakest party, the Liberals.

At times, coalitions are constrained by extraordinary exigencies that require wide alliances to meet limited aims and priorities. This was the case of the last government of the Fourth French Republic when the French parliament transformed itself into a de-facto constitutent assembly. This is also the case in the US congress where the existence of a two-party system does not impede the development of coalition dynamics across issues of great collective relevance. Between 1974 and 1979, even the British parliament experienced a *de facto* coalition led by Labour although it was not called a Labour government. Therefore, coalitions are the result and not the cause of the political instability that produces pluralism in society and its political culture. Moreover, this is a pluralism that is dangerous to restrain beyond a certain point through the artifices of constitutional engineering. This conviction is worth bearing in mind during this transition phase in the Italian political system when referring to a strategy of separating the functions of decision-making centres which distinguishes between the duties of government and instances of constitutional revision, or a more complex redefinition of the rules of the game. This position gives birth to the idea of a constituent assembly whose prerogatives are not a substitute for the elected parliament and which allows dialogue that is not prejudicial for or against the balance of forces between the majori y and the opposition.

The Logic of the Two-Ballot System

Like the hypothesis of creating a constituent institutional office free of direct and contingent political conflict, a two-round system is based on a critical reconsideration of Italy's first experiences of a majoritarian system. In particular, the difficulties encountered by the Berlusconi government in December 1994, when the Lega Nord withdrew from the coalition, were largely due to legislative strains caused by the adoption of a single-round voting system that allowed, through its proportional component, the survival of the old parties. Therefore, to sum up, there are defects with both the majority and proportional systems that compromise the identity and autonomy of political forces without helping to achieve their claims to self-sufficiency. Whether this later constituted an alibi for the Lega's disengagement, or actually helped to create a kind of blackmail of parliamentary institutions, is a cause for debate. However, this question does not alter the substance of the argument. In fact, it confirms it, demonstrating how a further consolidation of the one-ballot single-round majoritarian system (one of Pannella's proposals that was struck down by the Constitutional Court in January 1995) would have provided a pretext for the very forces which, on the basis of a calculation of costs and benefits, were not willing to change the electoral accord into a more organic and profound political loyalty towards one's chosen political alliance.

It should be added that if the hybrid electoral system currently in force helped develop the anomalous coalition and gave a *de facto* dominant role to a more radical and ideological force such as Alleanza Nazionale, then an appropriate response requires an efficient system of guarantees against the risk of regressing to the logic of the proportional system, if not to the actual return of proportional representation. Just like the French model, in a two-ballot system only those candidates who obtain a certain quorum in the first round (for example, 10 per cent of the valid votes cast) should go on to the second round. In this way, the competition would not be limited to the two contenders who win the most votes - as is the case in Italian mayoral elections. Instead, the contest would be widened to include all the actors who are truly representative. At the same time, calculations of expediency would prompt parties to form coalitions where fundamental lines of aggregation exist on a national scale. From this perspective, assuming the absence of conditions for a general consensus toward particularly prestigious candidates, or those who express an authentic political hegemony within a constituency, the first round of voting would take the role of a primary election where political forces could measure their social representation without exacerbating their conflicts and also gauge their influence (and thus, indirectly, their level of legitimate contractual power within potential coalitions).

A classic objection is that this type of system might produce alliances that are not homogeneous across different constituencies, thus greatly reducing the impact of the popular vote on a process intended to facilitate aggregation and simplify alliances within the political system as a whole. A response flows logically from our premise when one considers not only the partial and incomplete character of the electoral reform, but also the need to place the electoral innovations within the context of a more courageous and complex reform of institutional representation. To come to the crux of this argument, a two-ballot system of voting would inevitably lead to the direct election of the head of state or the head of the government (which, in this case, would mean the prime minister). And it is around the choice of the coalition leader who becomes the head of government, that we should be able to verify the convergence among parties and their policy programmes. We should not neglect the symbolic character and the drawnout impact of appealing to public opinion through a single leader, presented in advance by the party coalition. Together these elements - proof of political affinities, policy convergence and the selection of a leader who represents the entire coalition - seem more than adequate in removing any ambiguity and limiting any kind of power to veto, interfere, or blackmail.

It is also necessary to respond to another objection: the risk that a type of exchange market might develop between the two rounds of voting that would make us regret the exhausting and not always transparent 'mediation' that characterised the old proportional regime in selecting members of government. In reality, this danger is enhanced by a one-round system. The need to compete in a simple majority system actually produces the temptation to make choices behind closed doors, away from the influence of public opinion. The effects of this mechanism were partly apparent in the March 1994 elections when the Polo had to concede a considerable number of relatively safe seats to Lega candidates in order to guarantee support for a political programme in which they were indirect participants. Similarly, the Progressives undoubtedly paid a high price for the logic of prearranged alliances in terms of the quality and image of their candidates. On the one hand, the weight and distortions of the 'organizational rationale' of the party machine (especially, but not exclusively that of the PDS) brought candidates from traditional forms of organization to the fore, instead of figures who were an expression of local communities' demand for renewal and professionalism. On the other hand, the logic of a mutual veto was inexorably imposed, penalising the most authoritative figures. In the light of the above analysis, the systemic outcome has strongly redefined the innovative potential of the new rules of the game. And at the same time, it has impacted negatively on the quality of the parties in competition.

With regard to the constitutional aspect of the problem, it should be no surprise that the referenda aimed at transforming the entire electoral system into single constituencies were ruled to be inadmissible by the constitutional court. In fact, the eventual victory of those who wished to abolish the proportional representation component in the electoral law would have gutted the existing electoral rules without filling the resulting void. By abolishing the proportional quota, which currently assigns 25 per cent of the parliamentary seats, the candidates would have been chosen only from single member districts (474 in the chamber of deputies and 232 in the senate). In contrast, the constitution specifically states that 630 deputies and 315 senators should be elected in each house. In the absence of new regulations, which would have demanded relatively long parliamentary terms and laborious technical and administrative measures (beginning with redefining electoral seats), there would have been the risk of voting with the old rules and thus, in this case, violating the will of the electorate. But no constitutional organ, beginning with the parliament, can expose itself to the risk of not being able to exercise its essential functions. A totally different case (inappropriately invoked by the supporters of the single-round before and after the court's ruling) existed on the heels of the 1993 Segni referendum. After that referendum there was a need to urgently redefine the regulations governing the chamber of deputies in order to bring its electoral rules in line with those decreed by the referendum result for the senate. However, on that occasion the two branches of parliament could still function according to the constitution.

Added to these considerations of an apparently technical nature (but which are full of important implications nevertheless) is the fact that a single-round majority system which is tempered with a proportional component at least allows the survival of smaller political forces (the Popular Party, Patto Segni) that, had they been swept away, would have deprived the majority as well as the left-wing opposition of precious interlocutors in avoiding an exasperated radicalisation of the conflict; that is, avoiding the degeneration of competitive democracy into the self-destructive practice of a conflictual democracy where a congruent political culture does not correspond to majoritarian rules.

The Real Liberal-Democratic Challenge

As we have seen, considerations of electoral rules brings into question larger issues. What have been highlighted are the institutional outcomes that inspire analysis. No political transition can be realised without social costs (that is, without violence and without damaging civil order) unless it is done on a consensual basis. The competitive democratic paradigm serves to change the rules of the game, but in a way that is neither destructive nor reactionary. Its ideal goal is that of a modern liberal democracy, forcing itself to free this identity from the burden of outdated ideologies that belong to the old political culture and the obsolete political systems that accompanied them.

For this reason, in constructing rules of the game that are more functional for the exercise of democracy by the people and for the people (according to Lincoln's famous formula), it is essential not to lose the distinction between practices that act as an incentive and form of regulation of competition, and the recourse to conflict that became the preferred method of political action. To be sure, authoritive schools of thought have founded their own vision of representative institutions on the conflict and regenerative effects of political action. We can directly identify two currents which contrast due to ideologically inspired radical cultures. On one side are the metaphysics of conflict based on theories of social movements such as that of the French sociologist Alain Touraine. On the other side is the more aggressive version of a sort of right-wing political science that considers the exercise of a normal dialectic of responsibility between political actors as an unacceptable abdication of the rights and responsibilities of the majority to exercise its own prerogatives and wield power in its own name. This view forgets that the very essence of liberal-democratic thought - which is even by definition open to multiple experiences and which should always be willing to put its assumptions under concrete scrutiny - consists of the distinction between *the exercise of power* (a characteristic of authoritarian regimes) and *the practise of government* that requires the patient art of mediation and the acquisition of a consensus that is sufficient to produce effective services.

In the daily experimentation with government practices, there has been a constant disparity between the liberal-democratic model oriented toward consensus and efficiency and the option of emphasising political conflict. The victim has been the achievement of an ambitious reform programme. Citing an example that aptly illustrates the swelling of bureaucracy and the congested situation which institutions find themselves in, one needs to think of the need to de-legislate as much as possible, favouring instead, a more direct and comprehensive approach to the state machine. Italy can no longer remain the country of 150,000 statutes. A truly liberal government should be able to abolish at least 20 measures for each one that is passed. At the same time, it is unthinkable to entrust the public bureaucracy's recovery of efficiency to new technology. The computerisation of this bureaucracy leads to the delicate problems of managing personnel and providing stimuli, motivation and incentives. In other words, the modernisation and reorganization of the bureaucracy are the stakes in a political challenge that requires the ability to mobilise individual feelings, policy and creativity. Shortcuts of a brutally organizational kind do not exist, nor do magic solutions based on a prevailing 'directional' logic regarding corporative resistance (which is present and strongly conditioned).

A public administration that is a 'sleeping pachyderm' needs action that is courageous and specific, but which produces a willingness and consent among its staff and within the boundless social territory of public sector consumers. In addition to repealing legislation, there is a need to simplify all, or almost all, administrative procedures and adopt currently available technological resources, for adequate and updated personnel training, better communication with citizens and a drastic reorganization of departments. The very question of pension reform, which is absolutely indispensable in guaranteeing a minimum level of security for future generations, requires a strategy based on an agreed and negotiated combination of measures, avoiding wounds and conflicts that become difficult to control because, apart from concrete economic and material reasons, they deal with issues of a very deep symbolic nature. For good reasons or not, pensions are considered to be an absolute good, embodying individual expectations and need for security which defy a cold and rational economic calculation of costs and benefits. As demonstrated, it is consideration of very concrete issues which has given rise to *intra-organizational* tensions (internal to the bureaucratic machine and to its company and union representation) and *inter-organizational* tensions (between government and important social forces, but also between different interpretations of government action). These are tensions that a competitive democracy should not artificially hide or repress, but must equip itself to manage without producing a surplus of conflict that often creates a boomerang effect: a standstill in reform measures; adoption of paralysing compromises after phases of exacerbating contradiction; the prevalence of bombastic positions devoid of rigour and coherence. Similarly, the contested Biondi decree on protective custody, which was inspired by factors peculiar to the state of the law and which sought (not without some naivety and haste) to reduce the public evil of using incarceration as an inappropriate judicial tool, should have been preliminarily discussed with the opposition. In this way, the opposition would have been called to perform functions that lie outside those of pure 'vigilance', in order to flesh out the notions of collective responsibility foreseen by the constitution.

On the strength of these convictions rests the redefinition of a democratic strategy that hinges on the idea of a coalition government representing cultures and values that are not irreconcilable and are capable of efficiency and resilience. From this viewpoint, electoral mechanisms should be tested to act as proof of the liberal-democratic vocation of forces that may also be heterogeneous. Tools that associate the greatest possible governability with the greatest possible pluralism are needed, supporting - as implied in the above discussion - the prevalence of moderate portions (the 'half wings' of the two groupings destined to emerge from a bipolar logic). This is a need that responds to the urgency of making the Italian political system more stable and solid after the traumas it has experienced in the last few years and during the epilogue of a long period of erosion of the traditional logic of political action. The two-ballot system may represent an opportunity to meet this need (without miraculous expectations) in that it is precisely a 'virtuous instrument' at the service of the forces most aware of how deep the crisis is. In this sense, it is understandable that different political actors carefully value specific historical reasons (and also specific contingent factors of convenience). But we must not lose that sense of collective interest that really makes political forces representative and legitimate, no matter what their parliamentary grouping or ideology.

Reflecting on the trajectory of the Berlusconi government, we easily find confirmation of the preoccupations raised above about the dangers of anomalous coalitions. During this government, one could count the pulses of conflict and the pressure of a radical right which punctuated its attempts to survive under the mantle of the old political order. Therefore, this was an anomalous coalition that was not in a position to complete the transition to competitive democracy which is the natural result of a process of change inspired by a liberal-democratic model. In this coalition Forza Italia was not able (partly because of its unfinished organizational structure) to completely assume the political centre that the electoral result had potentially given it. In this sense, the growing dominance of Alleanza Nazionale (whose leadership achieved a courageous process of change at the Fiuggi congress, but which still harboured corporatist tendencies in a literal sense)[2] paralleled and mirrored by the Lega's growing intolerance of the governing coalition. Actually, the real or presumed dominance of Alleanza Nazionale added fuel to the Lega's aggression towards the cabinet, giving it a sort of ideological-cultural cover.

If the Polo was pushed to the right and if it prejudiced itself by its daily practice of entering into an indispensable dialogue with the forces that were less obstinately opposed to the majority, the predictable result was a crisis of equilibrium. It became less of a centre, not in the traditional political sense of the word (in any majority system the 'centre', as defined by proportional frameworks, cannot exist), but in a way that characterises systemic political theories. That is, the space for mediation and reason declines, leaving in its place a spiral of opposition and resentment.

Therefore, the real liberal-democratic challenge - and primarily the challenge facing those components of the majority and the Polo who wish to remain faithful to a culture of tolerance and dialogue - consists of cementing the Polo through the construction of a political order and strategic project consistent with the seriousness of the crisis of institutional transition and change in chronic cultural paradigms. This certainly means denouncing simplistic and miraculous visions of change. This is not a short process and is full of traps and 'challenges of complexity'. Concretely, it means that flexible rules and institutional mechanisms capable of self-correction must be invented. The battle of the two-ballot system, action for a diverse and more appropriate philosophy of coalition government, the choice to create an area of consensus aimed at overcoming old ideological schisms, but not open to extremist suggestions from some sectors of the right, are all part of this outlook, which is full of idealism and is terribly concrete. If the essential part of this objective were achieved, an important step toward authentic competitive democracy would be completed. In the opposite case, the road to a new and growing radicalisation would inevitably be opened, fostering a spiral of conflict that, at best, is destined to delay the confirmation of a more evolved and mature political system.

Notes

1. Editor's note: In reality the Good Government alliance brought together Forza Italia and Alleanza Nazionale in the South and the Freedom Alliance was composed of the Lega Nord and Forza Italia.

2. The reference here is to the polemics surrounding Bank of Italy, the attack on ENI, the concessions to state intervention in the economy, social security and the future of the welfare state.

References

Almond, G. and Verba, S. (1963) *The Civic Culture*, Princeton: Princeton University Press.

Dahl, R.A. (1971) *Poliarchia. Partecipazione e opposizione nei sistemi politici,* Bologna: Il Mulino.

Lijphart, A. (1988) *Le democrazie contemporanee,* Bologna: Il Mulino.

Lipset, S.M. (1963) *L'uomo e la politica,* Milan: Comunità'.

Urbani, G. and Carnazza, E. (1994) *L'Italia del buongoverno,* Milan: Sperling & Kupfer.

Warner, S. and Gambetta, D. (1994) *La retorica delle riforme. Fine del sistema proporzionale in Italia,* Turin: Einaudi.

three

The dilemmas of the majoritarian system[1]

Giuliano Amato

Historical Origins

Since my aim is to prove a thesis and not to limit myself to an analysis, it is my duty to warn the reader that I will use an axe where I should probably employ a scalpel. In the knowledge that I will exaggerate some arguments, simplifying them and making them problematic, my purpose is to make the thesis as clear as possible. But, I repeat, this is a thesis. I have read and re-read the writings of Ruffini (1920) on the majority principle and it has taken me some time to understand perhaps his most famous phrase: "the majority principle is not in itself a *raison d'être*: it may or may not acquire one depending on where and how it is applied". The sentence itself is clear. But what kinds of *raison d'être* was Ruffini referring to and what circumstances was he thinking of?

It is certain that whilst he wanted to eliminate the possibility of this principle being embodied by a juridical institution, it was a juridical conceptualisation, which is very ambivalent, that Ruffini used as a reference point. In fact, this conceptualisation postulates the majoritarian principle as a principle of representation as well as a principle of practice. And these are two different things. As a principle of representation it tells us who should be sitting around the decision-making table. As a principle of practice it tells us which actors at that table are crucial to reaching an agreement so that decisions may be considered final. But the problem is not limited to the plurality of juridical meanings, nor to the fact that the various meanings are often merged together without our realising it. Something else is wrong, something that strikes at the heart of the principle's problematic nature, demonstrated in history and in the history of thought that has influenced it. Let us not forget that Locke attributes the majority principle to nature, but Kant does not find a reason; he does not succeed in finding a justification for it. Starting from the premise of individual freedom he finds it difficult to evade unanimity as a conclusion. And even if he realises that unanimity does not work, this is not enough to make him rationally accept and explain the majority principle. *"Quod omnes similiter tangit, ab omnibus comprobetur"* (Whatever affects everyone equally will be sanctioned by everyone). This is the point and it is a very old point. How can we manage to rationally overcome it? With what risks? With what consequences?

History's response, indeed the response from political history, in which the majoritarian principle has always been essentially the same, unavoidably gives us two opposing answers. It was the instrument through which the majority could escape subjection by the few; and for this reason it appeared to correspond to nature because it forced the few to conform to the will of the majority. But it was also the instrument of the majority, or what was based on the majority, to oppress, or, more accurately, to suppress the few, that is the minorities.

This is the very dilemma that surrounds the majoritarian principle; it is also the dilemma that Ruffini was addressing and the dilemma he seemed to think the majority principle was incapable of freeing itself from. To conclusively prove this I could go a long way back in history from Sparta to Athens, from Rome to the medieval states, from the Polish Diet to our time. But, as I have said, my aim is to prove a thesis and thus I prefer to come directly to the point. Throughout history the majoritarian principle has effectively appeared under two different interpretations, both of which are children of the past and which have left a very deep mark on history to the present-day. Thus, it is these two interpretations that hold the key to our endeavour.

The first interpretation is Rousseauian, created by the Jacobins and successive revolutionary thought. It is based on the idea of the majority as the source of truth and rationality. As we know, Rousseau resolves Kant's doubt with a device that is absolutely insane on a theoretical level, but which is most effective on the political level. He states that the majority are right not because they are the majority, but because it is through them that we discover the general will. Therefore, there is a schism through which the majority does not dictate its law, but discovers the law, the truth. From this comes that element of Rousseau that has struck us since we were children: "I find myself in the minority, therefore I am at fault".

On the basis of this conceptualisation the Abbé Sieyés drew out the consequences: 'What is a minority? It is something without which things would be much better and problems would be resolved much more simply.' For him the minority embodies the past, privilege, the old that must be replaced, without obstacles, by the new. All revolutionary thought that followed embraced this idea: that democracy only works when there are no longer any minorities. It should be noted that this idea was to remain the same even in its most sophisticated forms, as Europeans of my generation cannot help but know. Even Gramsci himself maintains that democracy is achieved when everyone acknowledges that they form a single general will. This is not because the minority must be repressed, but because there is a need to operate mechanisms such as consensus *a priori*, to achieve citizens' consent. And the role of the party - the 'modern prince' - is precisely that of generating this type of consensus. There is no mention of revolutionary violence in Gramsci's thought, but it is crucial to remember that there is the idea that democracy exists without minorities.

There is a second and different interpretation of the majority principle, whose advocate in France was Condorcet. According to this version, the majority have the right not because they possess truth, but because they have strength and because there is no way to make the system work other than acknowledging the authority of the majority's greater force.

Therefore, in this interpretation the majority is not worth more than minorities in axiomatic terms: it serves only to make the system work, it serves to exercise power. This is the interpretation on which the American revolution was based and the difference between the two interpretations of the majority principle is also the difference between the French revolution and the American revolution.

It is not by mistake that in the United States, Calhoun was to emphasise the concurrent majority system, which today is called a qualified majority system, rather than the majority as such. As pointed out, this system confirms the principle of protecting the minority rather than the majority.

Where do these two interpretations come from? It is my conviction (and here

I begin to push my point) that the two interpretations are both children of the long battle that took place in the centuries before the revolutions and which had different outcomes in different countries. This battle was a reaction to the great tendency towards the recomposition and centralisation of power that the feudal period had previously fragmented and pluralised.

The rationales underlying this tendency were neither idealistic nor ideological; it was inspired only by practical exigencies such as the need to maintain an army and the first bureaucracies. Moreover, it is now doubted that those countries where centralisation was the most effective ever really eradicated their previous powers. According to some, there never has been an absolute state, but rather a state of the classes instead. However, it is true that absolutism gained greater headway in continental Europe than in England. It is also true that absolutism generated a new culture of power that was stronger and persuasive for its inability to concretely manifest itself historically.

This culture is not limited to the right of states, to the self-legitimation of power that has been released from both its imperial or papal roots and the contractual nature of feudal relationships. Above all, it is about the singularity of power, of Bodin's sovereignty which is, *per se*, exclusive and indivisible and allows for only one sovereign in each organised community.

I have always considered it to be an impediment in England, that the failure of the Stuarts at the beginning of 17th Century was accompanied by the failure to impose absolute power. Thus, the formidable cultural baggage that had helped absolutism in continental countries did not gain a foothold in Great Britain. It is of crucial importance that the Stuarts' attempt was stopped by a judge, albeit a very special sort of judge represented by the House of Lords and personified by Lord Coke, who in 1610 declared that a decree by the sovereign which contradicted the *lex terrae* (law of the land) was null and void. This constituted a negation of the singularity of power, a negation by a judge acting as the community's guarantee against political authority (rather than the discharger of such authority).

Both these precedents should be noted and at first glance we can read into their background one of the most important products of the two revolutions at the end of the 18th century: the separation of powers. We should realise that these two cases do not harbour the same separation of powers and that although this concept appears to be similar, two profoundly different interpretations are hidden within it.

The interpretation that arises from the French revolution posits separation as the division of a single power whose allotment is negotiated, but which has an inexorable tendency towards reconstituting itself. We shall see that this allows the maximum level of division between a complete and sovereign power and its sub-powers. The other interpretation refers to a separation of powers which are, in principle, separate, different and not derived from a partitioned single power.

Moreover, historically, the French revolution was about contestation - taking away from a single power. The theory to which I am referring, the Rousseauian general will, is a continuation of Bodin's thesis because investing parliament with the general will is tantamount to the same idea: someone must be sovereign and if it cannot be a king then it will be, with similar exclusiveness, a parliament. Because of this, there cannot be a system of law above the parliament's. Moreover, given that now sovereign power has to fit a 'separation of powers' framework, it becomes supreme and those other powers that surround it are not equally prescribed, but are executive powers.

With this system's glorification of the assembly, the government's power is executive. However, the judiciary is also executive. In many old textbooks on constitutional law one reads that there is a hierarchy with statutory power at the top and two ways of executing the law - the administration and the magistrates - below it. This hierarchy is not limited to a theoretical framework; note the development during the French revolution which saw judges of the time considered as guarantors of the privileges of the 'old' and for this reason they were used merely as executors, deprived of margins for interpretation, much less for creativity. The judges were to be vending machines, the automatic source of decisions entirely preordained by statute law.

This is not the only thing derived from this culture, which is itself a product of the absolutist conception of the singularity of power. Such a culture brings to mind Mortati's idea whereby monist forms of government are the only ones that are stable whereas dualistic governments are, by definition, unstable and transitory. Mortati's framework is dichotomous, theorised mostly from a marxist perspective which presupposes only one victorious social class and, consequently, only one holder of the only power that counts - political power (Mortati, 1972). From this premise arises the idea that if the government is dualistic it means (and it can only mean) that there is a social conflict that has yet to be resolved and when a victor emerges it cannot avoid taking everything. Thus, the resulting government becomes monist (and the majority becomes the holder of sovereignty).

The other interpretation of the separation of powers, reflected in the United States of America's constitution, is very different. Quite plainly, the idea is not one of supreme power with two executive powers under it. It is enough to exclude it by virtue of the fundamental concept of the supremacy of law that is the American codification of the *lex terrae* of 1610. The rule of law carries with it the idea of judges who are not subject to parliament and who defend citizens' rights, even before that body. Judges interpret the law directly for the community. They place themselves within the framework of the American separation of powers and give the system a very clear sense of separation between equal branches of government.

Moreover, those who wrote the American constitution may be considered the heirs of Montesquieu, but they also acknowledge that in addition to this the constitution is a product of federalism and that federalism alone would be enough to make any system in which it operates a truly plural one.

There is an extremely important passage by Madison in Number 51 of the Federalist :

> "...in a unitary state, all power given to the people is entrusted to the administration of a single government and this government is divided into distinct and separate powers to safeguard against any usurpations. In the federal state of America, power given by the people is first divided between distinct tiers of government and then is further subdivided into departments within each tier." (Madison, 1961)

Madison does not conceptually refer to the first (and primary) division between distinct levels of government as a separation of powers and actually calls it federalism. However, it is very clear that federalism enriches the separation and makes the whole system one in which Bodin's indivisible sovereignty is actually divided. Madison does not admit this and he cannot admit it because he is defending the Federation against the previous Confederation. For this reason, he says expressly that divided sovereignty is a political monster. But he does this because he has a political goal and he wishes to defend federal unity.

This results in what continental Europe has been unable to do - negate the singularity of sovereign power. Such a result includes an idea that differs drastically from that of the separation of powers: that it is a separation of powers that are different originally and not pieces of a single bloc that tends to reconstitute itself.

The Rejection of the Majoritarian Principle during the First Ten Years of the Italian Republic

The majority of institutions and principles belonging to contemporary democracies are rooted within two interpretations of power discussed earlier. The majoritarian principle is amongst them. A good starting point for understanding how it echoes the two interpretations and derives its meaning from them is provided by a subject that is rarely considered in this sort of discussion - the push towards proportional representation that began to appear alongside the growth of classes within institutional social substrata in the 1800s. This was a push that paralleled the social changes of the time and had results only in some countries, including Belgium, Italy and Germany, leaving the majoritarian system safe and sound in others, notably England and the United States.

The push for proportional representation - as Piretti (1990) reminds us - did not originally come from the popular or socialist parties, but from the conservatives who perceived that universal suffrage was imminent and wanted to avoid the *sanior pars* being swept away with the establishment of the majority. Attilio Brunialti, the founder of the Association for Proportional Representation in Italy, observed in 1871:

> "Where suffrage is universal, if numbers end up taking precedence over intelligence, the people dominating over the autonomy of originality, the stock-exchange, property and birth, then there will be a need for institutions which will stop the prevalence of numerical strength turning into tyranny... Justice and usefulness demand proportional representation of minorities as the most effective solution against the despotism that threatens them" (Brunialti, 1871).

The meaning of this passage is abundantly clear: the majoritarian principle (as a principle of representation) functioned very well up until the time when the homogeneity of the represented classes was guaranteed *a priori*. As soon as this homogeneity is reduced one can see it as a source of monolithic power that can crush the minority classes. Why? A response is provided by the fact that things are different in England and the United States where this surviving class conflict has been confronted, leaving the majority principle intact. The comparison lies in the two interpretive bases that characterise the two cultures. On one side, the singularity of power and on the other, its division. On the former side, the only way to break up the circle of singularity is to fragment political representation and thus the formation of parliamentary will. On the latter side, the circle's closure is precluded by the preconstituted and guaranteed existence of distinct and different powers.

Again, repeating my framework, from this premise I will go on to the dawn of our republic, a republic rooted in a society crossed by deep social and ideological cleavages and where the culture of monist power inherited from our past was seen as (or deemed to be) dominant.

On one side were the proletarian classes, represented by the Communist Party, who were largely convinced that after the resistance, and at the opportune moment, the revolution would come. On the other side were the reactionary bourgeois classes, inspired by hostility and even a desire to expel liberalism, who should have been attracted to democracy whose values and procedures they did not at first share.

Fortunately, this was not the only social and political panorama of the time, even if it is true that convergence on the choice for democracy was more convincing within the political elite than within the social strata they represented. Certainly, given such a situation and the expectation that its many influences should have been expected to lead to or consolidate a monist form of power and its consequences, (the Abbé Sieyés should be remembered), the majoritarian principle was an enemy principle and was inevitably perceived as the means by which minorities were suffocated. Few were able to see and propose it as a useful vehicle of democratic efficiency within a framework of separation of power whose general equilibrium would balance any potential disequilibrium.

The majoritarian principle, as a tool of representation, was first avoided in the constituent assembly and then rejected with growing conviction and vehemence. It is enough to note the pragmatism with which the assembly dealt with the question, favouring proportionalism but avoiding putting it in writing (and this is what allows us to say many years later that the constitution is neutral on this topic). Equally of note is the wide and convincing agreement that surrounded Carlo Lavagna's arguments against a majoritarian law in his famous parliamentary maiden-speech in 1952 at Macerata, after which the law became known as the "swindle law". In the following years, Lavagna's thesis became a sacred text, where any rivals doubting its validity were curtailed or accused of harbouring anti-democratic propensities.

According to Lavagna, the constitution contains a prohibition on majoritarian systems, not just those that do not give space to minorities such as the single national constituency, but also those systems based on local constituencies/

seats. This is because, firstly, political "competition" certainly does not require article 49 to enforce unanimity on decisions, but implies that everyone should be present in parliament during deliberations. Secondly, this obligatory attendance cannot be limited only to the strongest minorities, whoever they may be, as is the case with majority systems. Thirdly, in being present, the minorities should not be differentiated geographically, whereas geographically differentiated representation is precisely what is manifested by majority-system seats, violating both article 5 and article 67 of the constitution.

Using the constitutional prohibition of majority systems as his premise, with one of his typical and effective "crescendos" Lavagna goes on to demonstrate that proportional representation is actually prescribed by articles 3 and 48 which "require substantive equivalence between voters and, thus, equal value for the votes they cast".

Therefore, for years we grew up opposed to the majority principle as a principle of representation. This rejection also took effect on a functional level. The argument was perhaps supported by a minority when Gianni Ferrara (1972) postulated it, using the very concept of competition to deny the majority the right to express its platform or to make this platform count. He maintained that there was a need for the kind of competitiveness found in the Chilean system of government which imposes a requirement for wide consensus. With such consensus, a qualified majority becomes a simple majority and, as revealed above, negates the majority principle.

In fact, this argument has operated in real life and for many years the facts have increasingly lent it support. The parliamentary regulations of 1970 should be noted. So should the progressive enlargement of the concept of constitutional majority which has been extended to deliberations that are not formally of a constitutional nature and therefore do not require qualified majorities pursuant to article 138, but which nevertheless, by political convention, have been reserved for the parliament which needs the consensus of both the majority parties and the opposition. This was the case with the laws regarding the organisation of the regions or the local councils. The election of the head of state in 1985 was also done via such an extra-constitutional manner.

Once this tendency was confirmed, Gianni Ferrara was not the only one to share it. Using words that were very different to those used by the jurist, Joseph La Palombara (1988) wrote:

"The Italian system is one of reciprocal settlements which also include the opposition forces and therefore makes them part of the process.

Beyond the sound and fury of ideological exchanges, especially pre-electoral ones, one discovers that the continual search for peace and reconciliation is the norm. Even if it may seem to be a desperately fragmented system, it is sufficiently cohesive to allow most of society to legitimise it."

La Palombara added that some people were unhappy and forcibly maintained that the majority should govern and the minority should responsibly occupy itself in opposition. His conclusion was that, nevertheless, Italy worked well just as it was and actually demonstrated that, far from being the eccentricity that devotees of the Westminster model thought it, the consensual model could have results that were not only constitutionally necessary, but also politically efficient. Hence, Italy is seen as a triumph of that consociational model that Lijphart (1988) would have expanded (actually calling it consensual) beyond the original ethnic-religious cleavages that first gave rise to the model.

Pros and Cons

Was this really such an efficient model that it seemed to us then, as it does now, to be constitutionally necessary? It was certainly during the initial stage of the republic. Let us ask ourselves whether that dangerous cleavage which divided the two sides equally from democracy could have been civilly overcome if we had not adopted this kind of model. Having now adopted the majoritarian principle, we should ask ourselves what would have happened if we had found ourselves with an isolated minority in opposition whose extremist mood had been strengthened and reinvigorated by its isolation. Perhaps we would not have had that slow education in democracy that has brought us, without shocks, to a healthy institutional stability.

It is probably true that when the consensual model reached its apex and received the most ardent blessings, reason no longer mattered and its many dysfunctional characteristics began to emerge. In fact, the cleavage that made the model historically necessary had disappeared (which means that it had achieved its aim) and the procedural delays, the untiring negotiations, the torturous conclusions, the buried responsibilities of a system where everyone decided everything together began to weigh upon it.

An opposite tendency began to mature and there appeared the idea that the majoritarian principle was not only useful for achieving efficiency and responsible government, but, contrary to what Lavagna had written and what others continued to maintain (that is, that only proportional representation could guarantee democracy), a majority system did not contradict democratic principles.

Certainly, the beginning was cautious and the majority principle began to enter the arena not as a principle of representation, but only as a principle of practice. This was the case at the beginning of the 1980s and the clearest theorist of the time was Andrea Manzella (1977) who wrote that there was no reason for giving up proportional representation as the means of entering parliament, but parliament should function along majoritarian lines by introducing an open ballot and giving the parliamentary majority clear priority in setting the orders of the day and managing the allotment of parliamentary time.

This is exactly what occurred during that decade through continual modification of parliamentary regulations. It was precisely as these innovations were beginning to define parliamentary life with everyone's consent - that is, whilst the majoritarian principle was becoming entrenched as a functional principle - that the push to also confirm it as a representational principle gained strength.

The most striking thing about this historical process was that its motivation was of the most classic proportions. The driving force underlying the referendums on the electoral system (which, I admit, most people did not see), was clearly the widespread determination to take away power from the minority and give it back to the majority, to be able to form a majority and form a government. This was the collective sentence given to the parties that, in the meantime, had become a minority and whose power (a power that had legitimately belonged to them for over a decade) was reduced in the name of the majority.

And so we come to the present; a present where the majority principle has manifested itself in both its juridical interpretations. But what is the cultural *humus* in which it is immersed? Have we or have we not overcome the idea of the singularity of power? In the end this depends on whether this is really an instrument for rescuing the majority from the logic of the minority, or whether it still risks being the majority's tool (or the tool of those who represent the majority) to smother the minority. This is the real question. This is the dilemma that Ruffini saw in the majority principle. Therefore, we must ask ourselves what is our majority principle; what is our separation of powers; what is the qualitative and quantitative value we give to the majority; is our majority that of Sieyés or that of Condorcet? Have we made the right choice today? The answer to this question bolsters the institutional framework, giving meaning to its different parts, building them and constructing a balance between them.

I remain convinced by what I have been working on for the last fifteen years, naturally taking into account all the adaptations that have been necessary. My conviction is this: that a society such as ours is no longer governable without recourse to the majoritarian principle. However, precisely because we must turn to the majoritarian principle, we must ensure a commensurate, high fusion of independent powers and articulations that can guarantee that we do not allow ourselves to sanction an exclusive power through the majority principle. Instead, we must guarantee that only in cases that warrant it, we can promote the reconstitution of interests and groups that would otherwise remain unarticulated and self-referential. That entails a pluralism of power and articulations that are truly independent from one another and which have majoritarian opportunities through their recomposition. It is not the pluralism of parishes dependent on a single diocese. Actually, I might add that this model seems to be even more pertinent now than when I first began to think of it because then I was addressing the death of ideology, the growth of a series of categorical, economic and sporting interests of various kinds and thus, the start of the economic and social fragmentation that the old parties reflected, but did not embody. In addition to this, we now see in the future a pluralism that will also be made from ethnic and religious diversity, intermediate communities that are the bearers of cultures and identities that no longer refer to the national fabric. The crucial problem of this co-habiting organisation will be to find a common identity, safeguarding the right of each group to have its own identity. Already, less suffocating societies than our own, which has remained more provincial than others, are demonstrating this fact.

It is clear that this model veers towards a plurality of institutional tools. And reading our constitution through this framework, and thus liberating it from the duties of the monist culture, offers many of these.

Let us not forget that our constitution is the constitution of procedural quorums, strengthened laws, agreements and institutions that presuppose groups and communities who are allowed to negotiate their own status. Moreover, it is the constitution of regionalism, susceptible to many improvements, but already identified as a matrix for the possible vertical separation of powers. Legislation also exists that can offer precious points of departure. I re-read Marco Cammelli's book on the administration of constituencies which illustrates the recognised imperative of a qualitatively high representation so that a seat may be seen as invalid or will not place its holder in a position to make decisions, not because there has been a failure to reach the quorum, but because a specifically relevant interest is missing (Cammelli, 1980). Our administrative life is full of this type of phenomena. This is one of the most significant capacities of our social life; that is, the negotiated product between social parts that is not only a factor, but also a source of balance between interests.

The Italian transition

From this fundamental point of view, we are currently in a transition phase that is not very clear. Paradoxically, with regard to the interpretations of the majoritarian principle, this transition has been driven by the referenda. This is demonstrated by the electoral system, which is of some use to us. Hoping that I will be forgiven for my abuse of privilege, I can foreshadow the assessment of the electoral system that will appear in an as yet unpublished book by Giovanni Sartori (1995). Sartori writes:

> "The main justification of the majoritarian principle is that it promotes governability and, with this end in mind, it reduces political fragmentation. Using this scale of assessment, if fragmentation is a bad thing then localised fragmentation should be seen as an even greater and more devastating ill. It would be truly a supreme irony if the electoral system, seen as a vehicle for governmental efficiency, were to be transformed into the killer of every possible form of good government. Hence, the question is whether the system's localising tendency, with its single majority seats, is natural and inevitable. It is neither because it is a system of highly structured national parties and because it is an institutionally balanced system."

Sartori continues that this balance occurs in England where the strength and logic of the party-system guarantees it. It also occurs in the United States where the presidential system guarantees it. And Italy?

It is noteworthy that Italy appears in a specific passage of the book dealing with Italy, Russia and Japan all of which have turned to a mixed electoral system. However, Russia and Japan have adopted a mixed system similar to that found in Germany whilst in Italy, "the 75% majoritarian component does not produce any kind of bipolar realignment and the proportional component maintains fragmentation at dangerous levels".

The problematic nature of the current transition also emerges under different guises which I can only touch upon here. I am thinking of the crucial role played by the judiciary, the media and social interests in the name of pluralism. There is no doubt that the last few years have signalled a great cultural change for the role of judicial power in Italy. For the first time it has made itself the interpreter of the community's rights in the face of political power, introducing an element of security that is similar to the Jacobin separation of powers. However, it is a question of understanding whether or not the culture underlying the judiciary's independence is a product of the old monist conception of power. The difference between the two hypotheses is huge.

The media, social interests and their clients are, and will be an, excellent litmus test. As soon as we see that traditional clients run to the new victor and that this victor also runs the media, we know that the monist culture has invincibly survived.

Let us try to clearly understand what is happening now and what may happen. Ruffini presents us with the majoritarian principle as a dilemma, but I have reached the conclusion that it is possible not to remain its prisoner. However, to escape we need to move far away from the monist culture that has dominated continental Europe for the last five centuries and to promote an authentic pluralistic culture of the separation of powers. At its centre, the majoritarian principle should be as irrefutable as it is without dilemma, capable of acknowledging the authority of the majority without depriving the minority of the guarantees which are their right.

Note

1. A slightly altered version of this article was published in *Quaderni Costituzionali,* No. 2, 1994.

References

Brunialti, A. (1871) Libertà e democrazia, *Studi sulla rappresentanza delle minoranze*, Milan: Treves

Cammelli, M. (1972) *Il governo di coalizione*, Milan: Giuffrè.

Ferrara, G. (1972) *Il governo di coalizione*, Milan: Giuffrè.

La Palombara, J. (1988) *Democrazia all'italiana,* Milan: Mondadori.

Lijphart, J. (1988) *Democrazie contemporanee*, Bologna: Il Mulino.

Madison, A.J. (1961) *The Federalist Papers (or the New Constitution)*, Cambridge, Massachussets: Harvard University Press.

Manzella, A. (1977) *Il Parlamento,* Bologna: Il Mulino.

Mortati, C. (1972) 'La Costituente (1945)' in *Raccolta di scritti. I Studi sul potere costituente e sulla riforma costituzionale dello Stato,* Milan: Guiffre.

Piretti, S. (1990) *La giustizia dei numeri,* Bologna: Il Mulino.

Ruffini,F. (1920) *Guerra e riforme costituzionali (suffragio universale, principio maggioritario, elezione proporzionale, rapprestanza organica),* Turin: Paravia.

Sartori, G. (1995 - Italian edition forthcoming) *Ingegneria costituzionale comparata,* Bologna: Il Mulino.

four

The Berlusconi government

Marcello Fedele

The end of a cycle?

For more than forty years the Italian political system was characterized by the exceptional stability of its governing class. Viewed in a positive light, this trend was considered in the past by some observers to be a confirmation of the vitality of 'democracy Italian-style'. On the other hand, those who, quite rightly, sought to point out the costs of this stability looked at the same series of events from a quite different perspective. It had been clear for some time that this stability had its price.

The First Republic, as the entire period up to the 11th legislature is now called, had certainly achieved a strengthening of citizens' rights. However, Italy's institutions had remained in the shadows for a long time until 1991, when the system entered into a period of dramatic and irresistible change. Was this, as many have claimed, the end of a cycle simply because, from then on, any executive would have to be legitimised directly by popular will and not by top-level agreements formulated in the corridors of party headquarters? If only this were so! In reality, every political cycle lives off the illusions it succeeds in nurturing before it is brought to an end by the very problems it fails to resolve. In this case, the illusions did not last long.

It is easy to demonstrate, even to those who refuse to listen, that institutional changes are not created from one day to the next, by referenda, or by improvised electoral laws. In history there are many examples of revolutions that have ended in popular referenda, but only rarely has the reverse been seen. This is precisely what Italy has attempted in the last few years.

Generally, revolutions are a result of dramatic political crises which change the entire nature of public power and not just the criteria for the formation of such power. Instead, parliament and government in Italy now enjoy a different type of legitimation because the citizens have finally been able to choose their representatives by a system which is intentionally oriented toward a majority outcome. However, the institutional output and thus, the level of governability within the entire political system, has remained that of the past. This is because a majority-type system is not enough to increase the powers of government. Instead, what is needed are rules, procedures and political behaviour that never existed in Italy's First Republic and which the Second Republic has not been able to deliver. In fact, in order to have some effect on the relations between the legislative and executive branches, there would have to be either a radical strengthening of the present form of parliamentary government, or alternatively, a transformation of the system toward a presidential republic.

Naturally, not all the available solutions are of equal value and each presents some foreseeable problems. Even in the wake of the 1994 national elections, those who had won immediately realised the difficulties which still lay ahead because the capacity to govern is very different from the skills needed to 'try to survive'. Thus, the Berlusconi government revealed itself to be dependent on securing consensus when exercising its powers and majoritarian only with regard to how it was formed.

There is no need to look far for confirmation of this, nor indeed is it necessary to refer to politically controversial decisions such as the withdrawal of the Biondi decree (18 July 1994), which amended pre-trial detention provisions. One only needs to look at the problem of collective responsibility for decisions taken by the council of ministers. Shortly after the formation of the new government, the prime minister nominated the minister Giuliano Ferrara as the government's 'spokesman' to relay its official position of matters on state. What was the result? Every time a political problem arose within the majority there was hardly a single member of government who did not take the opportunity to give his or her personal opinion, even if it conflicted with the prime minister's office. And yet, in Italy there are still optimists who look open-mouthed to the 'Westminster model'. But in Britain, if ministers express an opinion that is contrary to that of the government, even on matters in which they have not directly participated, they are immediately obliged to hand in their resignation. In Italy, this rule of collective responsibility is something that no-one has even dared to suggest.

Sensing that a storm was brewing, the opposition went in search of a safe haven, thus avoiding the task of facing up to the perils of navigating in a majority system where the capacity to govern usually reaps greater rewards than the ability to merely represent opinions. Therefore, no political force seriously placed the creation of a 'shadow cabinet' on the agenda - and in any case it was not clear who could have put forward such a scheme. Should it have been the cartel of progressives which constituted the largest element in the opposition, or the more composite political affiliations represented by the Popular Party and other minor groups? Unable to overcome these political difficulties, the members of the opposition guarded themselves against reproducing the unhappy experience of the *'tavola comune'* (round table) which they had promoted as an electorally-expedient alliance forum. In this way, the institutional problem was deepened by the exigencies of the majoritarian system. The question of who was really the opposition and who was still waiting to be taken on board a new majority at the first opportunity was not resolved.

The entire political system was floundering in an institutional impasse no less profound than the one that led to the crisis of the First Republic. Given this, it was not easy to convince the voters that a new electoral system alone was not enough to govern. After having maintained at all costs that the earth was flat, the new political class would have to admit that the world was, in fact, round. But it was not clear who would be able to do this and launch what would amount to a total change of the political system. A real majority system cannot be constructed only through the adoption of new electoral laws. What is needed is a whole framework of new rules and, above all, an increase in the power of the executive. This was something that the right-wing was unable to do and which the opposition, for its part, was reluctant to support.

So everything continued as before and, in some cases, even worse than before. The Berlusconi government, which was strong only in the mandate obtained from its direct investiture, had to deal with difficulties linked to the survival of old operational routines which still dominated the workings of the 'legislative-executive subsystem'. The most striking confirmation of the continuation of the old system's unwritten rules, which tended to be flexible and adaptable to every change of direction, was the revitalisation of the majority groups' famous 'top-level summits', which characterized the First

Republic mode of decision-making. This mechanism, which was completely outside the formal institutional structure, ensured the necessary integration between the executive's need to promote its political line and the behaviour of parliamentary majorities that were often reluctant to give their backing to successive governments.

Those who have studied the top-level summits and their implications stress that they only disappeared a short time ago with the formation of the Amato and Ciampi governments (Criscitiello, 1993). In early 1992, Andreotti conducted a summit where Craxi and Forlani were summoned in great haste to Palazzo Chigi in their capacity as leaders of the two major governing parties. Together with the prime minister, the goal was to decide whom to elect as head of the government and whom to appoint as president in place of the incumbent whose mandate was running out. It was all a useless exercise because things were destined to go in a very different direction to what had been foreseen. The governments born in the 11th legislature made sure that they avoided any return to the summits. Amato even refused to take part in an important PSI meeting, though he had once been its deputy-leader (Fedele, 1993). And again in 1993, Ciampi said in reference to the budget: 'the parties will read about it in the newspapers. They have been kept in the dark about the measures to be taken'. What, then, did Berlusconi do when his government presented its package of economic measures? In great haste he called together an 'official' summit to discover whether the majority was prepared to enter into a conflict with unions over pension reductions on which the success of the budget depended. Had it not been proclaimed from the rooftops that the Second Republic had been created to overcome the vices of the First and to reduce the influence of the parties?

Thus, it is easy to understand why even those who have been studying these problems for some time may come to the conclusion that it is still 'too soon' to identify any real transformation in the relationship between the executive and the legislature. Cotta (1994) attributes the impenetrability of the old 'polycentric' system (in spite of the majoritarian change) to the survival of political factors such as 'the structure of the governing majority', or the ways in which the 'recruitment' and 'career-building' of Italian parliamentarians is carried out. The 'level of negotiation' which the government has always been obliged to undertake with both the majority and the opposition makes the Italian parliament more akin to the US Congress, where powers are divided, than to the experiences of comparable European institutions which operate on the principle of the 'fusion' of powers.

In general terms this evaluation does not pinpoint the heart of the problem. If one looks at the relationship between the parliament and the government from another standpoint, it becomes clear that there is also instability in the decision-making process, the origins of which are not so much political, but institutional and regulatory. The permanent uncertainty surrounding the outcome of both ordinary and extraordinary legislation has favoured a concentration of social reform decisions being made within the context of the budget and its attendant 'financial law'. If the power of the executive's initiative remains bound by parliamentary rules which belong to the 1980s, where the rules are typical of an institutional pattern in which representation is more important than governing; if the uncertainty of the law-making process continues to push the executive into issuing urgent decrees; if the procedures for the conversion of decrees into laws constantly upset the parliamentary schedule; if the ways by which it is possible to govern are not clear, then there are two consequences.

On the one hand, the government will 'tie' the most significant political decisions more and more closely to the financial measures which accompany the budget because, as they say in parliamentary jargon, this is the only 'train' that departs at a predictable time every year and manages to arrive at its destination, albeit following the imposition of some temporary emergency measures. On the other hand, to achieve its own ends, the executive will need to seek the consensus of social forces (unions and employers) above all else. Far more than parliamentary representatives, the latter are the only elements really interested in a policy of reducing the public debt in a way that will not worsen the already grave economic situation of the country. All this was made very clear by the measures launched by the previous Amato and Ciampi governments which 'arrived safely' thanks to aware and responsible public opinion, rather than the parties. This situation repeated itself in the case of the Berlusconi government which however, unlike its predecessors, did not benefit from consensus earned at summits with the unions.

In the absence of sufficiently incisive institutional innovations, the Berlusconi government saw the balance of power again shifted to favour parliament, not least because the political conditions which made possible the 'miracle' of the Amato and Ciampi governments in the First Republic had ceased to exist. In this way, the first real paradox of the majoritarian 'new road' took shape. Although it had a strong electoral consensus, the Berlusconi government did not reveal itself to be similarly solid on the political plain. It failed precisely where some governments of the First Republic had managed to succeed: in compensating for the chronic power weaknesses that afflicted the executive by having a strong political-institutional legitimisation.

Institutional Effectiveness

We have already signalled the inevitable return of top-level summits. But these, having made a comeback with the Berlusconi government, reflected only the vices of the First Republic and not its virtues. This was because in the intervening period the political and organisational stability of the parties, which is an essential prerequisite of the system, had diminished. Unacceptable, but at least understandable in the past, the summits proved to be completely useless in the new legislature because the new parties were still movements of opinion and not structured organizational entities. Indeed, the majority underpinning the Berlusconi government dissolved just as quickly as it had been formed.

Three other factors also help explain the weakness of the new executive. The governments of the First Republic were always able to gain legitimacy through parliamentary parties, even if they did not enjoy much respect in the eyes of the media and the public. On the other hand, though it achieved a vote of confidence from the electorate, the first government to be formed since the 'majority revolution' did not succeed in winning the same trust from the institutions and notably from parliament and the head of state.

There are numerous and understandable reasons for this outcome. Not only did the government not win the majority of votes in the elections (which is not uncommon in simple majority systems), but it did not even obtain the majority of parliamentary seats in the senate. Since the Italian system is a perfect two-chamber one, this means that the government did not enjoy an effective political majority to assist it in the ever uncertain relations between the executive and the legislature.

If this were the only problem, perhaps it would have proved possible to overcome because not only had there been excellent governments with restricted majorities in Italy in the past, but also because in Western democracies this type of situation is not altogether unusual. In England, the electorate has not delivered a clear parliamentary majority since 1945 (Beetham, 1995: 365). Moreover, several of the British governments of the 1970s were minority ones and the same situation has arisen in several European countries including Denmark and Belgium (Strom, 1990). Italy's first elected majority-system executive could have proved to be a 'good government' though it lacked a majority of the votes cast. However, Berlusconi failed to realise that failure to come to terms with the opposition ultimately weakens the executive.

It was far more difficult to set aside two other crisis-tendencies which appeared with some force in the international sphere before revealing their negative effects on the domestic arena as well. Immediately after its formation, the Berlusconi government was the subject of severe international criticism for two reasons: firstly, due to its inclusion of neo-fascist ministers from the Italian Social Movement (which was soon to be absorbed into the National Alliance) and secondly, because of the conflict of interests between Berlusconi's role as prime minister and his economic and financial interests as the owner of an extremely important industrial group. Naturally, the debate which erupted over whether or not the arguments were well-founded proved completely irrelevant because international 'friends' were free to judge the Italian 'revolution' in any way they pleased. However, the very airing of such preoccupations helped transform a government formed with the utmost legitimacy into a politically impotent executive that was continually subject to the scrutiny of other institutional bodies of the state.

As usual, the first signals came from the head of state, who for some time had assigned himself a function of primary importance in the Italian political system - that of 'guarantor' of change - despite the lack of constitutional provisions for such a role. During the formation of the new government, in a decidedly irregular exchange of letters, Scalfaro asked the newly appointed prime minister for guarantees on the composition and intended programme of the government and, by extension, on its intended political orientation. In fact, his request was more or less conceded as though the government's programme did not belong within that sphere of sovereign autonomy which is the privilege of any executive.

In reality, a government can only claim full legitimacy when the source from which it derives its power is clearly separated form the institution which embodies its authority. However, if the conviction that the government is capable of manipulating the direction of public opinion by controlling the media gains currency, it is inevitable that the legitimacy which, in a democratic system, is considered to be the 'governing mandate', should be seriously weakened. Having 'sniffed out the wind', the opposition lost no time and immediately began trying to discredit the Berlusconi government - it was kept in power by neo-fascist votes; it was full of former socialists and Christian Democrats; it was dangerous because of the concentration of power gathered in the hands of the prime minister; it was illiberal and therefore waiting to deliver the knock-out blow to pluralism in the country.

It is clear that in this political context the best institutional output which could be expected from the introduction of a majority system was paralysed by a circular argument. Governability, the benefit rightly held to be supreme and in whose name electoral reform had been introduced in Italy, can only mature if the government demonstrates that it is in a position to adequately control the country's main social and economic problems. This control can be exercised efficiently only if the government enjoys sufficient legitimacy to impose sacrifices for a limited period, (Wewer and Rockman, 1993 :447) in order to reap long-term benefits. As soon as this virtuous cycle becomes inverted because the government loses consensus at an international level, as well as within its own majority, the grip of the pincers inevitably tightens. The loss of legitimacy suffered by the Berlusconi government made the imposition of rigorous policies even more difficult. The internal divisions within the majority itself did the rest. Concomitantly, the benefits connected to the government's policies were also lost because it has always been difficult for parliament to ask the country for sacrifices.

There are many indicators by which a government's activity can be generally assessed. In fact, a fierce international debate has emerged on this subject because in the general crisis of the welfare state, what counts is not so much a government's ideological allegiance as its achievements. Cloudy discussions about the virtues of the state as opposed to the virtues of the market have been buried beneath the ruins of the Berlin Wall and they no longer interest anyone. On the other hand, what is important is the opportunity of finding a good job, securing health benefits when one is having a baby, getting a pension, or even the quality of transport services used by commuters. As for ideologies, if they exist, so much the better, though it is certainly possible to manage perfectly well without them because nowadays it does not take much to satisfy the imagination of the average voter.

Berlusconi managed to satisfy voters imagination during his electoral campaign with an all-too-famous promise of a million new jobs. The same was achieved just a month before with the referendum movement hammering the country with its promise of a 'change' if only the citizens could manage to 'elect the government'(Pasquino, 1992) directly. However, these are not the major problems because the very question of the new electoral system is not how to get votes but how to use them to ensure better institutional effectiveness.

Since there was no-one to look after the garden of the majority, the weeds began to grow freely, once again confirming the vitality of the old operative routines typical of the 'polycentric' power system that everyone thought had been overcome forever - draft bills presented with the general knowledge that they could be debated; decrees renewed over and over again; increased recourse by parliament to regulatory powers of very low political value when exercising its inspection prerogatives; and so on, following a ritual that has become all too familiar over the past years. The main difference between majority and consensus democracies is not in the content of their decisions, but in the way these decisions are formulated. Institutions belong neither to the right or to the left. Indeed, institutions can sometimes represent an opportunity, or an operative precondition for the development of one type of policy or another.

Thus, the Second Republic inherited the unbalanced relationship between the executive and the legislature that had existed for a long time in the Italian political system and it added something of its own. The reasons for this outcome become clearer as we examine the dynamic of the 'ordinary' and 'extraordinary' laws which characterized the initial stages of the 12th legislature. Amongst the many alternatives there is one indicator - the success or failure of legislative measures - which measures the technical 'output' of institutions (Griffith and Ryle, 1990) because it takes no account of the content of decisions and thus purges the assessment of all reference to the political composition of the majority, or the opposition. By reconstructing certain trends, the permanence of the 'polycentric' nature of the relationship between the executive and the legislature will be confirmed.

Government and Parliament

An observer who wanted to synthesise, by way of a graph, the impact of majority rule on the Italian political system would probably represent it with an extremely thin body and an incredibly long tail. It is not by accident that these new rules were immediately invoked by both the majority and the opposition; the former so that they could govern and the latter to defend the controlling powers and the constitutional prerogatives of parliament *vis-à-vis* the executive.

Initially at the margins of the political debate, this problem re-erupted when the leader of the government declared in a television interview in October 1994 that the parliamentary opposition 'would not let him work'. Naturally the opposition protested strongly, invoking arguments based not only on political order, but also on constitutional order. However, it was not expected that the government's stance would also be indirectly contradicted by the parliamentary speakers. Officially raising the problem of the government's excessive use of emergency decrees, both Irene Pivetti and Carlo Scognamiglio actually brought to light the other side of the coin. The reasons are clear. In fact, if it was possible (as unfortunately had been the case) for the government to issue an average of one decree a day with the exception of weekends, it was not possible for the chambers of parliament to ratify those decrees with commensurable speed. Far from being considered the cause of all delays in the decision-making process, parliament became the victim of the executive's activism, which engulfed the former's work and continually lengthened the list of measures waiting to be approved.

Regardless of whether the prime minister's and the parliamentary speakers' claims were well-founded, they exposed a discomforting situation which said a lot about the deep illness afflicting the Italian political system. However, we are far from reaching a cure because the problem exploded by the introduction of a majoritarian system cannot be solved by merely addressing symptoms such as the overuse of emergency decrees. In fact, the disease is much more widespread and it was born prior to, and independently of, the formation of the Berlusconi political coalition.

For years the relationship between government and parliament produced uncustomary procedures whose effects inevitably flowed onto the quality and punctuality of parliament's activities. For example, looking at the period of time needed for parliament to pass a bill, we know that during the last legislature it took an average of 125 days to secure final approval, which in turn was extended to about 150 days whenever a bill successfully gained the opposition's endorsement. But delays in decision-making are not the only factor against which the main problem of the new majoritarian system must be measured.

If we look at the statistics showing the success rate for ratifying legislation, the previous parliament scores only 4.1 per cent for the passage of bills, irrespective of their content and what powers put them forward. In the case of government decrees, 26.8 per cent were successfully ratified by parliament. The question which was first raised in the 1970s remains the same today: who governs Italy? Today we ask: what could a government, even a majoritarian one, ever do to rescue its own powers from that 'polycentric' quagmire which, until recently, had been sustained by the world's most exasperating system of proportional representation?

In reality, the Berlusconi government had rebalanced the action, resorting to the introduction of legislative proposals with greater frequency than, for example, the previous Ciampi government. However, at the same time, the methods employed in exercising powers of introducing legislative initiatives were not far removed from the past because even the Berlusconi government actually believed that it could make up for its decision-making paralysis through a generous use of emergency decrees.

For example, if we examine the first seven months of every other executive in order to make a legitimate comparison, the picture that emerges does not provide much to argue about. Let us disregard the Ciampi government which resorted to this strategy whenever there was an unfavourable forecast.

Where emergency decrees accounted for 24 per cent of all legislative initiatives under the seventh Andreotti government, it rose to 43 per cent in the case of the Amato government and to approximately 52 per cent with the Berlusconi government.

Figure 1

Percentages of legislative initiatives, by government. (First 7 months of office).

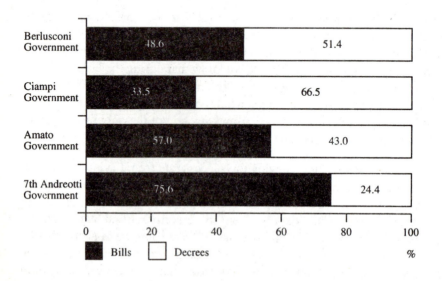

What initially appeared to be a solution soon turned into an illusion because even the capacity of institutional adaptation had its limits once all the procedures went awry. Indeed, rules do not exist to complicate the decision-making process, but to make that process more straightforward or at least more predictable. What happened then, when an institution like the decree, whose content should be 'specific and temporary' (for only in this way can we justify its legislative nature) is used on the same basis as any other ordinary act?

The response of the 'neoparliamentarians' is notable, if only because it has been repeated tiresomely for almost a decade. They object that by doing this, the government is exercising a sort of extra-constitutional power and treading on the prerogatives of the elected assemblies. Although worthy of attention in the case of single decisions, this assessment is generally unsustainable because it does not address the other side of the problem, which in recent years has assumed macroscopic proportions. Already the government is 'powerful', but 'impotent' to formulate its very 'political orientation', when the latter ought to be precisely its most sacred prerogative.

The continued recourse to emergency decrees resulted in two counter-productive effects, which, in the long run, weakened the constitutional effectiveness of such decrees. With a reduction in the mediation of interests secured by parliament via its activities, the government actually excluded not only the opposition, but also members of its own majority, from the decision-making process, and it is the latter who ensured the government's parliamentary legitimacy. Forcibly excluded from the framework of decision-making, groups within the majority coalition were among the first to oppose decisions, thus forcing further mediation during the period of ratification for decrees. In this way, the effectiveness of the emergency decree was increasingly eroded because the guarantees ensured by this type of constitutional tool were overturned by the dynamics of the political process.

To overcome the internal and external resistance that the executive faces in these cases, it can take one of two roads available to it. It can 'reinforce' its choice of decision by transferring it to the ambit of financial decision-making where, due to procedural reasons, the executive has greater scope for getting its own way. Alternatively, it can transfer the guiding principles of decrees into ordinary bills, thus implicitly confirming the absence of any real emergency.

During the Berlusconi legislature, the first case was verified with the decree granting an amnesty on illegal construction of dwellings (*condono edilizio*).

Having lapsed due to the criticism it attracted in parliament, its contents were reinstalled in a bill 'tied' to the 1995 budget by virtue of an amendment moved by the government concurrently with a confidence motion so as to better control the majority. An example of the second case is provided by the so-called 'Salva RAI'' decree (designed to keep the RAI solvent) which had to be introduced repeatedly until, finally, the provisions which caused considerable political division and which caused the dissolution of RAI's managing board, were removed and presented again through a specific parliamentary bill.

It is clear that the institutional effect illustrated by this dynamic is not so much the abnormal growth in the use of emergency decrees as the need to continually renew those decrees. During the past four years, the monthly average for renewing decrees reached levels that were not previously imaginable. In fact, Andreotti did not have to renew more than one or two decrees a month. The cabinet presided over by Berlusconi did so for approximately 17.

Figure 2

Monthly average for renewing decrees, by government. (First 7 months of office).

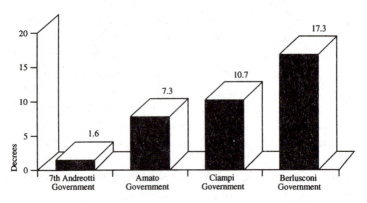

However, in this way, the Italian political scene assumed characteristics that were increasingly spectral because the dead seized the living and the past placed a heavy mortgage on the possibilities of the future. Today no-one misses the seventh Andreotti government. However, it left the Amato government 25 decrees waiting to be ratified. After ten months in office, Amato left Ciampi 44 decrees that had to be renewed. And finally, Ciampi, who was in office for as long as his predecessor, bequeathed to Berlusconi 66 decrees waiting to be ratified which strongly conditioned the government's agenda from the beginning of the new legislature.

Figure 3

Number of decrees still active at the beginning of each new government.

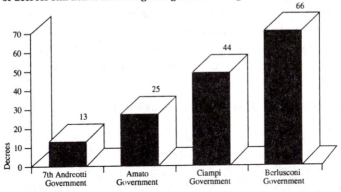

Initially conceptualised as a solution to the problem, the institutional strategy based on the renewal of decrees has itself been transformed into a problem that must now be solved. The more governments have used this instrument the less they have proved capable of guaranteeing the successful ratification of decisions within the given time-frame. Andreotti proposed an average of four decrees a month and succeeded in ratifying approximately two. Berlusconi issued around 23 during each month his government was in power, but was able to ratify no more than six. Therefore, there is no rational relationship between what has been a rise in legislative initiatives of an extraordinary character and the capacity of various executives to transform these into formally-ratified legislative acts.

Figure 4

Monthly average of decrees introduced and converted by each government.

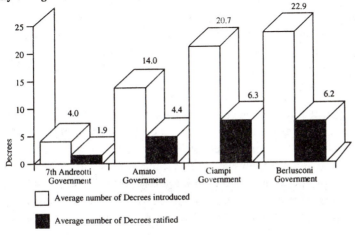

Therefore, all the indicators of institutional output strongly point towards the low end of the scale and the reasons for this are simple. The rules approved during the 1980s do not offer sufficient guarantees to ensure successfully ratified decisions and thus do not concede to the government powers which, in other democracies, have been exercised for some time either through the granting of explicit legislative jurisdiction, or through specific parliamentary procedures.

The Paradoxes of the 'Italian Revolution'

To clarify this primary paradox of the 'Italian Revolution' it is not necessary to follow the usual tendency and reopen the endless debate on what form of government is needed. Whether or not the government remains a parliamentary one, or is transformed into a presidential or semi-presidential system, is really of no importance. Indeed, the current 'policentric' nature of the system is not compatible with any hypothesis for improving the effectiveness of public powers. This is demonstrated by a few international examples, chosen randomly, but which are significant all the same.

For example, in France the constitution of 1946 allowed parliament to intervene in laws on any subject, establishing a hierarchical priority for itself with regard to the regulations promoted by the government. However, the constitution of the French Fifth Republic approved by referendum in 1958 profoundly changed the respective areas of intervention between parliament and government, with the latter exercising a regulatory autonomy in all areas where it was not expressly precluded by article 34 of the constitution which bestowed a reserve power to parliament. Moreover, the government was given the option of intervening, even in areas reserved for parliament, when it requests and receives the assembly's authorization. Substituting the traditional principle of having a hierarchy of legislative sources for that of delineating competence, the executive has become the bearer of ordinary legislative and regulatory powers based on law, but where the government cannot be limited in any way by that law.

One may object that France has a semi-presidential form of government. However, even in Spain where, like Italy, there is no division of competency between parliament's legislative powers and the government's authority, things are done in a different way. In fact, the Spanish constitution explicitly prohibits the principle of 'legislative hierarchy' between the sources of law (article 3, para. 3). Moreover, the government exercises an exclusive power whenever the Cortes invests it with a delegation of legislative authority and can therefore declare 'invalid' any bill or amendment that contrasts with a delegation that is already in force (article 84). Whenever the government proposes additional legislative decrees, the Cortes can make amendments through an emergency procedure, but parliament must ratify, or defeat, the decree within thirty days. Using a formulation which has obvious political worth, the Spanish constitution expressly does not allow the kind of damage inflicted by article 77 of Italy's constitution through the continual recourse to renewing decrees.

And in Italy? Naturally something was done. The court passed a judgement on the problem of renewing decrees (n. 302/88). Some articles of law (400/1988, Disciplining Government Activity and the Structure of the Council of Ministers, article 15) also apply to this kind of problem. These provisions prohibit the executive from conferring legislative delegations through decrees, renewing decrees that failed to be ratified in one of the chambers and finally, to regulate the legal relationships based on decrees not ratified by parliament.

In 1991, the Andreotti government presented (without success) a constitutional bill to revise article 77, which would prevent substantial amendments being made to decrees. However, these principal innovations were not introduced via legislation, but rather through practise, thanks mostly to the incisive controlling role exercised by the chamber of deputies' presidency during the last legislature.

Pinpointing emergency decrees as 'the most serious symptom of the growing difficulty of undertaking legislative functions', the presidency of Georgio Napolitano actually intervened on more occasions than the parliamentary committees and the government itself. The parameters governing the admissibility of parliament's powers of amendment were redefined according to criteria that were much tighter than in the past. The assembly's contingent ability to make decisions that differed from those of the budget committee on financing measures was burdened with further procedural restrictions. The government was invited to exercise its rightful prerogatives with utmost rigor and to re-organise the needs of various sectors into a united political programme, thus drawing them into a strategy of technical-legislative, financial and regulatory co-ordination that was considered necessary. And off they went.

On a political level, the outburst of this fragmentary initiative and other minor issues were balanced thanks, above all, to the actions of the Amato government. Through its use of direct legislative delegations to promote the reorganisation of entire legislative areas, this government managed better than any other to formulate an alternative institutional strategy to the worn-out recourse to emergency decrees. Throwing the executive's very *raison d'être* onto the other end of the scale, Amato succeeded in gaining parliamentary delegation to exercise powers that no assembly until then had ever given up. (Indeed, during one of his most difficult political moments the premier declared: 'we are here to govern, not just to hold out'.) The same institutional strategy was then followed by Ciampi, although only in part and in more circumscribed conditions, such as reforming the civil service.

However, not even the natural convergence exercised by these two different powers (the executive and the presidency of the chambers) proved to be sufficient to achieve a strengthening of the government's role. One only needs to think of the legislative delegations granted for the reorganisation of four fundamental social security sectors on which the government's budget strategies for 1993 were based. Although Amato repeatedly staked the confidence of his government in the assembly in order to secure the approval of all the measures, the text on which the parliament voted was not the one originally proposed by the government, but one which emerged after being examined in committee. Even though the government had never before exercised its prerogatives so decisively - and not without some strain as evidenced by the repeated recourse to a confidence motion - this case also confirmed the profoundly 'polycentric' character of the relationship between the executive and the legislature which the First Republic left to the Second.

One is forced to ask then, what is the use of continuing to invoke 'rules' that are typical of majoritarian systems, but which the majority cannot impose and which the opposition, for its part, has guarded against proposing. Naturally there is no logic to this. In fact, as demonstrated above, the relationship between the government and parliament worsened to such an extent during the course of the 12th legislature that it reached precarious levels. Thus, the conclusion is quite clear. Finding itself in this sort of dynamic, the majority system has paradoxically accentuated and worsened the institutional output and this output has reached a critical level. One can only add 'Rest in Peace' to that frequently, but inappropriately, invoked *Westminster model.*

Appendix - Data

The data used in this article are based on information provided by the senate archives on the legislative activity in both chambers of parliament. Below are the absolute values and time-frames upon which the statistics are based.[1]

The time-frame utilised is the first seven months of each of the following governments: the seventh Andreotti Government (from April 1991), the Amato Government (from June 1992), the Ciampi Government (from April 1993) and the Berlusconi Government (from May 1994).

Within this time-frame, the number of legislative initiatives introduces by the executives was as follows (in absolute values):

	Bills	Decrees*	Renewed Decrees
7th Andreotti Government	87	28	11
Amato Government	130	98	51
Ciampi Government	73	145	75
Berlusconi Government	141	149	121

* This figure includes the number of renewed decrees, but excludes those decrees that were 'reinstated' in one branch of parliament after first appearing in the other branch.

The approval of government bills and the ratification of decrees was as follows (in absolute values):

	Bills Approved	Decrees Ratified
7th Andreotti Government	36	13
Amato Government	71	41
Ciampi Government	17	44
Berlusconi Government	41	41#

This figure does not include five decrees ratified during the Berlusconi government, but presented by the Ciampi government at the beginning of the 12th Legislature.

This data was gathered by Polity, Osservatorio Istituzionale of the Department of Sociology, University of Rome "La Sapienza".

Note

1. For information on the methodology and criteria used in the statistical data on legislative

activity, refer to the methodological notes in M. Fedele and E. d'Albergo, 'Bilancio dell'XI Legislatura. Un'analisi del rendimento istituzionale', in *Sociologia e Ricerca Sociale*, N. 44, 1994.

References

Beetham, D. (1993) 'Political Theory and British Politics', in Dunleavy, D. et al. (eds.), *Development in British Politics,* London: Macmillan.

Cotta, M. (1994) 'The Rise and Fall of the "centrality" of the Italian Parliament: Transformations of the Executive-Legislative Subsystem after the Second World War', in Copeland, G. and Patterson, S. (eds.), *Parliaments in the World,* Chicago: University of Michigan Press, Ann Arbor, pp 59 - 65.

Criscitello, A. (1993) 'Majority Summits: Decision-Making Inside the Cabinet and Out. Italy, 1970 - 1990', *West European Politics,* Vol. 16, No. 4, pp 581 - 594.

Fedele, M. (1993) 'Il governo Amato', in *Il Ponte,* No. 1993.

Griffith, J.A. and Ryle, M. (1990) *Parliament, Functions, Practice and Procedure,* London: Sweet and Maxwell.

Pasquino, G. (1992) *Come Eleggere il Governo,* Milan: Anabasi.

Strom, K. (1990) *Minority Government and Majority Rule,* Cambridge: Cambridge University Press.

Wever, K. and Rockman, B. (1993) 'When and How do Institutions Matter?', in Wever, K. and Rockman, B. (eds.), *Do Institutions Matter? Government Capabiliites in the United States and Abroad,* Washington DC: The Brookings Institute.

II. politics

five

The Italian left between crisis and renewal

Martin Rhodes

In early 1994, the Italian left seemed to be on the brink of entering government. After over 40 years of Christian Democratic hegemony this would have a been remarkable event. And it was one that the secretary of the Democratic Party of the Left (PDS), Achille Occhetto, and his fellow leaders in the Progressive coalition had come to view as a virtual certainty. After all, in local elections in December, Progressive candidates had been elected mayors in six major cities (Genoa, Naples, Rome, Trieste, Venice and Palermo), apparently proving the utility - and invincibility - of the new alliance strategy. Flushed with that success, Occhetto baptised the alliance *'la gioiosa macchina da guerra'* - the 'joyous war machine'. But far from sweeping the Progressives to power, the 'joyous war machine' fell apart in the weeks before the national elections, the result of an undignified struggle amongst its members for constituency pole positions. Issues of leadership, strategy and programme fell victim to party fetishism, and the absence of a united front - and a clear candidate for premier - undoubtedly hurt the alliance at the polls.

The loss of the elections to the combined forces of the right sent the Progressives into a state of shock from which they have yet to fully recover. They appeared to learn little from the defeat and the party fetishists busied themselves in the spring with internecine disputes and skirmishes, reducing the coalition to four members by the end of April. But even among them there was little agreement on how to proceed. After the débâcle of the European elections in mid-June, the Progressive pole had for all intents and purposes disappeared. Then, after the resignation of Occhetto and under the new leadership of Massimo D'Alema, the PDS set off on an ultimately futile search for an alliance with the Partito Popolare Italiano (PPI), the less conservative of the two parties to emerge from the rotting carcass of Christian Democracy.[1] By early 1995 it was still unclear whether the Progressives could resurrect their fortunes, in alliance with a part of the catholic centre, under the putative leadership of Romano Prodi, the new 'man of destiny' for the moderate left. But it *was* clear that the Progressives had squandered a unique opportunity to put the left on a firmer footing, to create a new and credible pole of attraction for centrist as well as left-wing voters and to provide a clear and viable alternative to the 'soft' *peronismo* of Silvio Berlusconi.

March 1994: Seizing Defeat from the Jaws of Victory

In early February, the eight leaders of the Progressive alliance presented themselves to the country as a new, united political force, offering a clear left-wing alternative for government.[2] But there were problems from the very beginning. In the first place, although the form of the alliance was certainly novel, its component parts were certainly less so. They were, in order of parliamentary strength, the PDS, Rifondazione Comunista (RC), Alleanza Democratica (AD), Ottaviano Del Turco's wing of the Socialist Party (PSI), the Greens (Verdi), Leoluca Orlando's anti-mafia Rete ('Network'), the Cristiano Sociali (Social Christians)(CS) and Giorgio Benvenuto's PSI splinter group, Rinascita Socialista (RS). Led by eight middle-aged men and all, with the exception of the Verdi and Rete, representative of the old Italian establishment or 'counter-establishment', the 'new' (by contrast with the forces amassing on the right) was somewhat less than apparent. In essence, the alliance had been formed, *faute de mieux*, as a defensive response to the exigencies of the new electoral rules, rather than as an innovative, strategic force. The PDS expected to become the major pole of attraction on the left, making the smaller parties its obedient servants. The leaders of the latter, still acting according to the logic of the old proportional system, hoped to use the PDS to retain an electoral presence and sustain their own identities and political relevance.[3]

It was this basic tension which, in the weeks leading up the March elections, would deprive the Progressive alliance of both unity and credibility as a governing alternative. Forging the alliance in the first place had required numerous concessions by each of the partners and this process had gone someway towards creating a more cohesive alignment. Thus, at Rifondazione's Rome Congress in late January, Lucio Magri made a moderate speech to please the centrist Progressives that even swallowed the bitter pill of privatization as long as it did not extend to education and the welfare state. Under pressure from the Rete - which said that it would not sign up if the PSI, still tainted by corruption scandals, were also part of the alliance - the Socialist leader Del Turco pushed through the split between his Progressive-oriented group and the proud heirs of Bettino Craxi.[4] More generally, the leaders of the other, smaller parties recognised they would have to make some sacrifices for the sake of unity and electoral survival.

But this did not mean they were able - or even willing - to act as one. After the formation of the Progressive pact in the first week of February, the parties continued to jostle with one another. Their main concerns were to obtain the greatest possible number of secure constituency seats for their candidates and to guard against any assertion of PDS hegemony within the group. Thus, while in principle there were clear criteria for the distribution of constituencies (a quota more or less proportional to each party's presumed electoral strength), there was considerable conflict over the numbers and allocations. Thus, Rifondazione and the Greens fought hard - and with some success - to gain secure constituencies, while the latter also tried, but failed, to double their allocation. Orlando's Rete stood firm on its demand for a disproportionate number of seats in Sicily: it was eventually awarded one third of the total and refused to allow the PSI Progressive representation in the region.

In order to keep these parties on board, the PDS made a considerable sacrifice in terms of its own quota of candidates. In the Veneto, for example, the PDS had only 25 per cent of the constituency candidates for the chamber of deputies and 20 per cent for the Senate. In the 'red zones' of traditional left-wing strength in central Italy, the PDS had to cede 15 and 10 per cent of the seats, respectively, to Rifondazione and Alleanza Democratica - quotas exceeding their electoral strengths (Di Virgilio 1994: 514-520). PDS largesse did not, however, prevent outbreaks of conflict. There were open fights over the distribution of candidates in Liguria, where, in a fit of pique, the PSI abandoned negotiations; in Calabria where the Rete opposed certain candidates; in Puglia where there were divisions over quotas; and in Tuscany where the Rete accused the PDS of being 'hegemonic'. Numerous PSI regional councillors and party leaders in the centre-south, led by Claudio Signorile, were expelled from the party for seeking local coalitions with the Partito Popolare rather than toeing the Progressive line. In Sardinia the Progressives were split three ways: the Progressive group was limited to the PDS, Rifondazione and Alleanza Democratica, while the Socialists linked up with the regionalist Sardinian Action Party (PS d'Az), and a third group was formed by the Rete with a number of exiles from the PS d'Az and the PDS. Considerable disaffection at local levels was also created by an eccentric allocation to certain constituencies of key Progressive politicians.[5]

This unseemly conflict not only delayed agreement over the electoral detail of the pact, but, by contrast with the relatively rapid and consensual process of negotiations within the two right-wing poles - the *Polo della libertà* and the *Polo del buongoverno* - it projected a negative public image of the Progressives as 'hostile brothers'. It also absorbed a disproportionate amount of tactical energy that should have been invested in campaign strategy and in presenting a convincing team for government. Despite the considerable talent available for this purpose, it was hardly even attempted. Moreover, the pre-election skirmishes detracted from the coherence of the Progressive programme for government and, coupled with the absence of any clear leadership, or proposal for prime minister, produced an indistinct and muddled electoral profile.

The mainly PDS-inspired campaign programme contained a number of attractive proposals, many of which received the backing of all the Progressive partners.[6] But others divided them between the PDS and Alleanza Democratica on one side and their allies to the left. Thus, on taxes, although the Progressive's official position was in favour of the status quo - modified by a modest redistribution in favour of the most penalised, a reduction in income tax if tax privileges and evasion were eliminated and a rebalancing between taxes on property and those on income - Rifondazione wanted tax reductions for those earning less than the European average and increases for those above it. And while the PDS excluded taxes on treasury bonds (Bots) - a sure vote loser given the extensive investment in government paper by many ordinary Italians - Rifondazione's national secretary, Fausto Bertinotti, caused a storm by advocating taxes on Bot investments above 150-200 million lire. Employment was to be promoted via large-scale public works and greater employment flexibility: but the Greens were openly opposed to high-speed rail and highway construction and Rifondazione wanted a reduction of working hours with no loss of pay. In foreign and defence policy, while NATO remained of strategic importance for those on the Progressive right, Rifondazione and prominent Greens (Gianni Matteoli and Edo Ronchi) argued that the military alliance - and Italy's membership - needed serious rethinking.

It was not so much that positions on the left of the coalition were extreme: indeed, more than anything, this division reflected the extent of the PDS's rightward drift and its desperate quest for a responsible image. Hence the pains to which Occhetto and other leading figures such as Giorgio Napolitano went to secure the confidence of foreign governments and financial markets.[7] But it was, nonetheless, damaging. For it simultaneously weakened the Progressive's assault on enemy positions while leaving their flank exposed to attack: Bertinotti's ill-thought out statements on Bots, for instance, were grist for Berlusconi's anti-communist mill. Meanwhile, the Progressive's own campaign, alerting voters to the extremist danger of the Lega in the North and the neo-fascist MSI in the South, was derailed by Berlusconi's tactic of linking both of them to an apparently liberal project. The Progressives then turned their guns on Berlusconi, but this only seems to have increased his media exposure - to his own populist, political advantage. Furthermore, by contrast with the extravagant claims of Berlusconi (greater prosperity, efficiency, lower taxes and the creation of one million new jobs - all wrapped up, patriotically, in the Italian flag of the Forza Italia symbol), the Progressive's programme and campaign seemed lacklustre and over-responsible. This allowed the right to outflank them in traditional left-wing areas such as employment, while they, paradoxically, were more concerned to placate the financial markets.[8] All in all, a *noiosa* (boring) *macchina da guerra*.

All of this was extremely disorientating for voters. But, equally confusing, was the absence of a clear Progressive leader. Until fall 1993, many on the centre-left with experience in the referendum alliance (mostly grouped in Alleanza Democratica) had assumed that Mario Segni would provide them with leadership. These hopes were dashed when he and Occhetto failed to direct the momentum created by the reform movement into a joint programme for government. Segni returned to the centre (taking a number of prominent Republicans, Socialists and Liberals with him into the Patto Segni), while many of his former followers joined the Progressives (Rhodes, 1995b: 125-127). But this did not imply a transfer of allegiance to Occhetto. Far from it: one of their conditions for membership was that the PDS clearly renounce any hegemonic ambitions within the pact.

This was a further source of ambiguity. For while Occhetto was careful to avoid accusations of 'PDS hegemony', he was inevitably perceived as its key spokesman, and many simply equated the Progressives with the PDS. It was, after all, Occhetto who confronted Berlusconi in a televised debate on the eve of the elections. But Occhetto could not possibly become prime minister: the fragile coalition would have fallen apart at the very suggestion. Instead, and largely to placate Alleanza Democratica and the Socialists, the Progressive candidate appeared for a time to be Carlo Azeglio Ciampi - the existing premier and former governor of the Bank of Italy.[9] But even that choice was unclear and, in any case, Ciampi declared himself unavailable in the course of the campaign. The name of his budget minister, Luigi Spaventa was also mentioned, but only in passing. The fact of the matter was that the Progressives had no clear prime-ministerial candidate. In the televised debate on March 23, Berlusconi effectively exposed this leadership void when he asked Occhetto who the Progressives were proposing to lead the country. Occhetto's reply that they would decide after the elections not only helped Berlusconi emerge triumphant from the debate; it also revealed the ill-defined nature of the Progressive's alternative. This, in retrospect, was probably their greatest strategic error.

Defeat at the Polls

Signs that Progressive support was weakening in the weeks before the elections were evident from the opinion polls. From a peak of 44 per cent of the electorate in April 1993, support for the total left (including the PSI and Alleanza Democratica) was broadly sustained until October (when it stood at 42 per cent), but then slumped during the fall and winter, falling to 33.0 per cent in February. By the time of the elections, popular backing for the left had shrunk to its historic core of one-third of the electorate - most of whom were deeply pessimistic about the Progressive's chances.[10] A closer look at the components of the coalition indicates the source of defections. While backing for the PDS increased steadily between the April 1992 and March 1994 elections (from 16.1 to 20.4 per cent), and remained relatively stable (between 5.6 and 6.0 per cent) for Rifondazione, the smaller parties all declined. This was especially the case for the PSI and Alleanza Democratica: while the Socialists plummeted from 13.6 per cent in April 1992 to 2.2 per cent in February 1994 (the result of the fragmentation of the party and the schism between Del Turco and the former craxiani), support for Alleanza Democratica peaked at 8 per cent in April 1993 but fell following Mario Segni's departure in the fall to 2.0 per cent by February. As for the Rete and the Greens, while both acquired increasing opinion poll support during 1993, both also lost ground in early 1994.

As it turned out, this trend provided an early indication of the Progressive's principal weakness: their inability to capitalise on the creation of the alliance and use it to build electoral support. Thus, there was little in the way of 'coalition effect'. In the proportional vote, only in Basilicata, Campania 1 and the Marches did the Progressives as a whole perform better than the entire left-wing camp (including the Socialists) in 1992 (Lazar 1994: 84). The major gain over 1992 was made by the PDS, which boosted its vote from 16.1 to 20.4 per cent, while Rifondazione improved only marginally, from 5.6 to 6.0 per cent. These were creditable performances. Together, their total vote of 10,189,639 was equal to that of their predecessor, the Italian Communist Party (PCI), in the 1987 elections, although the aggregate result disguises a substantial decline in the North, compensated in part by gains in the South. Meanwhile, the performance of both the Greens and the Rete was rather mediocre and the proportion of former Socialist votes attracted to Del Turco's PSI was small. If the PSI is included, the Progressive parties' total vote fell from 39.9 per cent in 1992 to 34.4 per cent in 1994. If it is excluded - which provides a more accurate picture given the right-wing proclivities of the old PSI vote - their total increased from 26.3 to 32.2 per cent, all of which can be attributed to the PDS.

Contrary to their expectations, the leadership of the Alleanza Democratica attracted only a small portion of the centrist vote and even the Greens and Rete failed to mobilise their electoral potential for the coalition (Biorcio 1994: 164-5). Exit polls (CIRM/La Repubblica 31 March 1994) show that while both Rifondazione and PDS voters were faithful to their parties, the Greens and Rete only attracted around half of their previous voters to the Progressives, while neither they nor Alleanza Democratica succeeded in attracting voters from other parties. In terms of seats, one critical problem was the fragmentation of these smaller parties, none of which exceeded the four per cent threshold in the proportional vote. Some 3.6 million votes were, therefore, deprived of representation. So, while PDS and Rifondazione seats both increased marginally over 1992, the number of Green and Rete deputies fell, respectively, by a third and a half. Neither received a number of plurality seats proportional to their vote, while the PSI and the Alleanza Democratica (both of which performed poorly) were over-represented, due to the criterion of distribution according to presumed electoral strength (see Table 1).[11]

Table 1

Election Results, Chamber of Deputies, 1992 and 1994 (Parties of the left)

	1992			1994 List		Prop.	Plurality	Total
	Votes (in millions)	%	Seats	Vote	%	Seats	Seats	Seats
PDS	6.3	16.1	107	7.9	20.4	37	72	109
RC	2.2	5.6	35	2.3	6.0	12	27	39
Greens	1.1	2.7	16	1.0	2.7	-	11	11
PSI	5.3	13.6	92	0.8	2.2	-	14	14
Rete	0.7	1.9	12	0.7	1.9	-	6	6
AD	-	-	-	0.5	1.2	-	18	18
CS	-	-	-	-	-	-	5	5
RS	-	-	-	-	-	-	1	1
Ind.Sin.	-	-	-	-	-	-	10	10
Total	15.6	39.9	262	13.2	34.4	49	164	213

A number of explanations can be advanced for the absence of a coalition effect. The first is that the left was not sufficiently united inside the Progressive camp. Thus, separate Green candidates were presented for the chamber and the senate in Piedmont 1 and in Lazio; if their vote had been taken by the Progressive candidate it may have made a difference to the outcome in several cases. The same is true in Sardinia and Sicily where the PSI vote was lost to the alliance. But it is impossible to know whether the inclusion of either the rebel Greens or the PSI in the Progressive camp would have delivered the latter more seats. In any case, the difference overall would have been marginal. A more incisive argument is that the Progressives were too disparate ideologically to mobilise their potential electorate: thus, Rifondazione may have repelled moderate voters, while the Alleanza Democratica failed to attract the more radical. By contrast with their right-wing counterparts, Progressive candidates rarely performed better than their lists (Bartolini and D'Alimonte, 1994: 678). Organization was also important given that personality seemed to be of low significance in the vote and that the new majoritarian system placed a premium on sub-cultural roots and established networks: this clearly benefitted the PDS and Rifondazione, while penalising the more amorphous AD, Rete and Greens.

More generally, however, the Progressives failed to create a coalition that was in any sense larger than the sum of its parts; and it was this critical failure that prevented the mobilization of a larger proportion of the electorate. In part, this was unavoidable because of the failure to forge an effective link with the centre. Nevertheless, the argument that the Progressives lost because of the failure to bring Segni into the alliance is flawed. As it turned out, the Patto Segni only took 4.7 per cent of the chamber vote, while the PPI took 11.1. Given the conservatism of the catholic vote (and the animosity of the church hierarchy towards the PDS), few of the latter would have been attracted to the Progressives. Furthermore, a pact with Segni would also have lost the Progressives support on their left. Much more important was the failure to learn the lesson of the December 1993 administrative polls. Then, the Progressive mayoral candidates created what Anderlini (1994) calls a 'virtuous circle between two political realities' that could overcome the problems both of organization and of ideological distance between candidates and voters: the offer of representation managed by a party and the offer of government personalised in a leader. Handicapped both by their programmatic and leadership weaknesses, the Progressives achieved precisely the opposite in March 1994: a vicious circle linking a clumsily constructed coalition to an indistinct project for government. In sum, the Progressive pact was tactical and short-term. It fell far short of being an effective coalition for government and this, in turn, reduced its electoral utility.

But beyond the failure to turn coalition to their electoral advantage, the results reveal the fragility of left-wing support outside the traditional 'red' regions of former Communist Party (PCI) strength, both in the chamber of deputies and in the senate. In the chamber, while winning handsomely with strong majorities almost all (97 per cent) of the majoritarian seats in the Centre (Emilia-Romagna, Tuscany, the Marches and Umbria), the Progressives lost, equally impressively - and also by large margins - nearly all (90 per cent) of the seats in the North. In the senate, the vote was no less polarised: the Progressives won 98 per cent of the seats in the Centre and lost 84 per cent in the North. But they were much more competitive in the South where the elections were effectively fought - and won. There, and generally by slim margins, the Progressives won 34 per cent of the seats in the chamber and 46 per cent in the senate, while the right won 64 and 51 per cent respectively.[12] Nevertheless, only in the 'red' regions of the Centre did the Progressives perform like a popular force, attracting support from traditional working-class constituencies, as well as artisans and housewives. In the North and South, they received only around a third of the workers' vote (Biorcio 1994: 166).

A number of arguments have been put forward to explain the relative success of the Progressives in the South. These include organizational strength (Pasquino, 1994); their greater capacity than in the North to pick up former Socialist Party votes; and the anti-southern, anti-paternalist state rhetoric of the right which may have alienated some traditional Christian Democrat voters from Berlusconi (Bobbio, 1994). While some or all of these factors may have played a part, without doubt the most important factor was the dispersion of the vote in the South due to a division of the right in many regions[13] and the presence of numerous local and marginal candidates (Lazar, 1994: 77-78). Thus, while the Progressives had the largest number of marginal seats nation-wide (34 per cent in the chamber and 41 per cent in the senate), the situation was far worse in the South. There, 66 per cent of the Progressive's senate seats were marginal, as were 62 per cent of their chamber seats. This compared with 50 and 48 per cent, respectively, for the right (Bartolini and D'Alimonte, 1994: 651-670). In numerous cases, a united right could have easily defeated the Progressives. This suggests that, unless the political circumstances are considerably altered, the left will find it hard to improve on its performance in the South and thereby bolster its share of national parliamentary seats. The right, on the other hand, has considerable scope for increasing its strength by extending its alliance to all regions. This is especially true of the chamber where the left is less competitive.

The Summer of Discontent

Given the fragile unity of the Progressives before the election, it was inevitable that defeat should provoke further disarray. The reaction was predictable: as soon as work on the constitution of a single parliamentary group began, so did the bickering. While Rifondazione said the alliance had been too moderate, Alleanza Democratica said it had been too radical. Both, in a sense were right. For as suggested above, the ideological distance within the pact was hardly conducive to coherence. Referring to the factious nature of the coalition, Occhetto began talking openly of forging an alliance with the centre - an option he had rejected only two months earlier. Others, too, began to look longingly towards the lay, or social catholic centre. Leading members of Del Turco's PSI, such as Fabrizio Cicchitto, the leader of the Socialist group in the senate, argued that his party should have struck a common cause with centrist politicians like Giorgio La Malfa and Giuliano Amato. Gino Giugni, former PSI president and labour minister in the Ciampi government, advocated the creation of a structured shadow government, including the centrist opposition, as the prelude to creating a large *'partito del lavoro'* (labour party). In Alleanza, while Ferdinando Adornato strongly supported the creation of a single Progressive group in both chambers, former Republicans such as Bruno Visentini had already decided that their real political home was further to the right. Even the Greens, who were in favour of a parliamentary group giving considerable autonomy to its constituent parts, announced the creation of the *'Progressisti per la società sostenibile'* (Progressives for a Sustainable Society) which would be open to environmentally conscious, centrist politicians. Only the Rete - which had performed worst in regions where it had not been linked to the Progressives - firmly supported the PDS proposal for a single, united group. But even it was keen to ensure that this would herald the creation of a larger 'Democratic Party', less susceptible to PDS hegemony.

Behind these squabbles lay the same problems that had made the electoral pact so precarious. First, while the PDS has distanced itself ideologically from its communist past, it still bore the party form and party/movement vocation of the PCI. While this made it too large to make an alliance of equals with smaller parties, it simultaneously restricted its capacity for innovation. And second, the majoritarian shift in the electoral system had not been strong enough to force the smaller parties to abandon the defence of their own identities and traditions. Hence, the total disarray on the left in the lead-up to the June European elections. The Progressives were incapable of forming either a single force to contest the Berlusconi government, or presenting a coherent critique of its policies. Numerous voices advocated the creation of a strong shadow government, but in vain. This was not just a question of party fetishism, although that clearly played a role. It was rather that a series of further struggles had still to be played out before a new party form could be conceived. At the same time, a new intellectual project had to be devised, although in the months following the March elections, there was little evidence of either strategic or programmatic thinking. In sum, the reinvention of the left that began in 1993 was still far from completion.

The first struggle involved the smaller parties, each of which engaged in an agonizing reappraisal of its relationship with the PDS. This led two of them - Rifondazione and Del Turco's PSI - to abandon the alliance in mid-April. Despite misgivings on its more moderate wing, Rifondazione set out to reassert its radical identity under the close control of Armando Cossuta, the president and real leader of the party. Del Turco wanted to save face after his humiliation by the 'colonnelli craxiani' (Craxi's colonels) who, prior to joining forces with Berlusconi, had accused him of wanting to dissolve the PSI. Alleanza Democratica initially joined the new parliamentary group but then pulled out, unable to reconcile the Republicans and left-leaning Liberals and Socialists within its ranks. In early June, the latter, led by Ferdinando Adornato, returned to the Progressive camp as a 'liberal democratic area'. Thus, by May, the Progressives - now called the 'progressisti-federativo'- consisted of the PDS, the Social Christians, the Rete and the Greens. Of Occhetto's three partners, Orlando's Rete was the most enthusiastic; but even it had split over continuing the alliance, and a dissident group, including Nando Dalla Chiesa (one of the party's founding members), resigned over what it saw as a strategy of subservience to the PDS.

The second struggle involved the PDS itself which, during the early summer was torn apart by a contest which, although ostensibly about leadership, was really about the future of the party as an organization and movement. Relations between Occhetto and D'Alema had rapidly deteriorated after the March elections, and the other Progressives had been forced to indicate, at least implicity, their support for one or the other. This had further complicated the formation of the parliamentary group. While there was a tense truce - a *pax occhettiana* - until the European elections, a debate on the future of the PDS and the Progressives opened in mid-May. But neither D'Alema nor Occhetto figured prominently. The main participants were Massimo Cacciari, the mayor of Venice, who raised the issue of the PDS leadership right after the elections, and advocated a coalition led by a non-party leader (possibly himself); and the editor of L'Unità, Walter Veltroni, who, along with some prominent members of the Alleanza Democratica, made allusions to a broad-based Democratic Party on the US model. While D'Alema was clearly opposed to this idea, Occhetto's position was much less clear.

This, then, was where the Progressives found themselves in June: leaderless, rudderless and reduced to four member parties, the most important of which, the PDS, was now engaged in an undeclared leadership contest. It was hardly surprising, then, that the European elections were a catastrophe for the left: between March and June, the PDS lost 1.6 million votes, Rifondazione 300,000, the PSI and Alleanza 700,000 and the Rete 300,000 (a reduction of 50 per cent)(see Table 2). Only the Greens remained stable; but by comparison with their results in the 1989 European elections (when they stood as two separate parties), their support had been halved.[14] Exit polls indicated that of the 17 per cent of voters who deserted the left, 14 per cent went to Forza Italia and 3 per cent to the Lega Nord and Alleanza Nazionale. The PSI lost 44 per cent of its March vote to Berlusconi and the Rete 33 per cent (La Repubblica 14 June 1994). Although both the Lega and Alleanza Nazionale lost at least as many votes as the Progressives in what was, essentially, a benedictory plebiscite for Berlusconi, the cost to the centre-left was higher. Del Turco tendered his resignation from the PSI for the second time in two weeks (the first was turned down, the second accepted); Willer Bordon stood down as the spokesman for Alleanza Democratica; and Occhetto bowed to the growing pressure for a renewal of the PDS leadership.

Table 2

European Elections Results

	General Elections 1994		European elections 1994			1989			
	Vote	%	Vote	%	Seats	Parties	Vote	%	Seats
Forza Italia	8,136,135	21.0	10,123,990	30.6	27	DC	11,451,053	32.9	26
Lega nord	3,235,248	8.3	2,175,472	6.6	6				
Panella	1,359,283	3.5	706,000	2.1	2				
AN	5,219,435	13.4	4,132,093	12.5	11	MSI-DN	1,918,650	5.5	4
Ppi	4,287,172	11.0	3,299,456	10.0	9				
Patto Segni	1,811,814	4.7	1,076,660	3.3	3				
PDS	7,831,646	20.4	6,299,958	19.1	16	PCI	9,598,369	27.6	22
RC	2,343,946	6.0	2,007,651	6.1	5				
PSI	849,423	2.2	607,180[1]	1.8	2		5,151,926	14.8	12
Verdi	1,074,268	2.7	1,057,208	3.2	3		2,148,099[2]	6.2	5
PRI	456,000	1.2	243,311	0.7	1		1,532,388[3]	4.4	4
Rete	719,841	1.9	368,408	1.1	1				
PSDI	179,495	0.5	227,596	0.7	1		945,383	2.7	2

[1] PSI and Alleanza Democratica. [2] This is the sum of the results of the two separate Green Parties, the Verdi and the Verdi Arcobaleno, which merged in 1990. [3] Republicans plus Liberals (PLI).

Renewal or Stagnation?: the PDS from Occhetto to D'Alema

As pointed out above, the PDS leadership contest was partly also about its future as an organization. But the poverty of the debate suggested that few had any real idea about how to proceed with the party's renewal. To some extent the arguments were obscured by the attention given by the media to Massimo

Cacciari, who, although elected mayor of Venice on a Progressive ticket, was not a card carrying member of the PDS. But even once it was clear that the real contest was between Massimo D'Alema and Walter Veltroni, the terms of the debate became no more precise. Beyond the immediate problems confronting the Italian left, this is clearly related to the difficult task of renewal facing the European left as a whole. Everywhere the problem is one of redefining the policies and appeal of social democracy, while simultaneously adapting traditional organizational structures (Bosetti, 1994; Kitschelt, 1994). This is already a complex process. But in Italy it is further complicated by the fact that the PDS has still fully to escape from its old Communist Party past, not just in the perceptions of its allies and enemies, but in the way it perceives itself as an organization/movement. This is true regardless of the fact that the old organizational monolith no longer exists. It is also complicated by the fact that it is only now that the nature of the environment to which it must adapt is becoming clear, in terms of new cleavage structures, voter preferences and electoral competition. The latter problem clearly afflicts all political forces in Italy, now that the previously closed, static and oligopolistic electoral market has become more open and competitive (see Diamanti and Mannheimer 1994). But the PDS is the only major party to have remained intact during the turbulence of the last few years; caught half-way between the old and the new, this renders its adaptation - and the task confronting its leaders - much more problematic.

The process of adaptation should have been addressed directly by the two competitors for the party leadership in the summer of 1994. But neither had a clear manifesto for party management and change and neither was especially eloquent about their respective alternatives. While either would have been capable of leading the party, neither appeared fully to understand the challenges confronting it. But what the contest did reveal early on was a divorce between large sections of the party's regional base - which had at least a strong sense of the future they didn't want (a preservation of the existing party structure and hierarchy) - and the aspirations of Massimo D'Alema. Veltroni (a man clearly less encumbered by respect for party tradition) was their preferred alternative. Two issues were at stake: the future of the PDS (should it remain intact and preserve its heritage, or become part of a wider, more viable opposition?); and the nature of party democracy (should the local leadership acquire greater influence over the central apparatus?).

The response to these questions effectively split the party in two. In the PDS stronghold of Emilia Romagna, the secretary of the regional federation,

Antonio La Forgia, backed the call made by Massimo Cacciari for a special congress to elect a new party leader. But La Forgia (an *occhettiano*), was outvoted by five provincial secretaries to three, the majority opting instead for the immediate election of Occhetto's replacement by the PDS National Council, in line with party regulations. This represented in microcosm the widening rift in the party. More generally, the leading *occhettiani* in the party, such as the PDS mayor of Bologna, Walter Vitali, Walter Veltroni, Piero Fassino (who had run the party organization for five years) and Claudio Petruccioli (the mastermind of Occhetto's *svolta*) wanted a leadership referendum, as, by and large, did most supporters of Veltroni.[15] By contrast, the D'Alema camp wanted a special congress. Both were rejected. The compromise found between the two was a consultation, conducted largely via fax, whereby the views of around 2000 officials and elected representatives were considered prior to the National Council vote. The result of the consultation was that while the party federations favoured Veltroni over D'Alema by 64 to 42, the national leaders favoured D'Alema by 129 votes to 118.[16] In the National Council vote, however, D'Alema won by a large margin of 294 to 173. Occhetto voted for Veltroni. To many local *pidiessini* in central Italy this indicated that there was now a *partito reale* quite distinct from the *partito legale*; and that the leaders in the party apparatus had lost touch completely with their base.

For the party's allies in the Progressive Federation, this was all a distracting side show and contributed little to resolving the strategic issues now confronting them. However, with D'Alema firmly in charge of the party, it soon became clear that while he may have been the more conservative of the two candidates in organizational terms, there was little difference between him and Veltroni when it came to tactics and ideology. By the fall, D'Alema had abandoned the notion of an alliance on the left for a resurrection of the 1993 strategy of alliance with the catholic centre, this time with Rocco Buttiglione, the leader of the PPI, rather than Mario Segni. In the interests of boosting its electoral competitiveness, the PDS now seemed ready to abandon Rifondazione to its fate. Distinct policy changes began to appear to back up such a strategy, including a more tolerant attitude towards private, religious schools and the beginnings of a dialogue with the 'pro-life', anti-abortion movement. At the same time, Veltroni began work on building a bridge between the left and the catholic church, by giving away free copies of the scriptures with the party's newspaper, L'Unità (Togliatti must be turning in his grave!) and by meeting high ranking clerical figures, including the Pope. The longer term plan suggested that there had been at least a partial reconciliation between the heirs of Occhetto and the party's new leadership. In February 1995, both D'Alema and Fabio Mussi (an occhettiano and deputy leader of the Progressives in the chamber) began talking of plans to change the party's symbol and structure. While the hammer and sickle would be removed from the party's flag altogether (it was relegated to the base of the *quercia* (oak tree) at the time of the 1989 *svolta*), what remained of the old organizational traditions (ie. centralism) was to be abandoned. All of these changes were being driven by the electoral imperative. But will they work?

The way forward: do all roads lead to the centre?

As discussed already, the plight of the left in Italy is similar to that of its counterparts in other European countries: the collapse of the egalitarian ethos, and with it the close organizational and ideological links with the aspirations of a politicised labour movement; its growing dependence on themes that are also articulated by the right, due in large part to the fact that the economy is no longer a 'positional' issue (which divides parties on fundamental principles) but rather a 'valence' issue on which they are differentiated by technocratic capacity (Kitschelt 1994: 296); and the need to redefine itself and its message in terms of post-materialist and communitarian concerns that are also being contested (and quite blatantly in Italy) by an individualist, right-wing neo-materialism.

But in Italy this plight is compounded by the fact that, unlike other mainstream European socialist parties, the PDS has had to make a quite radical transition to post-communism within a five year period, even if it already bore many of the traits of a social democratic party. It has also had to adjust to the erosion of its position and role as a counter-establishment (some have described it as a counter-church) in Italian society, even if it also had a tradition of participation within conventional political structures - as its involvement in numerous corruption scandals attests. This multifaceted process of adjustment is producing a far from monolithic, fragmented party-movement which bears the traces of what Michael Walzer (1994) has called the 'post-modern left' - one that combines elements of the old sectarian left, the traditional proletarian left of the union movement, the left of the new social movements and the communitarian left. The struggle to contain these elements is a monumental one that could easily - and most likely will - give way to disintegration. And to add to these problems, the PDS is being forced to forge a relationship with a centre which, in addition to a large lay component, is predominantly catholic and historically linked to Christian Democracy. This, too, will contribute to the unravelling of the traditional Italian left.

Church meets Counter-Church: a Catholic-post-Communist synthesis?

The relationship between the Italian communists and the Christian Democratic left has always been one of mutual fascination combined with repulsion. In national politics it underpinned the attempted reconciliation between Aldo Moro and Enrico Berlinguer in the so-called 'historic compromise' of the mid-1970s. In local politics, many communist militants have also been strongly religious and, ignoring the dictates of the church hierarchy, many priests have openly sympathised with the communist left. Now that the left has moved into a post-communist era, the mutual suspicions that have always prevented a full embrace between socialism and social catholicism may be abating. Indeed, there is a powerful argument to suggest that Italian neo-materialism, coupled with the laicization of the electorate and the party system (as epitomised in Forza Italia), may in some respects be driving the church and the counter-church closer together.

This argument can be buttressed in a number of ways. The first is that the left, like the catholic centre-right, still has difficulty in accepting the legitimacy of the search for individual wealth and consumerism and it still adheres to a form of paternalism which has its counterpart in a jacobin moralism and conception of democracy. This is linked to some extent to the legacy of marxist intellectualism. Remarking on the success of the left throughout Italy among the more highly educated component of the labour market, and the new class divisions introduced by the triumph of Forza Italia, Diamanti (1994) talks of 'a right of producers confronting a left of intellectuals'. And in a fascinating analysis of the left's reaction to defeat, Bellardelli (1994) draws attention to the left's inability to understand the aspirations of the masses, believing that the collective good is superior - rather than complementary to - the individual interest. The distaste for consumerism, for example - which is also a feature of social catholicism - was clear in the discourse of left-leaning analysts of Berlusconi's victory. The dominant tone of an interview with Norberto Bobbio in the Progressive monthly, *Reset* (May 1994), was dismissive of mass society and the media as one of trivia, sport and spectacle, in short, 'the *natural* society of the right'. Whereas the society created by television could not relate to the great principles of the left and its identification with human suffering.

Secondly, there are signs that the church itself may be moderating its view of the PDS, after decades of depicting the PCI as the communist lucifer. At the highest level, there is still a great deal of suspicion about the PDS and the left in general. This was made clear in the local elections of November 1994 when D'Alema and Buttiglione experimented with alliance in 14 communes and two provinces. The PPI allied with the PDS in 36 per cent of cases, with the parties of the right in 21 per cent and with the Lega Nord in 9.4, and the increase in support received by both the PPI and the PDS appeared to confirm the utility of such alliances. However, shortly after the elections, the bishops' daily Avvenire and the official Vatican paper, L'Osservatore Romano, warned Buttiglione against a plan for government with the PDS or the Lega Nord because this would be a betrayal of the Roman Catholic electorate. And this was regardless of efforts by Mario Segni and Buttiglione to convince the Vatican that the Berlusconi-Fini pact - with which it had been reasonably happy - might not be in the best interests of peace and solidarity. It was this suspicion of even the post-communist left that led the church in 1993 to apply pressure on Segni to back away from the PDS after the success of the referendum movement (Rhodes 1995: 126). Yet, outside the Vatican there is a conviction in many quarters that the communist leopard really has changed its spots. In early 1995, numerous senior figures, including Cardinal Giovanni Saldarini, the Archbishop of Turin, urged the church to accept that the PDS was no longer the PCI; and local bishops in areas where PPI-PDS alliances have been struck have generally given them their blessing.

Emboldened by the results of the November elections, D'Alema forged ahead with his strategy of opening to the centre. In the second week of December, when the PDS National Council met in Rome, D'Alema stated openly that the strategy of a united left-wing front against the right had been a mistake in March and one he was not prepared to repeat. On December 12, the National Council approved the *chiusura* (end of the dialogue) towards Rifondazione Comunista and sanctioned the move towards the centre by the party and alliance with the PPI and, if necessary, with the Lega Nord as well. The reaction from the other Progressives was decidedly cool: Gianni Matteoli, the vice-president of the Progressive group in the chamber, stated that D'Alema was foolish to believe in alliance with Buttiglione and Umberto Bossi just because the latter were distancing themselves from Berlusconi. Anticipating an eventual pact between the PDS and the PPI, Ferdinando Adornato, the leader of the liberal-democratic area in the Progressive camp remarked that the PDS had still no idea about how to rebuild the left; and suggested that D'Alema was still convinced that a historical wave would eventually bring his party - intact and in a tactical alliance - to power. For Adornato - and many others - the priority should have been on redefining the PDS within a broader reconstruction of the left. Salvatore Biasco, the president of the PDS research centre Cespe (Centro studi di politica economica) agreed. He resigned on September 28, stating that the PDS had taken no notice of Cespe's programmatic advice in March and that it was now evident that the PDS had no strategic sense of direction (La Repubblica 27 September 1994). It was true that the PDS had given little thought to the Progressive alliance since the summer and that it was putting all of its eggs in the centrist basket. But going beyond local alliances to a national-level pact with the centre was bound to be difficult. And so it turned out to be.

The prospects for a Centre-Left Alliance

The first obstacle derived, once again, from the confessional character of the centre and the position of the Roman Catholic Church. This will continue to complicate alliances between the left and the catholic centre for, as mentioned above, there is still a reflex opposition in church circles to anything beyond a tactical short-term alliance between the descendants of Christian Democracy and the PCI. At the same time, many practising catholic voters will continue to take their cue from the religious press and will be repelled by the heirs of atheistic communism, regardless of the free distribution of the scriptures with L'Unità. Their religious faith continues to be an important influence on their voting behaviour, regardless of the substantial erosion that has occurred in Italy's catholic subculture. A second obstacle is created by the ambitions of former Christian Democrats. Many leaders of the catholic centre (and of the church) still clearly believe in the prospect of rebuilding the Christian Democratic party, in one form or another, if necessary from within the right-wing alliance of Forza Italia and Alleanza Nazionale. Hence the split in the PPI in March 1995 when Buttiglione changed strategy. Ending his flirtation with D'Alema and the centre-left, he embraced Silvio Berlusconi and Gianfranco Fini instead, repudiating criticisms that social catholicism was incompatible with the illiberal right. He was backed by the ultra-conservative catholics in Opus Dei and other sections of the church. But others deplored the division this created in the catholic political movement and Buttliglione alienated the left of his party and probably a good proportion of his voters. Many of the latter may now be attracted to the new centre-left project of Romano Prodi which D'Alema is also supporting. Nevertheless, by early 1995, D'Alema was looking rather foolish: Buttiglione had only had an opportunistic interest in a relationship with the PDS and broke it off as soon as he received a better offer.

Beyond short-term tactical manoeuvres, the third obstacle to a successful centre-left project for government derives from the electoral arithmetic. Although it is difficult to make electoral predictions for either the right or the left - due to the rapidly evolving party system, electoral volatility, shifts in alliance strategy, and the prospect of yet further electoral reform - it is clear that combining the votes of the left and the centre will not necessarily provide an electoral fix. First there is the problem of 'summability'. As occurred within the Progressive coalition in March 1994, the stand-down system for candidates would mean that former Christian Democratic voters could find themselves voting for former communists and vice-versa. There is thus a danger of a haemorrhage from both the left and the right of any prospective coalition. More generally, there is the problem of linking two quite different electoral cultures: the practising catholic centre-right which, according to recent socio-cultural surveys, is predominantly composed of rather conservative, socially isolated, older voters and housewives, inspired by religious principles; and a secular centre-left of more politically active, middle-aged employees. In both there is a low degree of vote transferability beyond the immediate political area (i.e. the number of voters willing to support an alternative party to their own) (Calvi and Vannucci, 1994).

The PPI vote is distinguished by the fact that it is not attracted to any great extent by any other party, whether to its right or its left, the sympathies of its elite notwithstanding. Indeed, there appears to be a substantial gap in this respect between the PPI leadership (whether leaning to the right or the left) and its base. The degree of openness to other political parties that does exist is clearly oriented towards the right of the political spectrum: while 13.9 per cent in the Calvi-Vannucci survey were prepared to vote for Forza Italia and 8.6 per cent for Alleanza Nazionale, only 4.7 per cent would consider supporting the PDS. In the case of the left, the greatest degree of transferability is between the PDS and Rifondazione; while only 3.1 per cent of PDS and 2.1 per cent of Rifondazione voters could conceive of voting for the PPI. In both cases, more were likely to vote for Forza Italia (Calvi and Vannucci, 1994: 147). This suggests that even were a way to be found of linking the two electorates programmematically, it might not be much of a vote winner: indeed, it could send centrist voters into the open arms of the right, while a proportion of left-wing voters, released by the erosion of their own sub-culture, might also follow them. Ricolfi (1994: 627) goes further, and argues that an alliance between traditional PDS (and PCI) values and social catholicism would sink both parties given that the electorate is moving in the opposite, secular and individualist, direction.

But even were it possible to combine the two electorates, including the reformist catholic and lay centre of the Patto Segni, the numbers do not add up to a centre-left victory. Simply adding the 6.1 million centre votes in the March 1994 elections (Segni plus the Partito Popolare) to the 13.2 million won by the Progressives gives a total of 19.3 million - more than the 17.9 million won by the right, including Marco Pannella and his supporters. But as Anderlini (1995) illustrates, the geo-political factor - i.e. the territorial distribution of votes and seats - in a majoritarian system prevents such simple calculations. As discussed above, Italy is divided between a North dominated by the right, a Centre dominated by the left, and a South in which the greater success of the left was critically dependent on a large number of marginal seats where its opponents were divided. Adding the votes of the centre to those of the left does not compensate for the latter's southern weakness, because the 15 per cent of the national vote won by the Partito Popolare and the pattisti is overwhelmingly concentrated in the centre (Emilia-Romagna and the Marches) and those parts of the South where the left already does well. Thus, in Anderlini's simulation of the performance of a left-centre coalition in the March 1994 election, 50 per cent of the national vote would have delivered 41.5 per cent of the seats - just 29 seats more than the Progressives and the centre groups achieved divided. Where both the centre and the left need seats, they are both too weak to achieve the necessary critical mass (Anderlini 1995).

Conclusion: the oak, the olive and the future of the left

This discounts, of course, changes in electoral rules combined with new and effective innovations in political alliance and leadership. With a double ballot system (which now has wide political support) and a new leader of the centre-left, the results could conceivably be very different. In principle, Romano Prodi - who in the early months of 1995 was rapidly adopted as a future coalition leader by centrist and left-wing forces - could perform the same trick as Berlusconi: launching a project in the media, building an electoral coalition around it, and attracting votes from right across the spectrum, as well as from that 20 per cent of the eligible electorate that is currently composed of non-affiliated, non-voters. With his sensible, centrist manifesto for government - which appeals to the common sense of the average Italian and promises a maintenance of the welfare state, greater public sector efficiency, a judicious injection of privatization into the health and pensions systems, and an active policy for education and the labour market (Prodi 1995) - the new man of destiny could conceivably attract widespread support, even if he lacks the charisma, media resources and extravagance of Silvio Berlusconi (who has alienated a growing proportion of his erstwhile electorate). But his problem remains that of attracting the vote of the moderate centre, rather than that of the left which, according to opinion polls, has flocked readily to his cause.

For the time being, it is impossible to do anything other than speculate on the future of the Prodi project. But it is legitimate and possible to consider the future for the left within it. The small centre groups - Alleanza Democratica, Mario Segni and his *pattisti*, members of Giuliano Amato's Italia Domani and the Socialists - all aligned themselves rapidly behind Prodi's so-called Olivo (Olive Tree) project in early 1995.[17] Among the leading deputies identifying with the cause were Mario Segni, Enrico Boselli, Gianni Rivera, Gino Giugni, Ottaviano Del Turco, Willer Bordon, Giorgio Brogi and Giuseppe Ayala. Rifondazione Comunista has been split between its old guard and its 'new left' faction by the prospect of collaboration with Prodi. As for the PDS, the presence of figures such as Segni in the Prodi camp suggests that some distance will be kept between the olive tree and the quercia (oak tree) of the PDS. It is said that the two grow well together, but not if they are too close since the shade of the oak will stifle the olive. I would suggest a different outcome: that, given the sorry condition of the oak, its weakened roots could be strangled by those of the olive.

The main problem for the PDS is one of identity after years of ideological drift and programmatic stagnation that the *svolta* has so far failed to reverse (Minucci, 1995). It is all too clear that D'Alema is seeking an electoral fix in linking up with the centre and backing Prodi after the failure of his tactical manoeuvres with Buttiglione. But this may prove to be electorally dangerous unless he can provide the PDS with a new and more definite profile. If the party follows its present course - which is one of refraining from developing an alternative for government, lest it alienate potential allies - then it could well lose support to a more credible pole of attraction to its right. Major opportunities have been wasted due to the timidity bred of 40 years in opposition. For example, the success of the demonstrations against the Finance Bill in October 1994 was not exploited by the development of an alternative budget. More generally, D'Alema's strategy is to refrain from making concrete policy proposals until after he has entered government. This strategic caution has prevented his party from deriving any real benefit for itself from the string of errors committed by the Berlusconi government: only a professional, structured shadow cabinet could have taken advantage of that probably unique opportunity. In 1993, it seemed possible that the former communists could shape their own future, as well as that of their country, by reinventing the Italian left. By 1995, the PDS had become the victim rather than the master of its fate.

Notes

1. The other, the more conservative Centro Cristiano Democratico, became a member of the Berlusconi-led Polo della Libertà. For the March elections, the Partito Popolare joined forces with the Patto Segni. The latter combined an array of forces, including Mario Segni's Popolari per la Riforma, elements of Giorgio La Malfa's Republican Party that had not joined the Alleanza Democratica and centrist Socialists and Liberals such as Giuliano Amato and Valerio Zanone.

2. For an analysis of the background, see Rhodes (1995b).

3. The resulting lack of renewal was reflected in the high number of Progressive candidates in the March elections who were outgoing deputies - 21.5 per cent, compared with 17.1 per cent for Mario Segni's Patto per Italia and 12.2 per cent in the case of the Polo della Libertà.

4. While Del Turco's group abandoned the old symbol of the carnation for that of the rose, received the blessing of Socialist International president, Pierre Mauroy, and allied themselves, with some trepidation to the PDS, the *craxiani* in the Federazione Liberal-Socialista joined forces with Silvio Berlusconi. This cemented an alliance which had had, in fact, *de facto* status since the days of the Craxi-Berlusconi entente cordiale.

5. This was the case in the Rome 1 senatorial district where the formerly influential Christian Democrat, Bartolo Ciccardini (who left the DC to join Mario Segni's Reformists and then Alleanza Democratica) was the candidate; in Rome 15 where the candidacy of Roberto Villetti, the former editor of the PSI broadsheet, Avanti!, under Bettino Craxi, was opposed - for reasons of old PSI/PDS animosity - by local *pidiessini* (PDS members); in Abruzzo 3 where another Socialist, Alberto La Volpe, the former director of Telegiornale 2 (a Craxi appointment), led the Progressives; and in the heavily PDS Emilian constituency of Bologna 18 where PSI leader Ottaviano Del Turco was presented.

6. Among these proposals were: a single pension insurance system, ending the regime of privileged treatment and separate management; the preservation of a public health system and a range of free basic services; family allowances determined by the number of family members and old people; allowances for women on maternity leave or on leave to look after the sick; incentives to return to work for those who leave employment for family reasons; schools to remain lay and public and the leaving age to be increased from 14 to 16 then 18. As for institutional reform, the Progressives backed a double ballot system, a reduction of the number of ministers and a transformation of the senate into a regional chamber.

7. On 11 February, while Napolitano was reassuring the IMF in talks with its director-general, Michel Camdessus, and stressing the importance of a new Ciampi-led government of technicians, Occhetto was at a conference in Milan conducting a confidence-building exercise with around 60 investment fund managers.

8. A month before the election, a CIRM opinion poll revealed that while 52 per cent of voters thought unemployment the most important theme of the campaign, only 25 per cent thought that

the Progressives could deal effectively with the problem, compared with 42 per cent for the right.

9. At this stage, as in number of European countries, many on the Italian centre-left were obsessed with the Clinton victory in the United States and intent on emulating that example. For the spokesman of Alleanza Democratica, Ferdinando Adornato, Ciampi was Italy's closest equivalent: 'He's the only Clinton we have. And certainly not Segni, that Bush who won the Gulf war of the referendum campaign but who failed to understand the needs of the country, and still less Berlusconi-Ross Perot...' (cited in La Repubblica, 11 February 1994). After the election, Adornato admitted that the choice of Ciampi had been an error, a defensive rather than an innovative choice, trapping the Progressive's in the old order rather than propelling them forward into the new.

10. Just prior to the elections, only 44 per cent of left-wing voters thought probable a Progressive victory. 76 per cent of supporters of the Polo della Libertà thought the right-wing alliance would win (see Biorcio 1994: 161).

11. A second problem, this time for the left more generally, was the distorting effects of the electoral system. While the new right-wing alliance received less votes than the old *pentapartito* government in 1992 (42.9 per cent of the proportional votes as against 49 per cent), it won 58 per cent of the seats in the chamber. It won just under 50 per cent of the seats in the senate with 40 per cent of the vote. The centre parties were more penalised than the left: with 16 per cent of the vote in the chamber and 17 per cent in the senate, they won 7 and 10 per cent of the seats (see Bobbio 1994).

12. These figures come from Bartolini and D'Alimonte (1994) who define marginality as a less than 8 per cent gap between the vote of the winning candidate and that of the runner up.

13. Generally, the right was divided by Forza Italia and Alleanza Nazionale presenting separate candidates (this was the case in Campania 2 in the senate and Abruzzi in both the chamber and the senate elections), or by the Pannella List breaking away from the right-wing pact (as in Campania in the chamber and in most parts of Puglia and Lazio in the chamber and senate elections). The presentation of joint candidates could conceivably have won a further 24 seats in the chamber (10 of which became Progressive safe seats) and four in the senate.

14. The Greens in Italy face an uncertain future. Their inability to mobilise more than a small section of the vote, the aging of their electoral base (which it shares with the left more generally), and their failure to counteract the neo-materialist allure of the right are likely to prevent any revival of their fortunes in the foreseeable future (see Rhodes 1995a).

15. Fassino was the driving force behind the Veltroni campaign in the party and Petruccioli the propagandist. Petruccioli said that D'Alema would only be able to create a second Rifondazione, a ghetto party that would face certain defeat at the hands of Berlusconi (La Repubblica, 29 June 1994).

16. While Veltroni won nearly all the 'red zone' federations, D'Alema conquered the south. For some *dalemiani*, however, the success of Veltroni in the consultation suggested that the figures had been manipulated. But even amongst the party elite, the result was less clear cut, at least before the final National Council vote. In the consultation, 130 members of the National Council chose D'Alema and 120 Veltroni, while 55 indicated no preference and 54 proposed alternatives. Although the higher party ranks (regional and federation secretaries) also favoured D'Alema, a slim majority of deputies, regional presidents and trade unionists backed Veltroni (La Repubblica, 29 June 1994).

17. These groups are better described as political clubs rather than parties. Not only are they small but also the affiliation of their members is rather fluid. Thus, when Giuliano Amato launched Italia Domani at the end of September 1994, a variety of reformist, lay and catholic politicians and trade unionists signed up. Among them were Luigi Spaventa, Gino Giugni, Antonio Maccanico

and Fernando Contri (all former ministers in the Ciampi government), Umberto Rainieri (PDS), Valerio Zanone (Liberal), Marco Boato (Green), Silvia Costa (PPI), Cesare San Mauro (Patto Segni) and numerous former Socialists. The latter's own political home had fragmented even further throughout 1994. In April, those socialists that did not side with Del Turco in the Progressive pact linked up within the *Federazione dei socialisti italiani* led by Franco Piro (the secretary) and Margherita Boniver (the president). Following them dutifully into Berlusconi's Polo della Libertà were the illustrious heirs of the Craxi order. In mid-November, Del Turco's wing of the old PSI was relaunched as the Socialisti Italiani (SI) and Enrico Boselli was elected its secretary. Party fetishism continued to characterise this group: on 13 November, Enrico Manca broke away from the SI to create the Partito Socialista Riformista!

References

Anderlini, F. (1994), 'La razionalità del voto e il modo di cambiarlo', *Politica ed Economia*, 2, April.

Anderlini, F. (1995), 'Partiti: elezioni', *Politica ed Economia,* 1 January.

Bartolini, S. and D'Alimonte R. (1994), 'La competizione maggioritaria: le origine elettorali del parlamento diviso', *Rivista Italiana di Scienza Politica,* Vol. 24, No. 3.

Belardelli, G. (1994), 'Sè alla sinistra non piacciono gli italiani', *Il Mulino,* 5, September-October.

Biorcio, R. (1994) 'Le ragioni della sinistra, le risorse della destra', in I. Diamanti and R. Mannheimer (eds.), *Milano a Roma. Guida all'Italia elettorale del 1994,* Roma: Donzelli Editore.

Bobbio, L. (1994), 'Dalla destra alla destra, una strana alternanza', in Ginsborg P. (ed.), *Stato dell'Italia,* Milano: il Saggiatore; Bruno Mondadori.

Bosetti, G. (1994), 'La crisi in cielo e in terra' in G. Bosetti (ed.), *Sinistra punto zero,* Roma: Donzelli Editore.

Calvi, G. and Vannucci A. (1994), *L'Elettore sconosciuto: Analisi socioculturale e segmentazione degli orientamenti politici nel 1994,* Bologna: Il Mulino.

Diamanti, I. (1994), 'Perchè perde la sinistra', *MicroMega 5,* November-December.

Diamanti, I. and Mannheimer R. (1994), 'Introduzione', in Diamanti I.and Mannheimer R. (eds.), *Milano a Roma: Guida all'Italia elettorale del 1994,* Roma: Donzelli Editore.

Di Virgilio, A. (1994), 'Dai partiti ai poli: la politica delle alleanze', *Rivista Italiana di Scienza Politica,* Vol. 24, No. 3.

Kitschelt, H. (1994), *The Transformation of European Social Democracy,* Cambridge: Cambridge University Press.

Lazar, M. (1994), 'I Progressisti', in Diamanti I. and Mannheimer R. (eds.), *Milano a Roma: Guida all'Italia elettorale del 1994,* Roma: Donzelli Editore.

Minucci, A. (1995), *La sinistra da Craxi a Beluscoui,* Rome: Edizioni Sisifo.

Pasquino, G. (1994), 'The Unexpected Alternation: The March Italian 1994 Elections and their Consequences', *Bologna Centre Occasional Papers,* 97, The Johns Hopkins University, July.

Prodi, R. (1995) *Governare l'Italia: Manifesto per il cambiamento,* Rome: Donzelli Editore.

Rhodes, M. (1995a), 'Italy: Greens in an Overcrowded Political System', in Richardson D. and Rootes C. (eds.), *The Green Challenge: The Development of Green Parties in Europe,* London: Routledge.

Rhodes, M. (1995b), 'Reinventing the Left: The Origins of Italy's Progressive Alliance', in Mershon C. and Pasquino G. (eds.), *Italian Politics: Ending the First Republic,* Boulder, Colorado: Westview Press.

Ricolfi, L. (1994), 'Il voto proporzionale e il nuovo spazio politico italiano', *Rivista Italiana di Scienza Politica,* Vol. 24, No. 3.

Walzer, M. (1994), 'La sinistra che c'è', in Bosetti G. (ed.), *Sinistra punto zero,* Roma: Donzelli Editore.

six

The new catholic parties: the Popolari, the Patto Segni and CCD

Carolyn M. Warner

"If it must break apart, the DC will not do so in two but in a thousand pieces, like a crystal." Giulio Andreotti.[1]

In 1945, the Italian Christian Democratic party, Democrazia Cristiana (DC), vowed to become "the sail and rudder of our national community"(Gonella 1959:30). By generating a strong electoral wind from catholicism, anti-communism and patronage, it did - for a time. Not quite 50 years later, the DC ran its own ship aground. When it first fractured, it split into three catholic political parties, the parties which are the subject of this essay.

The DC built itself on the use of patronage, anti-communism, and the Catholic church.[2] Aside from the fact that the strategy has had grave social and economic consequences for Italy, in the collapse of those pillars, the DC had nothing to stand upon - nor did its successors. The DC had adapted to the increasing secularization of Italian society by relying upon patronage, while the Catholic Church's influence over the electorate had weakened. In the late 1980s, the actions of leaders and activists in the Soviet Union and Eastern Europe rendered anti-communism an irrelevant campaign battle cry. The conjuncture of these two factors reduced significant barriers to voter and politician exit from the DC. The DC, ensnared by its own patronage web, could not use its policy record as a substitute for the role of anti-communism in getting votes. Thus, when communism was no longer a practical problem, the DC had to portray as demonic another party: the Lega Nord.[3] But with norms shifting against patronage, it was too late.

What is of note also is that the DC set up a patronage system which drew in all the political parties. The use of national level patronage enabled the DC to remain the dominant party as the church's influence over Italians lessened in the 1970s. Yet that strategy let the mafia go unchecked, prevented beneficial policies from being implemented and so weakened the government and the DC that when some DC politicians finally wanted to change the system, they could not without themselves becoming victims of the overhaul.

The DC's old strategy produced such a massive rejection of the political class that where previously the prime minister was a seasoned, long-time politician, the latest prime minister entered politics only two months before the elections in which his new party was victorious. Where previously the neo-fascist movement was excluded from cabinet participation, neo-fascists were in the Berlusconi government. While the DC anti-communism strategy appears to have led to the perpetual exclusion of the left from government, other politicians, notably Umberto Bossi and his Lega Nord, Silvio Berlusconi and Forza Italia, and Gianfranco Fini and his neo-fascists, seized, and even created, the opportunity to re-structure the Italian political and economic system.[4] In their wake trail three catholic parties: the Partito Popolare Italiano (PPI), the Patto Segni, and the Centro Cristiano Democratico (CCD).

In the March 1994 legislative elections, the three catholic parties between them did not get more than 16 per cent of the vote. Hindered by association with the DC and by a lack of the DC's vote-getting methods, the parties have had to put alternative strategies to work. In order to understand the catholic parties' actions, one needs to consider how parties in general attract voters. After discussing various strategies, I will sketch the DC's demise and the major events of 1994 concerning the catholic parties and those parties' options. Following that, I will argue that one can best understand these parties and what they are doing in terms of the differing fundamental strategies of each party. I will conclude with a discussion of the Church and other catholic organizations' relations with the PPI, the Patto Segni and the CCD.

Strategic options

Political parties are directed by politicians with particular ideas about how to run a government, about what should be done in politics. Politicians are not just office-seekers responding to the preferences of an electorate and the incentives and constraints of the electoral system. Politicians come to politics with ideas, with norms of organization and behavior. This is not to say that incentives and constraints are irrelevant, and never impinge upon politicians' intentions and ideals. Rather, leaders' beliefs will colour the choice of strategy. The leaders' actions will be taken with an eye toward how those actions cohere and resonate with their goals and ideas. This analytic point is particularly important when the creation of new electoral rules and new parties coincides. Such a situation is characterized by great uncertainty as to the consequences of a given action.[5] Ideas and the struggle to give primary place to them, influence the types of internal and external party coalitions which politicians try to build, and how politicians go about building them.

With this in mind, each of Italy's three catholic parties can be thought of as embodying a strategy for building an electoral following. The DC's actions had foreclosed certain options. The parties had to build themselves in the absence of a dominant catholic block, in the absence of a communist threat and in the presence of anti-corruption prosecutions.

To bring about their policy and career ambitions, politicians in democracies need organizations. Principles alone will not get politicians into office. They need a political party and they need votes.[6] So how do they construct vote-winning organizations?

Politicians can try to monopolize an issue which has deep resonance in major organizations and in the electorate. The party can portray itself as the best solution to a serious threat, while the threat itself can be manufactured. Party leaders can create an enemy: as in 1992, when the DC demonized the Lega Nord. Party leaders can make programmematic appeals. The party can portray itself as the best solution to a pressing problem.

Patronage, or material resource distribution for the purpose of getting votes, can be particularly useful. Resource distribution fosters links to social forces and individual voters. Patronage coopts both voters and rival politicians. (Shefter, 1977). These factors make it difficult for another party to obtain a larger market share, or even to break into the political market in the first place. Yet, significant for the new catholic parties, the moral and judicial tide has turned against patronage.

Another means of attracting and retaining voters is for a party to rely on authoritative organizational allies - allies which provide useful endorsements and campaign resources. To attract organizational allies, the party might exploit a particular threat, emphasizing dire consequences of exit, and it might also withhold material benefits. In turn, the organizational allies could emphasize to their members the importance of supporting a particular party. Also, the organization could make membership and organizational benefits contingent upon voting for a particular party.

Given all that occurred between 1989 and 1993, the pillars upon which the DC had built itself - catholicism, anti-communism and patronage - were no longer available. Those factors, including the substantial resources of catholic organizations and of public enterprises, as well as a much publicized "communist threat", had enabled the DC to contain disparate, competing factions within itself. The electorate had strong incentives to vote for the DC and remain within the party. Absent those and the DC had few levers of control. So it was not surprising that when the DC folded, the political expression of Christian Democracy would be split into various fragments, each one now a party carrying a separate name.

For the first time, any attempt to attract voters and to renew Christian Democracy would have to be based upon programmatic appeals, policy proposals and results. The shrinking influence of the Catholic Church over catholics' political choices limits the utility of appealing to the DC's traditional electorate. Forza Italia, the Alleanza Nazionale (AN) and the Lega Nord are all, even for catholics, fairly credible parties. All votes for the centre-right need not go to the catholic parties. The catholic politicians must now concentrate on producing tangible results through policy initiatives and accomplishments (roads, jobs, reduced taxes, increased family subsidies).

For this, the party must have a sufficient numerical presence in the cabinet and/or parliament in order to get funding for its district-specific, or economic-group targets and to be able to make a credible claim that it was indeed the party responsible for the procurement of the benefit. Presently, this option is a difficult one for the catholic parties to exercise: their party politicians are an insignificant force in the Italian parliament and the emphasis is on budget cuts.

One response to such difficulties is for a party to negotiate a common legislative programme or electoral strategy with other parties. Party leaders can see which alliances have the most voter appeal. The party may gain visibility and influence by positioning itself as the central link in an alternative majority. It is this strategy which the PPI has pursued.

Another tactic is for a party to give unswerving support to the government, getting whatever rewards the majority agrees to send the party's way. This is what the CCD has done. Even the Popolari were able to exercise some leverage in the Senate, where the Berlusconi Government was three seats short of a majority.

In contrast, parties can be part of an adamant opposition, vocally attacking the government for alleged or real failures. They can take advantage of being in the opposition by presenting their party as the solution to citizens' disenchantment. It is this which the Patto Segni has done.

The catholic parties have pursued different strategies. In essence, they represent an interesting case of parties from the same starting point pursuing different strategies. It is too early to assess "what works." The intent of this chapter is to describe the parties, exploring what has become of Christian Democracy in the DC's absence.

Demise of the DC, creation of separate Catholic parties

"It is paradoxical that while we speak of alliances with those who are far from us, here we divide ourselves from those who are near." Gerardo Bianco, (Corriere della Sera, 19 Jan. 1994.)

It was in the summer of 1993 that DC leaders and activists began speaking seriously of folding the party and creating an ostensibly new organization - one which would somehow represent more than a name change, but less than a complete disbanding of Christian Democracy as a political organization.

Discredited by *Tangentopoli*, lacking both a strong communist enemy and a large obedient catholic voting bloc and its vote percentage dropping dramatically,[7] the DC disbanded on 18 January 1994. Its secretary, Mino Martinazzoli, immediately proclaimed the formation of the Partito Popolare Italiano. Simultaneously, several ex-DC leaders formed the CCD. Ironically, just when the electoral system is such that individual parties are encouraged to unite with others, thereby creating larger all-encompassing organizations, the catholic parties find it impossible to unite.

For the March 1994 legislative election, the PPI and the Patto Segni did find a platform upon which to agree. Linking also with the Liberals and Republicans, their Patto per l'Italia was to be a "liberal-democratic reformist" bloc. Its general propositions included a "reduction of government subsidies, a revisiting of the fiscal question" and increasing the efficiency of the civil service (Corriere della Sera, 23 February 1994). The Patto per l'Italia advocated a foreign policy which pushed the ideals of liberty and Western democracy, thinking this would counter "the resurgent spectre of ethnic, religious and racial hatreds"

(Corriere della Sera, 2 March 1994). It was both lay and clerical, the "backbone" of a "wide aggregation" which sought to contrast its seriousness with the televised glossiness of Forza Italia.

The election was an utter defeat for the various catholic parties. The Patto per l'Italia won only 15.7 per cent of the vote. Martinazzoli immediately tendered his resignation and withdrew from politics (to return as the successful mayoral candidate of Brescia in the autumn). The CCD, for its part, won less than one per cent of the proportional votes. Linked with Berlusconi's northern and southern alliances, the CCD fared better on the majoritarian ballots, winning a number of deputies equal to the Patto's.

Partito Popolare Italiano: opportunistic alliance strategy

One might recognize in the PPI's strategy much of the DC's politically opportunistic alliance policy, with a dose of catholic social and economic values. Though they agreed that catholics were now to be found in all political parties, the PPI insisted that their voters were in the centre, where, by their definition, catholicism and economic, political and social solidarity meet. This appropriation of the political centre coincided with the former DC leaders' efforts to renew Christian Democracy. That effort to leave behind the discredited DC began with a controversial claim to the heritage of Don Luigi Sturzo's Partito Popolare Italiano (1919-1924). The PPI's home base continued to be at the DC's old headquarters in the Piazza del Gesù, Rome. Other claims to the DC's patrimony were unsettled.

The North dominated the party membership. As of the July congress, the PPI counted 233,377 members; 43.4 per cent of them in the North, 19.1 per cent in the Centre, 28.2 per cent in the South, and 9.3 per cent on the islands. The members tend to be middle-aged, active professionals. Of those members, 17 per cent were in the tertiary sector; 16 per cent in industry; 14 per cent in public service (La Repubblica, 28 July 1994).

Programme

With a vision of maintaining the catholic social heritage, the PPI pushed a programme which, while reducing some taxes, includes a thick social safety net, particularly for families. It was unvarying in its opposition to abortion, divorce and birth control. It supports the financing of catholic schools, strict rules on genetic research and engineering, and morals in line with the teachings of Pope Wojtyla. Obviously, it was a programme which would render alliances with the secular left difficult.

Social "solidarity" was the keynote of the PPI's economic platform. The PPI endorsed a "tax pact" with self-employed and small businessmen which would reduce taxes on investments and income used to create new jobs. Regarding social welfare, the PPI has advocated reforming the system by allowing citizens to choose their own medical suppliers. On this, the Patto Segni agreed. The PPI would raise pensions so as to guarantee retirees a decent standard of living. All but those below the poverty line should have an obligatory pension, chosen from a public or private supplier.

The PPI proposed tackling unemployment by exempting industries which hire youth from various social security taxes for two years and by reducing those contributions for another two years. In so doing, the PPI estimated it would create 300,000 new jobs per year. The PPI also emphasized economic rigour so as to be in the "hard core" of the European Union, all the while stating that adjustment burdens must be equitable.

On the institutional reform question, the PPI advocated a differentiation of functions and powers of the chamber and senate, a strengthening of the Government's powers and a "profound re-organization of the regions" (Corriere della Sera, 26 March 1994). The PPI, in contrast to the Patto Segni, contended that the prime minister should continue to be elected by the parliament. It concurred with the Patto that the president should be directly elected. In contrast to the Lega Nord, it was against federalism. On foreign policy, the PPI stated only that Italy should be at the centre of efforts to extinguish the Mediterranean and European wars.

The PPI's programme, while perhaps pragmatic, was hardly dramatic or new. The party's job creation proposal was nearly three-quarters of a million jobs short of the number promised by Forza Italia. The PPI's platform, being more cautionary than enthusiastic in tone, was unlikely to elicit votes from an electorate tired of Italian politics as usual.

Elections

The PPI used the legislative elections to eliminate the image of a party with something for which to apologize. Martinazzoli declared, "enough suffering, the time of repentance is over. Whoever would like to expel us will not do it because of our mistakes, but because of our policies" (Corriere della Sera, 22 March 1994). Unfortunately for the PPI, only 11. 6 per cent of the electorate found reasons to vote for the party.

Indeed, the PPI's programme and its difficulties in appealing to the electorate can be seen in its alliance with the Patto Segni for the March 1994 legislative elections. The two parties formed the Patto per l'Italia and negotiated the placement of their respective candidates in the single-member districts. In the key constituency of Rome 1, the PPI found itself represented by the Patto Segni's Alberto Michelini. Michelini, running against Luigi Spaventa for the Progressisti and Silvio Berlusconi for Forza Italia, stressed that the Patto per l'Italia was, first of all, a "pact for the family", secondly, a "pact for the elderly and young", and lastly, a "pact for Rome". Because those factors found echoes on the left, Michelini could only distinguish his candidacy by an emphasis on catholicism, with its now limited vote appeal, and by saying that a vote for the centre would avoid the success of a contradictory left and an unstable right-wing bridge. In Rome as in most of the country, the Patto per l'Italia was decimated by the left and right: 11.7 per cent against the Progressisti's 39.9 per cent and Forza Italia's 47.7 per cent. The Patto was damaged by Forza Italia turning the tables on the catholics. As the DC used to do, Forza Italia in 1994 claimed that it was the only logical barrier against the left, and it worked for the support of the Roman clergy. (True to Berlusconi's audiovisual campaign, Forza Italia sent not just letters, but promotional videotapes to parish priests)(La Repubblica, 29 March 1994).

The PPI fielded candidates who found little positive to say: a candidate in Rome's periphery could only say that he spoke with the people and tried to make them think, while he tried to avoid falling between right and left. Adding to its problems, the Patto per l'Italia was far out-spent by Forza Italia. As Michelini noted, if it were the Patto and not Berlusconi which owned half the Italian TV channels and could run forty television advertisements per day, the Patto may have been ahead in the polls. Conveying the Patto's message by modest means, emphasizing catholic solidarity, the PPI could not compensate for the secular corruption of its predecessor.

Surveying the results, the PPI's former President, Rosa Russo Jervolino, nevertheless asserted that the PPI was a viable, important entity. The party "has more than ever a role to play in order to avoid the country sliding definitively to the right, making individualism and egoism prevail"(La Repubblica, 30 March 1994). Yet the party has had to do so with only 33 deputies in the chamber and 27 in the senate.

Alliances and internal divisions

Rocco Buttiglione summarized the party's problem, "the fundamental fact that one must understand is this: in Italy there was a large right-wing wave which we did not know how to intercept and which has carried away a substantial part of our electorate"(Corriere della Sera, 30 March 1994). This had left the PPI facing two questions. The first is whether it should recover that electorate; the second question is, if so, how?

Here the party divided and the division was epitomized in conflicts between the then secretary, Rocco Buttiglione, and Rosy Bindi, PPI leader of Veneto. Rocco Buttiglione, elected secretary in July 1994, tended to represent the centre-right of the old DC. This politically moderate group was willing to consider working with the Berlusconi majority.[8] Buttiglione was in agreement with Berlusconi's controversial stance on the judiciary and on budget proposals. This appears to have been an effort to appeal to the catholic right. On the PPI's formation, Buttiglione indicated that an alliance with the former communists, the Partito Democratico della Sinistra (PDS), was not of interest - the left was not, according to this wing of the PPI, where the PPI's electorate was to be found.[9]

Instead, he noted that Forza Italia had managed to express the desires of an emerging middle class and that now one cannot govern without that class. Christian democracy could extend itself to this class. After taking the secretariat, Buttiglione held talks with all leaders of the Berlusconi government and seemed willing to work with the Lega. Only Alleanza Nazionale, the neo-fascists, and Rifondazione Comunista, the hard-line communists, were excluded from consideration. "It is necessary to see the programmes (of the governing parties)." In December, Buttiglione let it slip out that he was interested in an alliance with Forza Italia. When a substantial outcry over this coincided with the questioning of Berlusconi on corruption issues, the PPI leader issued a disclaimer. Buttiglione had tried to appropriate for the PPI, the claim of being the only party with a "culture of governing", hence its effectiveness as a mediator.

Rosy Bindi, PPI leader of Veneto, represented the side which emphasized autonomy for the party, yet sees the PPI's natural electorate more on the left. This wing consistently opposed the government, having harsh words for Berlusconi's attacks on the judiciary, and on the influence of his private economic power on politics. It emphasized "solidarity" over the prevalence of market economy logic. This wing viewed Forza Italia as a business enterprise which had gone into politics and was critical of what it saw as merely opportunistic alliances with the right. Citing the opposition behavior of the Patto Segni, Giovanni Bianchi, ex-Catholic Action labour president, noted that opposition does not entail adoption of the PDS's platform. This wing argued that "our identity orientates the alliances," rather than the reverse (La Repubblica, 29 July 1994). With ideals that were in opposition to the right, it contended that alliances with the right would merely reinforce the latter's upper hand.

Under Buttiglione's leadership, the PPI was a party in search of the best deal. The PPI, for general parliamentary affairs and for mayoral elections, played the DC's Janus-faced role. Buttiglione emphasized preparing legislative programmes for the time when Forza Italia failed, with the intent of enabling the PPI "to inherit the electorate of Forza Italia" (La Repubblica, 22 July 1994). When asked about a PDS-PPI-Lega alliance, Buttiglione rejected it - this wasn't what the voters wanted. Yet later, in several mayoral races, the PPI did form such alliances.

Buttiglione's PPI did this while at the same time declaring that an electoral alliance with the PDS was "premature" and that a permanent blending of the centre and left was "out of the question". Yet Martinazzoli's mayoral victory in Brescia came via centre-left political support. The PPI leader defended his party's tactics by saying the situation was fluid; the moment of decision had not yet arrived.

In December, that moment did. The PPI opposed the government's initial proposals on pension reform; then, after it supported the revised budget, the PPI joined the Lega in tabling a no-confidence vote. Ironically, after the fall of the Berlusconi government, Buttiglione negotiated an alliance with Berlusconi and Forza Italia - the very person and party the PPI had opposed. These actions appear to have been aimed at de-coupling Forza Italia from the Alleanza Nazionale. The PPI's left wing, in contrast, had been pushing an alliance with the PDS, the Greens and former socialists. Both wings expressed a preference for a technical government, with elections after institutional reforms.[10]

Patto Segni: strident opposition strategy

The Patto embodies the firm opposition strategy. Formed on a strident, reformist platform in 1992, the Patto Segni is to the old DC what Lutheranism was to the Catholic Church. DC leader Mariotto Segni, son of former President

Antonio Segni, led an attack on the corruption of the DC and argued that not just the DC, but Italy's political institutions, needed to be reformed. He was ejected by the DC and for a time in 1993 it was the Patto Segni which was known as the Popolari.

The Patto Segni's definition of the "centre" is one which is more liberal (in the European sense), less catholic and statist, than that of the PPI. It is to be an organization which can win on its own. Alliance tactics are to be dictated by that goal. Segni has emphasized that both the left and right alliances were nothing but electoral expediencies, poles for battle, not for governing. Though sharing the left's opposition to the Berlusconi government, the Patto has been critical of the PDS and other parties of the left.

Segni's reformist crusade turned first to the electoral system. It was Segni who spearheaded the successful campaign for direct election of mayors and the nearly successful drive for an end to proportional representation in legislative elections. The irony of his fate in the March 1994 elections has been often noted: losing to a Forza Italia candidate (Carmelo Porcu) by 6,000 votes in the single-member majority rules he had supported, but gaining a seat in parliament via the proportional representation rules he had opposed.[11] The elections left the Patto Segni with only 13 deputies in the chamber and only four senators.

The Patto Segni leadership, with a determination to make "liberal-democratic" Italy emerge under a centrist alliance, has not given up its opposition strategy. The Patto sees "small businessmen and artisans" as the "natural" constituency for the liberal-democratic centre. It was one of the interests which were in conflict with those of Berlusconi. The latter, according to Segni, "does not interpret real liberalism: he wants only to transfer the advantages of state control from one part to another". The Patto Segni contends that the middle class was "seduced" by Forza Italia, but has become deluded. When asked if Segni would ally with Berlusconi, were Berlusconi and Fini to part company, the answer was no: "what is there in common between the culture of 'TV movies' and the great catholic and lay tradition?"(La Repubblica, 20 September 1994).

Programme

The Patto's electoral programme differed from the PPI in several respects. The Patto emphasized liberalism and free market competition, save for state intervention on behalf of the weakest. First, on fiscal policy, the Patto proposed a constitutional ceiling of 40 per cent on tax rates and a structure of taxation such that overall no individual or corporation would pay more than 33 per cent.

Other policies include an emergency plan to control organized crime and ridding public entities such as the RAI of party control. While the Patto Segni targeted a growth rate of three per cent, with inflation to be kept at two per cent, and raising productivity so that 300,000 new jobs would be created yearly, it did not say how these goals would be achieved.

The party is quiet on traditional catholic issues. On the institutional issue, the Patto advocated direct election of the Prime Minister and the two-ballot system, as in France. In foreign policy, the Patto shared much with other catholic parties: an activist stance, working in "strict union" with the Atlantic and European allies. Like the PPI, the Patto favoured the European Union and its expansion.

Elections

Though the Lega ultimately rejected a proposed spring 1994 election alliance, based on their common views on "the anti-trust law, on freedom of information, on defence of small business, the institutional question beginning with the second ballot and direct election of the prime minister," the Patto and some in the Lega Nord signed an electoral alliance. Despite the unwillingness to form an electoral alliance, Bossi's unrelenting criticisms and final rejection of Berlusconi's premiership renders the Lega a potential ally of the Patto Segni. The two parties concured in support of a "technical" government.

The March election was a resounding rejection of the Patto Segni, which won only 4.6 per cent of the vote and 13 seats in the chamber. Then, in a policy dispute in late April, five of the deputies joined the Berlusconi coalition. The dissidents, led by Alberto Michelini, who had been offered the newly created Family Ministry, reasoned that it was time for cooperation and compromise rather than sterile opposition. Segni's determination to push for the implementation of reforms and policies he did not believe the Berlusconi government would support impelled him to remain in the opposition.

Set on a platform of adamant opposition, yet lacking the financial backing to canvass the country, lacking governing positions that would influence the distribution of resources and lacking the endorsements of significant organizations, the Patto Segni faced a hard struggle for existence.

What effect has this strategy had on the Patto's fortunes? In December 1994 opinion polls indicated the electorate's interest in the Patto for national office had been halved (Corriere della Sera, 5 December 1994). In the November to

December mayoral elections, the Patto was relatively invisible, while the PPI tended to do best where it had the support of the PDS. Nevertheless, the Patto Segni improved with the collapse of the Berlusconi government and the formation of the Dini government. Like the PPI, the Patto endorsed the no-confidence motions and President Scalfaro's search for a non-partisan prime minister and government.

If strident opposition has had limited electoral success, what of the opposite strategy - unwavering support? It is this which the CCD has demonstrated.

Centro Cristiano Democratico: unwavering support strategy

The Centro Cristiano Democratico (CCD) was formed by dissident ex-DC parliamentarians when the DC was transformed into the PPI in January 1994. The CCD's secretary, Pier Ferdinando Casini, made it clear that the CCD would lean to the right, and not be "prisoners" of the left (Corriere della Sera, 19 January 1994). This view has been seconded by the southern CCD, with Clemente Mastella as spokesman. The party represented the third option: pursue votes and policy goals via participation in and support of the governing majority.

Viewed by the Church as the unnecessary manifestation of an unnecessary split in the catholic political movement, the CCD has been consigned to struggle largely on its own. The CCD formed a separate parliamentary group, starting with 23 deputies, and then joined the Polo alliance for the March elections. Francesco D'Onofrio is president of the group. The CCD was in a perpetual battle with the PPI over the political "rights" to Christian Democracy. The party has insisted that it was not an apology for the DC. Membership figures are not available, though from electoral returns, one can deduce that the CCD's support is strongest in the regions of Veneto, Liguria, and Lazio, followed by Calabria, Abruzzo, and Sicily.

Programme

The CCD's programme was scarcely distinguishable from that of the PPI. Where it differed most was in the CCD's determination to stay on the centre-right, in the Berlusconi majority and far from anything smacking of "catholic communism". More so than the PPI, the CCD was supportive of Berlusconi's fiscal and social policies and also of his attacks on the judiciary. One CCD leader, Carlo Giovanardi, went so far as to equate the *Tangentopoli* investigations with the Spanish inquisition.

Where the CCD seemed most like the PPI was in its stressing of continued government support of the Mezzogiorno and, rather vaguely, for the family. The party opposes abortion and divorce. Being quite critical of Bossi's federalist proposals, the CCD is pro-national unity. The CCD claims to support educational, cultural and "informational" pluralism and to be, at heart, a liberal and popular catholic party. The CCD claims it is the "centre of the centre." However, with its firm commitment to the conservative governing majority, such a claim hardly seemed credible. On the electoral system, even though as a small party it would barely have survived had it not linked with the Polo in the elections, the CCD supports single member majority district elections. Casini explained: "Bipolarity is an irreversible given and there is no need of a third subject which remains in the centre and befriends now the right, now the left" (La Repubblica, 9 August 1994). He neglected to add, so long as one of the dominant poles accepts superfluous allies.

Elections

For the parliamentary elections, the CCD ran as part of the Polo della Libertà, winning 32 seats in the chamber and 12 in the senate under its own name. The party, itself, claimed that during the election it allied with the Polo della Libertà in order to block the anticipated victory of the left. Given the Polo's results, the CCD was not a necessary part of the governing majority. It appears, however, that the other leaders of the Polo invited the CCD into the cabinet in order to make a goodwill gesture towards catholics. In attempting to convince voters that the CCD served some purpose, Casini and other CCD leaders have been stressing their role as a brake on extremist tendencies in the Berlusconi majority. The image is that of a CCD rescuing the far right and those who voted for it from themselves. Berlusconi, for his part, has belittled the party.

The CCD's coalition strategy was rewarded through various government posts. Ombretta Fumagalli Carulli became the under-secretary of civil protection; Francesco D'Onofrio the minister of education; and Clemente Mastella became minister of employment. Given the fall floods and the labour and student protests stemming from proposed budget cuts, none of these ministers was in a position to bring electoral favors to the CCD's potential voters.

Has there been any positive effect on voter support from the CCD's firm involvement in the majority? Casini would argue yes. The party, testing the waters, decided to run alone in a number of cities in the November to December mayoral elections. Where the CCD ran alone, it averaged three per cent, with a peak of nine per cent in Pescara. Casini expressed satisfaction with these results, noting that, after all, "we are a young party" (Corriere della Sera, 21 November 1994).

In 1994 the CCD chose to build a Christian Democratic political party through alliances with the right, where it saw its electorate and policy preferences as being. While the lion's share of that electorate was usurped by Forza Italia, the Lega and the AN, the CCD leadership has been optimistic about the party's future. Deposed from government with the Berlusconi coalition's collapse, the CCD has held to the conservative orientation which motivated it to join Berlusconi's government in the first place.

While the catholic parties appeal to the catholic sensibilities of voters, have the parties had any assistance from the organizational expressions of Italian catholicism?

The Catholic Church and Catholic organizations

"Me? I yell 'Forza Italia' only when the national soccer championship is played." Cardinal Florenzo Angelini (La Repubblica, 26 March 1994).

The Church's main political effort in 1994 was to push for catholic unity. Fearing that a change would lead to dispersal of catholics into different parties, thus diluting catholic influence in politics, the Pope argued that there was "no need to start over from the beginning." The DC, and christian democracy, could be renovated without "breaking with the experiences of the past" (Corriere della Sera, 27 June 1993). Yet in January of 1994, the Church was forced to grapple with three separate catholic parties.

As with previous legislative elections, the Church emphasized the importance of the vote for catholics. The Bishops' union told catholics to vote for "the force of Christian inspiration," for a "coherent and united presence" in the government. The Church was worried that the right's view of liberty was "liberty to do as one likes" and that the right saw "solidarity and progress as contrary to liberty". Even granting that "the catholics (candidates) are now found everywhere," the spokesman for the Bishops noted that catholic politicians are not found "with the same intensity in the various (political) organizations" (Corriere della Sera, 22 March 1994).

Taking aim against Berlusconi, Fini and Bossi, the Church argued that "the country needs not power conquerors, but servants of the people". Ironically, it is precisely because the previous catholic party so long supported by the Church proved itself to be little more than a power monger that the rival "conquerors" succeeded.[12]

One notable exception to that view was an editorial published the Sunday prior to the vote in the catholic daily, Avvenire. Written by Cardinal Ruini, the editorial seemed supportive of Forza Italia (La Repubblica, 5 April 1994). There are some indications that the Church's stance was pragmatic: when Forza Italia appeared on the verge of dominating the elections, the Church considered it a force to acknowledge. This was done without a clear endorsement of Forza Italia's politics. The catholic hierarchy's general view was that Berlusconi's party stood only for blatant consumerism and that Forza Italia's policies would widen the gap between rich and poor. Monsignor Ersilio Tonini went so far as to state that the Polo's victory was the "euthanasia" of democracy.

Recently, the Church has spoken optimistically about the potential for the PPI's enlargement and for a "network of agreement" between the catholic parties for the next election. The goal is to foster an explicit catholic bloc. Having similar concerns about aspects of Italian society and politics, the Church is available to the PPI as an ally. Whether such an alliance will be exploited is uncertain. Just as there was in the DC, there is in the PPI a dispute over the extent to which the party should be associated with the Church and beholden to its support.

Moving on to consider briefly the various catholic organizations so important to the DC's early successes, the catholic trade union - the Confederazione Italiana dei Sindacati dei Lavoratori (CISL), and Azione Cattolica, it is clear that these were both less involved with the new catholic parties and saw those parties as less useful to them. The CISL has focused less on the catholic parties than on coordinating action with the other two major unions. The goal seems to be to create one trade union. Even though the CISL's economic concerns would find expression and support in the PPI, the CISL has not proposed support for one of the catholic parties. Instead, the CISL stresses "pre-political, cultural" efforts to put these themes together. The general political concern has been, as CISL president, Sergio D'Antoni, said, with re-creating Italy's "grand catholic-democratic and laic-reformist patrimony" (La Repubblica, 15 September 1994). The interest in such a union has more in common with the Patto Segni than with the PPI. Azione Cattolica, while being favorably disposed toward the PPI, particularly since its ex-president is now president of the PPI, has been preoccupied with its own organizational fate. In a classic Catch-22 situation, were the PPI to have more political influence, Azione Cattolica might find it more rewarding to serve as a catholic electoral machine. Yet to gain influence, the PPI needs the prior campaign support of the catholic organizations. An added complication is that the PPI is unlikely to agree to the CISL's more leftist policy and alliance tendencies.

Conclusion

"The Catholic split is not necessarily definitive." Arnaldo Forlani (Corriere della Sera, 25 March 1994).

Despite Forlani's observation, the catholic parties will remain split so long as they insist on pursuing the divergent strategies of opportunistic alliance negotiations with, adamant opposition to, or unswerving support of what was the right-wing majority of 1994 in Italy. Changes in the electoral system have yet to elicit "rational" responses to alliance incentives; changes in the nature of political enemies and in opportunities to use patronage have, in turn, altered the incentives for politicians with differing interpretations of Christian Democracy to remain united in one organization. Contrasting views of political catholicism can continue to find separate organizational expressions.

Notes

1. Giulio Andreotti, quoted, no date, in Damato, F. (1979), *Dc contro Dc. Splendori e miserie di un partito di gomma*, Milan: Editoriale Nuova, p. 5.

2. See Casella M. (1992), *18 Aprile 1948: la mobilitazione delle organizzazioni cattoliche.* Lecce: Congedo, and Warner C. (1994), *Priests, Patronage and Politicians: the role of political party strategies and of institutions in the construction of the French and Italian Christian Democratic Parties, 1944-1958* (unpublished Ph.D. thesis, Harvard University).

3. The DC's April 1992 parliamentary campaign slogan was; 'They want to destroy Italy.'

4. The Lega Nord was originally called Lega Lombarda, for the region in which it was established. Fini's party was the Movimento Socialista Italiano (MSI); it now calls itself Alleanza Nazionale.

5. Other scholars have characterized such a situation as a "multi-level chess game". O'Donnell, G. and Schmitter P.C. (1986:66). On situations in which rational choice explanations are most powerful, see Taylor, M. (1989:115-162 and especially:149-153).

6. For an account of the development of parties as features in political democracies, see, to begin with, Lipset, S.M. and Rokkan, S. (1981:27-62).

7. The mayoral elections of May-June 1993 were one factor in the decision to fold the DC. The party averaged 18.5 per cent in the larger towns (15,000 or more), Corriere della Sera, 8 June 1993.

8. Buttiglione is a philosophy professor, born in Gallipoli, pupil of Augusto Del Noce, ex-ideologue of Comunione e Liberazione and presumed to be on good terms with the Pope.

9. Buttiglione's assessment may be validated by a *Directa* survey which found that while 30 per cent of Forza Italia's voters go to mass every Sunday, only 17.5 per cent of the PPI's do. Another 11.5 per cent of AN's do and 11 per cent of PDS's do (Corriere della Sera, 7 April 1994).

10. Editors note. In the aftermath of the Buttiglione-Berlusconi pact the PPI disintegrated into two new groups. The bulk of the old PPI joined the new PPI led by Gerardo Bianco while Buttiglione's new group is called CDU (Unione Democratica Cristiano).

11. Some attribute Segni's loss to the absence of strong parish support, where it normally was forthcoming, and to the resentment of local DC leaders, who did not forgive Segni for abandoning the DC in 1992. La Voce, 30 March 1994.

12. Monsignor Riboldi, who was 25 when the DC first came to power, commented that "we also made mistakes, we trusted people without knowing who they were. We were not poor; we were allied with power. We did not have the courage to chase away the temple merchants". La Repubblica, 29 March 1994.

References

Casella, M. (1972) *18 Aprile 1948: la mobilitazione delle organizzazioni cattoliche*, Lecce: Congedo

Damato, F. (1979), *DC contro DC. Splendori e miserie di un partito di gomma*, Milan: Editoriale Nuova.

Gonella, G (1959) 'Per a Nuova Costituzione' in Dane, C. (ed.), *I Congressi nazionale della Democrazia cristiana*, Rome: Cinque Lune.

Lipset, S.M. and Rokkan, S. 'Cleavage Structures, Party Systems, and Voter Alignments: an Introduction,' and Charles Maier, '"Fictitious bonds...of wealth and law:"on the theory and practice of interest representation,' in Berger, S. ed.,(1981) *Organizing Interests in Western Europe*, Cambridge: Cambridge University Press.

O'Donnell, G. and Schmitter, P.C (1986), *Tentative Conclusions about Uncertain Democracies*, Baltimore: Johns Hopkins University Press.

Shefter, M. (1977) 'Party and Patronage: Germany, England and Italy', *Politics and Society*, Vol. 7, No. 4, pp 403 - 451.

Taylor, M. (1989) "Structure, Culture and Action in the Explanation of Social Change" *Politics and Society*, Vol. 17 No. 2 (June).

Warner, C. (1994) *Priests, Patronage and Politicians: the role of political party strategies and institutions in the construction of the Frrench and Italian Christian Democratic Parties, 1944-1958*, (unpublished PhD thesis, Harvard University).

seven

Forza Italia: an American party for Italy?

Laurence Gray and William Howard

Introduction

Italian democracy in the post-war years of the First Republic always represented a convergence of interests and coalitions where compromises were necessary and where a much discussed consociative rapport was said to develop between governing and opposition parties (Hine, 1993). For much of the Italian left, the appearance of Forza Italia - the "American party" created by the entrepreneur Silvio Berlusconi - represented a kind of mass-democracy viewed with diffidence. Forza Italia seemed to represent the Americanization of mass politics in Italy and, as a consequence, a threat to the culture that had long been the preserve of the left. That culture outlined what was politically acceptable by defining a "constitutional arc" of parties that excluded the neo-fascist Italian Social Movement (MSI). The general elections of March 1994 which witnessed the affirmation of Forza Italia and its coalition partners, the Northern League and the MSI-dominated National Alliance, in effect ended the isolation of the MSI and broke one of the taboos of the Cold War.[1]

The victory of Berlusconi's "American party" succeeded in opening up a debate in Italy on fascism and breaking not only one of the taboos of the Cold War, but questioning the assumptions of the left regarding anti-fascist political culture. Berlusconi was perceived by some to represent one form of the culture of modernity - a political style connected to a high-tech rapport between capitalism and democracy - a form of the "new" feared because it represented the abasement of the left's historic role among the masses. For others, the advent of Forza Italia, if unheeded politically and organizationally by the left, would herald the loss of the left's historic role in developing culture in Italy, reflecting the fear of political cultures that, in turn, fear political decline.[2]

The results of the March elections seem to have brought concern and discussion within Italy over the very future of terms like left and right, parties and movements. The terms do not fully and accurately reflect the full impact of the results of the March elections. The traditional post-war battle of left/right, anti-fascist/anti-communist, has been supplanted, in large part, by a different dynamic - a dynamic that revolves not around policy (or purported policy) but around the essence of the viability of the political system and its accompanying elites - the conflict between what is and has been, and what is and would like to be. Moreover the very example of Forza Italia shows how citizens have been receptive to non-traditional organizational forms.[3]

For the past half-century Italy was ruled by a wasteful and destructive regime that appealed to Cold War logic for its legitimacy. The country had the lowest turnover of any democratic parliamentary system in the world meaning the same parties and individuals had a habit of holding onto government power.[4] It is not surprising that the Italian electorate would sooner or later become fed up. What is striking is how long the First Republic lasted. The overwhelming desire to see change, a change of new faces and political identity, sums up the March 1994 vote.

A most important matter for the electorate was that the Forza Italia candidates represented "change".[5] In the minds of voters, Forza Italia became a symbol of the desire for a "new order" that was free of corruption. For many voters the opposition of other parties to Forza Italia was viewed as opposition to change itself. Berlusconi plugged into the widespread distrust of established political classes that pervades the world. Some in Italy are concerned by this trend, viewing it as an eventual encouragement to the enemies of democracy.[6] But distrust of the old political class can also be a cathartic process, purifying the political system.

The March 1994 general election marked the end of the old political system - the party politics of the First Republic - which existed from the fall of fascism to *Tangentopoli*. But it did not signify the beginning of the Second Republic. Nor did it signal the beginning of a transition period leading away from the

First Republic. If the First Republic was deficient it was mainly because it was not governed. The results of the March elections seemed to offer the possibility of a cure, that is, a solid government. But a revolution there has not been. And if the contours of a much-desired Second Republic are unidentifiable then the country can not be in a state of transition.[7]

Berlusconi ran a presidential-type election campaign using his persona as the symbol and identity of a new force in national politics. Forza Italia supporters surely considered this identification appropriate; unusual for a parliamentary democracy where there have always been problems with a weak executive.

In Italy there has always been an incestuous rapport between business and politics, the offspring often being corruption.[8] But while Berlusconi the businessman was himself a product of this system, he was also one of the few top businessmen not directly touched by the *Tangentopoli* scandals. The Fininvest network was used by Berlusconi to organize the Forza Italia network which, in turn, was modelled on the organization of fan clubs for Italian soccer teams, the most successful of which, AC Milan, is owned by Berlusconi. The name of the movement and the clubs, "Forza Italia" is even a soccer chant. Many of the adherents of Forza Italia were, in turn, members of the soccer clubs. The Forza Italia theme song had a Reaganesque "morning in America" appeal with the words "it's time to believe". Approximately 40 executives from Fininvest devoted themselves to the March 1994 campaign.[9]

Does Berlusconi respond to a real need in Italian society at this historical moment or is he just a creation of his media empire? The March 1994 elections were both a case of adaption of Italian politics to modern medium-is-the-message Western politics and yet, at the same time, may be a foretaste of what is to come elsewhere in Europe. A true media pioneer, Berlusconi made the connection between *mani pulite* (no corruption), no past political experience and candidacy in Forza Italia lists for the March general elections. The 267 Forza Italia candidates for office were given crash courses by Publitalia, a Fininvest company. Berlusconi's business interests were clearly used to the advantage of his political ambitions as the Forza Italia structure was heavily dependent upon Fininvest.

Forza Italia was formed in October 1993 and seemed at the time to be a movement through which political challenges might be orchestrated by using traditional politicians. But the Forza Italia that eventually emerged was new and strongly identified with a new style in relations with voters. The Forza Italia electorate was spread throughout Italy, but was especially concentrated in the urban North and in Sicily. More women than men voted for Forza Italia, most of them young housewives. Religion, family and the free market were important values for these voters. Forza Italia drew away voters who, in the 1993 administrative elections, voted for the Lega Nord and the MSI.[10]

Berlusconi also discovered that Italian voters did not pay much attention to politicians making formal speeches on television but they did listen to "ordinary people" and watch talk shows. Forza Italia organizers realized that many people in Italy felt excluded by Italy's political establishment. The Forza Italia clubs allowed and encouraged political debate and participation much as soccer clubs encourage fans to follow the success of members' favorite teams. Therefore, 13,000 Forza Italia clubs were formed in four months and all was made possible by the resources provided by Publitalia.

The language of Berlusconi was disarming and simple. He was less like a Ross Perot than a Ronald Reagan given his grasp of modern marketing techniques, enthusiasm, and ability to communicate with people.[11] Like Reagan, the language of Berlusconi was clear, with politically uncluttered phrases, selling a mix of anti-communism and free market economic solutions.

But Berlusconi's movement or "American party", was a loose cast of relatively undisciplined deputies and senators. They all had only one trait in common and that was a debt to Berlusconi for being elected to parliament in the first place. Moreover the Forza Italia component in parliament, with 37 senators and 112 deputies, was far from an absolute majority. Forza Italia was but one part of the Freedom Alliance coalition along with the Northern League and the National Alliance. Given the tumultuous relationship between Forza Italia and its former Freedom Alliance partner the Lega Nord and the continuing tie with the National Alliance, the "clear victory" of March 1994 translated as something less than clear in programmematic terms.

Candidate Selection

The candidate selection process used by Forza Italia was unique. During the First Republic the typical parliamentarian was a product of a political party machine. Forza Italia used the private assets of Berlusconi. The task of searching for and finding acceptable candidates for the movement fell upon Publitalia. Using their expertise in modern marketing techniques, Publitalia found potential candidates and conducted initial evaluations of their acceptability.[12]

The manner in which candidates were found and selected was informal and hurried and took place in an atmosphere of great political uncertainty in Italy. The summer of 1993 witnessed bomb attacks in Florence, Milan and Rome by unknown individuals. The two largest centre parties, the Christian Democrats (DC) and the Italian Socialist Party (PSI) were being destroyed by corruption investigations. Only the left, represented by the Democratic Party of the left (PDS - the former Communist Party, or PCI), seemed immune to the mani pulite investigations and were benefiting from it in the polls. But the greatest uncertainty was when, not if, the President of Italy, Oscar Luigi Scalfaro, would call for early elections.

Forza Italia became an official political "movement" on 25 November 1993. Parliament was dissolved on 15 January 1994 and new elections took place only two months later in March. In a few short months Forza Italia and Publitalia put together a political movement represented by candidates that were, as compared to their political opposition, political novices and came out the big winner in their first electoral contest. The following evaluation of the elected men and women Forza Italia sent to parliament can give a picture of Forza Italia itself and, more importantly, a suggestive profile of its constituency.

Forza Italia sought candidates that were not tainted by the corruption of the old system and were not from the political left. In order to fulfill this formula, Publitalia searched for people with three essential traits: youth, business experience in the private sector and no prior experience in politics. These three characteristics were mutually supportive in the Forza Italia quest for untainted candidates on the centre-right. With so much of the Italian political elite under suspicion, if not indictment, having political novices became a boon, not an oddity. Youth works hand in hand with the reasoning behind choosing novices. The younger a parliamentarian, the less opportunity to have been a part of the massive corruption that developed in the First Republic. Seeking candidates who were active/successful in the private sector of the Italian economy was useful in two ways. First, an entrepreneur/business person/manager was more likely to agree politically with a new movement on the centre-right. Second, the selection of novices reinforced the decision to distance Forza Italia from the corrupt practices of the past.[13]

In attempting to field young candidates, Forza Italia met with little success. The average age of Forza Italia senators was just over 53.5 years, roughly a year and a half younger than non-Forza Italia senators. In the Chamber of Deputies, Forza Italia representatives did no better. With an average age of just over 46.5 years they were, again, only a year and a half younger than non-Forza Italia.

Forza Italia also looked for people with experience in the private sector; entrepreneurs, business people, managers and directors who were successful in private enterprise. An evaluation of Forza Italia parliamentarians shows a good match between goals and results. In the senate, 54 per cent of all Forza Italia representatives had backgrounds in private industry including small-business owners, consultants, managers, directors and salespeople. All had experience in the private sector of the Italian economy. This compared with only 25 per cent of non-Forza Italia senators with prior business experience in the private sector. This percentage decreased somewhat in the chamber of deputies, but the results are no less striking. Forty-nine per cent of Forza Italia deputies had business backgrounds compared to only 22 per cent of non-Forza Italia deputies with the same working experience. In both chambers of parliament, Forza Italia had more than twice the number of representatives with business experience than the rest of parliament.

An examination of the level of political experience of Forza Italia senators and deputies raises a number of questions (see Figures 1 & 2). Of the Forza Italia candidates elected to the senate, 51 per cent were active in party politics while 82 per cent of non-Forza Italia senators had political backgrounds. The chamber of deputies showed a still greater contrast. Only 34 per cent of the Forza Italia deputies were politically active prior to their election. The non-Forza Italia deputies held steady with their senatorial counterparts - 83 per cent having prior political experience. This data illustrates the concerns of Silvio Berlusconi and Forza Italia in choosing and then electing faces new to politics. Forza Italia was represented by a percentage of political newcomers unprecedented in Italian politics. However, the data reveals that a significant number of Forza Italia parliamentarians had a consistent history of prior political involvement. While Forza Italia promoted political neophytes, it also inserted a high percentage of political veterans within its candidate lists. In other words, a certain degree of expertise and experience in First Republic politics was programmemed into the "new" Forza Italia political movement.

Figure 1

Italian Senate - Forza Italia/non-Forza Italia Comparison

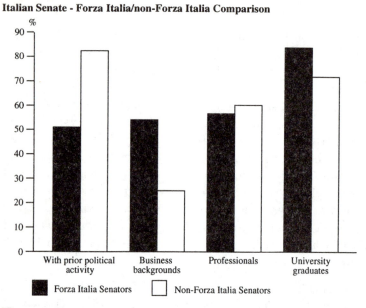

Figure 2

Italian Chamber of Deputies - Forza Italia/non-Forza Italia Comparison

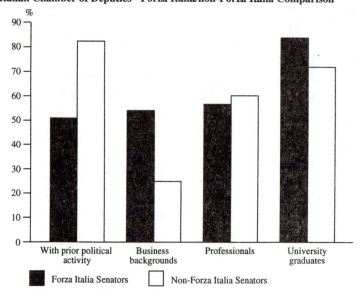

It is noteworthy that Forza Italia parliamentarians with prior political experience come from across the Italian political spectrum.(See Figures 3 & 4).

Forza Italia elected senators who had been active in the DC (Christian Democrats), MSI, Radical Party (RP), and the Liberal Party (PLI). This picture becomes even more muddled when examining the prior political affiliation of the Forza Italia exponents seated in the chamber of deputies. There were Forza Italia deputies who had been active in the DC, PR, PLI, PSI (Italian Socialist Party), Lega Nord, PCI/PDS and the Republican Party (PRI). Clearly Silvio Berlusconi was able to convince a very diverse group of politicians that he and his movement represented something to which they could relate. It is no small feat that former adherents of parties from the left to the extreme right could be found within the Forza Italia parliamentary group. Forza Italia explained the involvement of these First Republic party activists by stating that they were *riformatori* (reformers) in their prior political lives.[14] However the presence of parliamentarians in the ranks of Forza Italia who were active politically in the First Republic shows that while Forza Italia may have sought political novices as parliamentarians, it settled for a good number of experienced activists from the First Republic.

Figure 3
Previous party affiliation - Forza Italia Senators

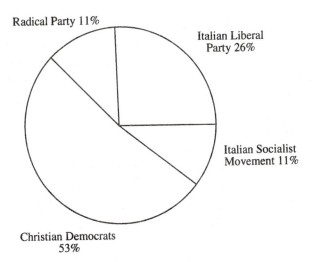

Radical Party 11%

Italian Liberal Party 26%

Italian Socialist Movement 11%

Christian Democrats 53%

Figure 4

Previous party affiliation - Forza Italia Deputies

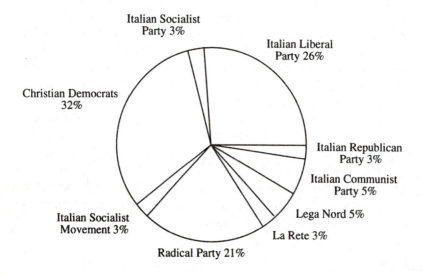

There was also the issue of the presence of a significant number of former Fininvest employees in the chamber of deputies (there are none in the senate). Of the 12 former Fininvest employees (including Silvio Berlusconi), only two of them were elected by popular vote. The other ten took their seats by means of the 25 per cent of seats awarded on a proportional basis and selected by the party. Of the 24 Forza Italia deputies that entered parliament in this manner, ten were ex-employees of Fininvest. As a group, former Fininvest employees made up a small percentage of Forza Italia deputies - 11 per cent. However, the fact that 42 per cent of all proportional seats went to Fininvest employees and that of the former Fininvest employees in the chamber, only two were popularly elected, adds evidence to the charge that Forza Italia is closely tied to the Berlusconi business empire.

The three main criteria for choosing candidates for parliament - youth, political novices, background in the private sector - reflected a desire to create a movement not linked to the practices of the First Republic. By targeting candidates without political pasts, Forza Italia went a long way in selecting parliamentarians who had not been active in the corruption of the First Republic and had a professional background that would place them politically on the centre-right.

But these efforts, taken together, show less than full success. For example, an examination of the typical "profile" of a Forza Italia deputy or senator showed a parliamentarian only slightly younger than the rest of parliament. The contrast between Forza Italia and the rest of parliament was more marked when comparing the high percentage of private industry backgrounds and political neophytes in Forza Italia to the rest of parliament. However, the success of these contrasts was muted by questions related to the still significant percentage of Forza Italia parliamentarians with links to the First Republic and the number of former Fininvest employees (and the manner in which they gained their seats) in the chamber of deputies.

A more complete picture of the typical Forza Italia parliamentarian will consider education level, professional background and the participation of women. (See Figures 1 & 2.) The percentage of Forza Italia professionals in the senate was slightly less than non-Forza Italia senators, 57 per cent to 60 per cent.[15] In the chamber of deputies this difference increased from three per cent to 10 per cent with 51 per cent of Forza Italia deputies with professional qualifications compared to 61 per cent for the rest of the chamber. In the area of education, a higher percentage of Forza Italia senators had earned university degrees than the rest in the senate, 84 per cent to 73 per cent. However, in the chamber of deputies they were on a par with the rest of those seated in the lower house, with 69 per cent having completed university degrees. Forza Italia suffers when comparing their percentage of women representatives to the rest of parliament, but only just. In the upper house eight per cent of Forza Italia senators were women while the rest of the senate was made up of nine per cent women. In the chamber the difference increased, but not significantly. Women made up 12.5 per cent of Forza Italia deputies. The rest of the chamber seated 15 per cent women.

In many ways the representatives of the Forza Italia movement looked much like the rest of parliament.[16] Their age, the number of certified professionals in their ranks, their level of education and their gender was not significantly different, if different at all, from their counterparts. The difference lay in their relative lack of political experience, as a group and the preponderance of parliamentarians with backgrounds in the business world. Forza Italia parliamentarians with political experience did not contrast with others in parliament, but with the stated goals of Forza Italia in seeking new faces. The benefits of having political novices were a result of the corruption investigations of the past two to three years and, politically, could be expected to be only short-term. However, the other contrasting characteristic, the mobilization of individuals from private enterprise as parliamentarians, had the trappings of a long-term phenomenon.

The PDS was the counterweight to Forza Italia in the Italian political spectrum, leading a coalition of centre-left parties, some the shards of the discredited PSI and DC. Current PDS representatives reveal a high degree of political activity during the First Republic. (See Figures 5 & 6.) In the senate, 51 per cent of Forza Italia members had political experience prior to their election in March 1994, compared to 94 per cent of PDS senators. The difference increased even more in the chamber of deputies. While 34 per cent of Forza Italia deputies were politically active prior to their election 90 per cent of PDS deputies could claim the same distinction; a 56 point difference. This is a startling contrast and one that illustrates the high rate of carryover within the PDS of party elites from the First Republic.

Figure 5

Italian Senate - Forza Italia/PDS Comparison

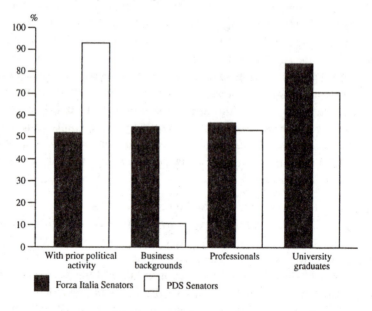

Figure 6

Italian Chamber of Deputies - Forza Italia/PDS Comparison

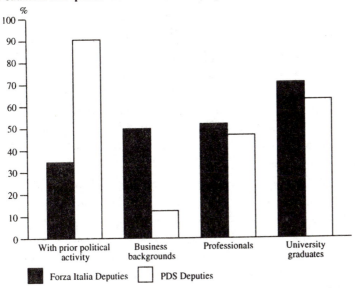

The contrast is no less severe when evaluating their level of economic activity in the private sector. As previously stated, Forza Italia is represented by a high number of men and women with experience in private industry, much higher than the rest of Parliament as a whole. The contrast grows when comparing Forza Italia to the PDS. In the senate 54 per cent of Forza Italia adherents had a business background while only 10 per cent of PDS senators had the same type of experience. In the chamber the difference was only slightly less dramatic with 49 per cent of Forza Italia deputies enjoying business backgrounds and only 12 per cent of PDS representatives coming from the private sector.

The contrasts are marked when comparing Forza Italia and PDS parliamentarians who had backgrounds as party functionaries and teachers. Eighteen per cent of PDS senators and 25 per cent of their deputies could be classified as party functionaries - all with prior political experience. In the senate 28 per cent of PDS professionals were teachers, all having prior political activity. Thirty-eight per cent of the PDS deputies who were professionals held teacher certificates, 84 per cent of them with prior political experience. On the other hand, Forza Italia reflected a decidedly less statist character. There were no Forza Italia senators who would qualify as party functionaries while less than three per cent qualified in the chamber of deputies. Only five-and-a-half per cent of Forza Italia senators and a minuscule 1.8 per cent of the deputies held teaching certificates.

Organization, Structure and Programme

It is clear from the previous data that Forza Italia was the political formation that best took advantage of the new majoritarian electoral law put in place before the March 1994 elections. The "centre", an area that many politicians claim, was largely squashed by the emerging bipolar nature of the electoral system. The triumph of the Forza Italia-led Freedom Alliance coalition - receiving nearly 43 per cent of the votes cast - was also a result of the new electoral system (Bobbio, 1994:654-655).

A classical Italian political party Forza Italia was not, but well organized it is and the majoritarian electoral system privileges organization. The lesson was that flexibility and simplicity were needed in forging electoral alliances and that Forza Italia must remain an electoral movement tied to local needs and, especially, reflected in the example of its own leaders. Forza Italia's structure was, by comparison, very fluid and light, holding together millions of adherents by way of loose local interaction tied, also loosely, to a nation-wide media/marketing infrastructure. This interactive infrastructure served Forza Italia well and the "looser" Forza Italia remained - truly an American-style party - the better chance it would have of winning future elections.[17]

The March 1994 election results were bolstered by the improved showing of Forza Italia in the June European elections. Of course, the June vote was not about Europe, but very much about Italy. It is noteworthy that European issues were not even raised in the campaign. Forza Italia won almost one-third of all votes cast, raising its share of the vote by 10 per cent. The vote for Forza Italia stood out even more since only 75 per cent of the electorate voted. Forza Italia obtained 30.6 per cent of the vote, up from 21 per cent in the March elections, giving it 27 representatives in the European Parliament.[18] Moreover, Forza Italia demonstrated a new quality of becoming a respectable alternative for voters who could not identify with the Lega Nord, but who would support a renewed form of the DC.[19] However, this was followed by the poor showing of Forza Italia in the November 1994 partial local elections which prompted a minority of Forza Italia members to demand a stronger organization. Some made an unsuccessful appeal for a fusion with the rightist National Alliance to create a new movement, a truly traditional party to be named Alleanza Italia.

The mandate received by Forza Italia in March 1994 was also a special opportunity to help bring Italy's public spending under control. The extent of the Forza Italia victory reflected a broad agreement in the country on the need for a radical economic and political break with the past. But the advantage of a fresh start seemed to wither with time and the perception of lost opportunities and inaction.

Unfortunately, the procrastination of the Berlusconi government regarding budget matters was typical of many preceding governments. Promises of an early 1995 budget before the end of the 1994 summer were not kept. While the government's financial targets included the admirable goal of a 45 trillion lire deficit reduction, government documents were vague on how this would be achieved. While cuts in spending on the public health system were discussed, the far greater problem of reforming Italy's costly pension system was considered too sensitive an issue to be earmarked for anything except postponement. The government mainly distinguished itself by offering pardons and amnesties - in return for the payment of generous fines - to violators of building codes and tax evaders. However, the 1995 budget was ultimately passed in December 1994 even though it was immediately acclaimed as flawed and insufficient. Spending cuts totalled 29 trillion lire and the budget deficit was to be trimmed by 50 trillion lira or just under nine per cent of GDP. The spending cuts would hit pensions, health care, defence and public administration. The tax amnesties and pardons, as well as the closing of some tax deductions, were slated to bring in 21 trillion lire in new revenues.

The dynamic that overtook events with the victory of Forza Italia in March 1994 was largely centred around the labels of "old" versus "new" rather than the framework of anti-communism versus anti-fascism within which many policy issues were debated and much of the political discussion was developed during the First Republic. The issue of pension reform is illustrative of this dynamic. In 1994 the Berlusconi-led government put together a pension reform package, the architect of which was the then Minister of the Treasury, Lamberto Dini. The plan was decried by the leftist opposition, notably the PDS, and was accompanied by work stoppages and demonstrations. When the Berlusconi government resigned in December 1994, to be replaced in early 1995 with a government of "technocrats" led by Dini, the PDS supported the new Prime Minister, the same Lamberto Dini pilloried only two months before. With an electoral base heavily dependent on organized labour, their stance during the Berlusconi government is easily explained. But their flip-flop in supporting the Dini government revealed their primary concern as being that of mounting opposition to Forza Italia and its allies first and foremost, even at the expense of policy favorable to their constituency.

This dynamic, that supplanted any real debate on pension reform or other issues regarding the way Italy may reduce its significant level of public debt,[20] was also a struggle between two elites. On the one hand there were the remaining elites of the First Republic that include the left and who, until 1993, were firmly entrenched socially and were now seeking to maintain leverage within the political system. On the other hand there was a second group made up of an alliance of elites that were either new to politics or composed of defectors or non-participants from the First Republic. Led by Forza Italia and its political allies, this second group was seeking to depose the First Republic system of political interaction, but in so doing, raised many questions. Can the remnants of the First Republic reform themselves fast enough to salvage the First Republic itself? Or can the alliance led by Forza Italia demonstrate enough cohesiveness and determination to lead a transitional period away from the First Republic? If the Forza Italia-led, centre-right Freedom Alliance coalition manages to hold together as a political alliance will it stay together if returned to power and faced with difficult policy choices? Or would a new Forza Italia-led government portend the return to the factious politics of the First Republic, albeit with new players? These questions will be answered in time as Italy continues through a cycle of elections.

As Prime Minister, Berlusconi often appeared out of touch with the public mood in spite of his much vaunted marketing gift for knowing the public's tastes. For example, restoring the writ of *habeas corpus* was an admirable idea, but was promoted badly when it appeared that many of the suspects in the *Tangentopoli* cases would be advantaged. However, the merits of Berlusconi's ideas regarding the need for judicial reform should be acknowledged if indeed, as one observer remarked, there was the risk that "Italy, the cradle of law has become the graveyard of justice" (The Wall Street Journal Europe, 23 July 1994). The poor handling of the *habeas corpus* issue was just one of the political stumbles committed by Forza Italia. The worst political mistake Forza Italia made, and perhaps its first, eventually led to Berlusconi's resignation in December 1994.

The national elections of March 1994 saw not only a new political force, Forza Italia, but also a new electoral law that gave favor to the "first past the post" ideal in the electoral system. This encouraged alliance-building prior to the election, instead of after, as was the norm in the First Republic. Forza Italia, in their alliance building, turned to the CCD (Democratic Christian Centre), the MSI-AN and the Lega Nord. In the complicated give-and-take of determining their alliance candidate lists, Forza Italia erred badly in its agreement with the Lega Nord, giving too much, so much so that when the Lega Nord defected late in the year, Berlusconi had no choice but to resign.

The Lega garnered 8.4 per cent of the vote in the March 1994 elections. But the deal cut with the new Forza Italia in constructing the candidate lists resulted in Lega Nord gaining 18 per cent of the seats in the senate and the chamber of deputies. Forza Italia, with just over 20 per cent of the popular vote claimed 18 per cent of the seats in the chamber and only 11 per cent in the senate. In other words, the Lega, with 8.4 per cent of the vote, seated 59 senators while Forza Italia, with 20 per cent, had only 37. In the chamber, the Lega took 111 deputies - Forza Italia a total of 112. The initial alliance with the Lega Nord can be explained as a political necessity of the moment. However, the agreements hammered out regarding the candidate lists not only disproportionately favored the Lega Nord, but created for Forza Italia, a state of political dependency upon the Lega Nord to back the Berlusconi government. This was a fatal political error the consequences of which may not have been immediately evident. But it allowed the temperamental Lega Nord leader, Umberto Bossi, to sway the coalition, wielding undue influence and ultimately sealing the fate of the Berlusconi government by withdrawing from the coalition in December 1994.

It is also ironic that the mass media, which carefully launched Berlusconi's career, was also frequently the instrument of his embarrassment. By July 1994 the cracks in Berlusconi's seductive appeal became evident and a crisis of credibility quickly developed into a question of survival for his coalition government. In part, the crisis of Berlusconi's leadership reflected the quality of his inner circle of advisers - associates who were effective in winning for Berlusconi the businessman a marketing battle in promoting Forza Italia during an election campaign. But that same circle of advisers proved less adept at advising Berlusconi the prime minister. In short, Berlusconi and his advisers, all without political experience, were capable of protecting Fininvest interest, but less effective in maneuvers to guard Italy's interests.[21]

Again, there was a problem of method. Forza Italia was constructed as a company movement to the extent that business criteria were used to establish it. Both Fininvest and Forza Italia used - and still use - the most advanced forms of technology and communication techniques. In terms of their organization and leadership Forza Italia and Fininvest are very much images of one-another, a political development previously unknown in Italy. Of course Forza Italia and Fininvest are fundamentally different, but they are similar in style, function and image. At the same time, Forza Italia success is also the result of the collapse of the centrist parties.

Much attention was given to the conflict-of-interest issue which arose when Berlusconi refused to divest himself of any proprietary interest in Fininvest.[22] The management of Fininvest as such was not the issue, but many questions were raised.[23] Rightly or wrongly Berlusconi was identified as a defender of Fininvest, a complication which involved the very role of Forza Italia as it was largely created and staffed by Fininvest employees. But did the conflict-of-interest problem make any difference and was political information that was available to the public truly affected? What difference did it make to the voting public when political parties controlled the RAI? Do the *telegiornali* really make a difference in influencing voters? How does Berlusconi's proprietary position relate to the electoral influence of 'Dallas' and 'Beautiful', with their simplified cultural models, easily understood, and played on the dialectical edge between rich and poor, winner and loser?

Conclusion

Forza Italia filled a "market gap" created by the disappearance of the DC. Berlusconi represented the emergence of business in the political world in contrast with the dominance of politics in the business world so characteristic of the First Republic. In tune with much of the Western democratic world where there is a general mood of scepticism toward established political groups, Berlusconi offered an alternative to the country as it appeared to be on the verge of being seduced by the Left.[24] Instead of a traditional professional party, Berlusconi offered something never before seen in Italian politics, a free market alternative with Forza Italia.

Berlusconi and Forza Italia were symptomatic of changes taking place in Italian social structures whereby privatization and economic liberalization became dominant themes. This trend did not start with Berlusconi, but it appeared most closely associated with the Forza Italia-movement created by and supportive of him.

The break-up of Italy's First Republic political system and the affirmation of Forza Italia begot strange bedfellows. National political realignment is taking place within and between political parties. New parties and movements sprung up while new associations have formed between old politicians. Forza

Italia represented the possibility of voter realignment with its support coming from a variety of social groups encompassing mainly the middle classes, but also including low-wage workers. These voters include refugees from the defunct catch-all DC. The next election could be decisive in determining whether there has been a realignment of the centre. The next general election will likely see the emergence of a two-coalition system made up of, respectively, centre-right and left-centre aggregates.[25] Italian voters may then have a clear electoral choice for a stable coalition government with the prospect that the future Prime Minister may be identifiable during the campaign as leader of one of the coalitions.

Notes

1. The only taboo greater than the Cold War taboo of keeping the Italian Communist Party (PCI) out of power was the one that kept the MSI in the closet. Unlike the PCI, the MSI was not a "constitutional arc" party. But unlike the PCI's successor of self-mutation, the Democratic Party of the Left (PDS), the MSI successor party, the National Alliance, succeeded in joining a national governing coalition following the March 1994 elections.

2. Economic opportunity and job security are always key issues and, as such, can be threatened by protectionist sentiment. The political message of Forza Italia was viewed by some as the harbinger of a "rightist New Deal" founded on an ambiguous dual fear - a fear of Italy losing its competitive trading edge and fear of accepting the measures necessary in order to make Italy competitive with countries where net family incomes are less than half of those in Italy. On the suggestion that a wave of rightist "New Deal" sentiment may be engulfing Europe, finding in Italy an advance point, see the article by Giorgio Ruffolo in La Repubblica, 23 June 1994 as well as the article "Ed ecco s'avanza il New Deal di Destra", La Repubblica, 25 June 1994. Competitiveness is the subject of a study by the World Economic Forum reported in La Repubblica, 30 September 1994, where Italy is sandwiched between Indonesia and the Philippines, ranking 32nd in the study of 41 countries.

3. The value of a post-political analysis is questionable, as in Nathan Gardels, 'From Italy a Postmodern Overture for a Raucous Political Era', International Herald Tribune, 14 April 1994, even if Berlusconi is a foretaste of things to come. For intellectuals of the First Republic Berlusconi seemed to represent the new barbarians once feared by Edward Gibbon. See, for example, Statera (1994). For his supporters, Berlusconi seemed to create a media-designed refuge where Italy could re-emerge and flower again. For a description of these supporters see Paolo Madron (1994).

4. See Kaare Strom (1990). In addition, Italy has had the governments with the shortest life-span of any democracy in the world. See King, Alt, Burns, and Laver (1990).

5. Some may ask what "change" can mean in Italy, a country where history has worked against making hard policy choices. Yet the "costs" of the First Republic were high in spite of the comfortable lifestyle built up over the post-war years.

6. See Eugenio Scalfari, La Repubblica, 4 March 1995, and for the same concerns amplified from abroad, Frankfurter Allgemeine Zeitung, 28 March 1994.

7. For a discussion of this point see Urbani and Carnazza (1994:15-18).

8. For an explanation of *Tangentopoli* see Allum (1993). For the various reactions to the bribery scandals within Italy, see W.V. Harris, "Italy: Purgatorio", *The New York Review of Books,* 3 March 1994, pp. 38-41.

9. See the account provided in Corrias, Gramellini and Maltese (1994).

10. According to CIRM (Centro Internazionale Ricerche di Mercato) the Forza Italia electorate in the March 1994 elections was made up of the following percentage of voters from the 1992 general elections: 24 per cent from the DC, 31 per cent from the Lega, 13 per cent from La Rete, and 27 per cent from the PSI electorate. See Diamanti (1994:665-667).

11. Some of the foreign press have attempted comparisons between Italian and American political reformers. See Leslie Gelb, International Herald Tribune, 23 April 1993. For the Ross Perot - Berlusconi comparison see the International Herald Tribune, 31 March 1994.

12. Once the "candidates-to-become-candidates" cleared this first hurdle they were evaluated by Domenico Lo Jucco, an executive from Publitalia and now a member of the chamber of deputies. Those that passed beyond this point were then evaluated by Berlusconi for final approval. See Dilioli (1994:13 & 19).

13. The statistical profiles and comparison used in the following pages were constructed by the authors from data obtained from the Istituto Nazionale dell'Informazione, *La navicella. I deputati e senatori del dodicesimo parlamento repubblicano,* 1994/1995, Editoriale italiana, Roma. For a statistical comparison of all the candidates competing in the 1994 elections see Mattina (1995).

14. See "Io, l'azzurro di Forza Italia", L'Espresso, 14 January 1994 and "Voglio settecento Berlusconi", Panorama, 19 December 1993. This has been reinforced by a direct interview with Antonio Palmieri, an official of the Ufficio di Comunicazioni e Immagine di Forza Italia, Milan.

15. Professionals are defined as lawyers, medical doctors, magistrates, teachers, journalists, etc.

16. A useful comparison of the elected parliamentarians is found in Verzichelli (1994).

17. In Italy the tradition is to set down roots and create a professional party structure. On Forza Italia as a *partitio leggero* see the interview with Gianni Pilo, the Forza Italia poll-taker, former senior official of Publitalia and current member of the chamber of deputies, in La Repubblica, 22 November 1994. The very short life and quick success of Forza Italia could qualify it for the label of "instant party". See Revelli (1994:667-670).

18. Forza Italia European parliamentarians label themselves "Forza Europa" and can be roughly divided into two tendencies. First, there is the pragmatic, entrepreneurial tendency of those who identify closely with Berlusconi and want to inherit the centrist role and votes of the DC. A second, minority tendency within the Forza Europa are the European DCs that operate in Strasbourg under the banner of the German Christian Democratic Union-dominated European Peoples Party (PPE). See the article by Franco Papitto in La Repubblica, 13 July 1994.

19. The Lega polled 6.6 per cent in European elections down from 8.4 per cent in March 1994. See the data in the article by Robert Graham, Financial Times, 14 June 1994.

20. The Italian public debt is over 2 quadrillion lire which equals about 1.3 trillion dollars, putting it close to 125 per cent of Italian GDP. See The Wall Street Journal Europe, 14 February 1995.

21. The "inner circle" includes Gianni Letta, former editor of Il Tempo; Marcello Dell'Utri, manager of Publitalia; Fedele Confalonieri, chairman of Fininvest; and Berlusconi's lawyer Cesare Previti. Previti became defence minister and Letta chief of staff when Berlusconi became prime minister. See Financial Times, 24 July 1994.

22. However Berlusconi did agree to have Fininvest managed independently of him and under a

transparent series of controls. See the articles in the Financial Times, 18 November 1994 and 28 July 1994.

23. Given the complicated ownership entanglement between Fininvest, Berlusconi and his family, it is difficult to know - and Berlusconi has never revealed - just how much of Fininvest he personally owns. It is, therefore, hard to know what, if anything, Berlusconi is distancing himself from if, as he claims, he is truly willing to distance himself from Fininvest. See Financial Times, 1 August 1994.

24. Speculation on a possible victory by the left was especially prominent in the foreign press. For example see Alan Cowell, International Herald Tribune, 21 December 1993.

25. Timing of the next elections is uncertain at the time of writing. The current government of moderate "technicians", led by Lamberto Dini and installed on 25 January 1995, seems to be preferred by much of the left in order to avoid new elections before 1996.

References

Allum, P. (1993) 'Cronaca di una morte annunciata. La prima repubblica italiana', *Teoria politica,* Vol. IX, No. 1, pp 31 -55.

Bobbio, L. (1994) 'Dalla destra alla destra , una strana alternanza' in Ginsborg, P, (ed.) *Stato dell'Italia,* Milan: Mondadori.

Corrias, P. Gramellini, M. and Curzio, M. (1994) 1994. *Colpo Grosso,* Milan: Baldini & Castoldi.

Diamanti, I. (1994) 'Forza Italia: il mercato elettorale dell'imprenditore politico' in Ginsborg, P, (ed.) *Stato dell'Italia,* Milan: Mondadori.

Dilioli, A. (1994) *Forza Italia, la storia, gli uomini, i ministeri,* Ferruccio Arnoldi Editore

Hine, D (1993) *Governing Italy: The Politics of Bargained Pluralism,* Oxford: Oxford University Press, Clarendon Press.

King, G. Alt, J.A. Burns, N.E. and Laver, M (1990) 'A Unified Model of Cabinet Dissolution in Parliamentary Democracies', *American Journal of Political Science,* Vol. 34, pp 848 - 871.

Madron, P. (1994) *La gesta del cavaliere,* Milan: Sperling & Kupfer Editori.

Mattina, L. (1995) 'I candidati', in Bartolini, S and D'Alimonte, R (eds.) *Maggioritario ma non troppo*. Bologna: Il Mulino

Revelli, M. (1994) 'Forza Italia: l'anomalia italiana non e' finita' in Ginsborg, P, (ed.) *Stato dell'Italia,* Milan: Mondadori.

Statera, G. (1994) *Il volto seduttivo del potere,* Rome Edizioni SEAM.

Strom, K (1990) *Minority Government and Majority Rule,* Cambridge: Cambridge University Press.

Urbani, G. and Carnazza, E. (1994) *L'Italia del buongoverno,* Milan: Sperling & Kupfer.

Verzichelli, L. (1994) 'Gli elletti' in Bartolini, S and Alimonte, R., *Maggioritario ma non troppo,* Bologna: Il Mulino

eight

Getting out of the ghetto: the case of Alleanza Nazionale

Marco Tarchi

Taking part in democratic politics in the Italian post-war period was not an easy task for those who looked upon the fascist past as a symbol of honor. Giorgio Almirante, who led the Italian Social Movement (MSI) for over twenty years, from the foundation of the party to 1950 and then from 1969 to December 1987, had already raised the issue during the 1956 MSI congress and sought, thereafter, to find a solution. Neither he nor the other party secretaries who preceded, or followed him - De Marsanich (1950-1954), Michelini (1954-1969), Fini during the first phase (1987-1989) and Rauti (1990-1991) - succeeded in resolving the contradiction prior to the beginnings of the 1990s.

This did not mean that during the course of its history, which was finished in January 1995 with the 17th congress decreeing the party's end, the MSI did not achieve tangible gains even before 1994, the year that consecrated its political triumph with 13.5 per cent of the vote. This electoral result and the subsequent spill-over into the manoeuvring for the formation of the right-wing government coalition translated into 109 deputies and 48 senators present in parliament, 11 Euro MPs in the May 1995 European parliamentary elections and five ministers and 12 under-secretaries in the new Berlusconi government. Another positive aspect of the electoral result was that it helped the party to consolidate its organizational structure and avoid a slide into the lunatic fringe or a move from one split to another, as had been the case with other European right-wing parties.

In the past, the MSI had played a substantial role, providing support for the election of Giovanni Leone as president of the republic (1972-1976) and capturing a substantial amount of the protest vote between 1972 and 1992 to transform it into the fourth largest party in parliament. Nevertheless, until recently, the lack of democratic legitimacy inscribed into its fascist chromosomes served to severely limit the party's political ambitions. On several occasions the party's attempts to achieve legitimacy within the system were rejected and served to mobilize mass reactions (such as in 1960 when the MSI backed the Tambroni government, sparking civil demonstrations and riots throughout the country). On other occasions, it was held at bay due to the actions of the centrist political forces in the system. These actions included the Scelba law of the 1950s, which banned the reconstitution of the National Fascist Party (thereby placing the MSI in a legal and constitutional limbo) and the creation of the "constitutional arc" which legitimized political bargaining and cooperation on legislation among parties from the centre-right (DC and PLI) to the left-wing (PCI). The MSI was not considered a legitimate political party supporting parliamentary principles and the dictates of the 1947 Italian constitution.

In addition, the very nature of the MSI as a self-declared anti-system party (more so in its culture and political programmes rather than its methods) was essential in creating a "triangle of illegitimacy" (Chiarini, 1991) that made the political centre (i.e. the DC) the linchpin of Italian politics. In this context the MSI was assigned a subordinate role, being occasionally co-opted when it served the DC's purposes. However, on the whole it was excluded from government and political legitimacy due to the Christian Democrats' need to appear as the main political bulwark against the left. Despite the modest coalition potential and the leverage it had in the system, the MSI's presence gave substance to the paradigm of "polarized pluralism" (Sartori, 1982). The party undermined the credibility of any possible alternation in government between the left and right and it favored the existence of a blocked system of party competition based on a conditional co-option of one of the "extremes" - in general, the PCI - in decision-making processes. The objective was to create a form of consociationalism that used anti-fascism as its cornerstone.

Given these characteristics and the nostalgic bent of the MSI after its unsuccessful attempts to insert itself into the dynamics of coalition building, it may seem odd that the party never renounced the prospect of making a comeback, especially in the two years between 1993 and 1994. This phase was particularly difficult because of two internal developments: the death of two historical leaders of the party (Almirante and Romualdi) and their succession[1] and the party's less than brilliant result in the 1990 regional elections when its share of the vote dropped to 3.9 per cent, its worst electoral result since 1948. However, due to its consistent exclusion from power at national and local levels and its general image of being a different party from the others, the MSI underwent a rapid change in its fortunes. Its forced abstinence from power, which had limited its resources and prevented it from establishing solid relations of exchange with economic and social interest groups, was transformed into fortunate coincidence when the cyclone of moral indignation hit the ruling class of the First Republic in connection with the clean hands investigation. The weight of anti-fascist discrimination, already eroded by the passage of time, was further reduced because many leaders who had paid lip service to this principle were implicated in the corruption scandals. In addition, the growth of the anti-politician[2] backlash brought on by *Tangentopoli* favored the re-admission into the national political arena of those political "exiles in their own country" (Tarchi, 1993) who in December 1946 had gathered around the symbol of the tricolored flame to keep alive the memory of fascism and the Salò republic.

The disruption of many of the adversary parties under the blows of the magistrates certainly provided the MSI with the essential pre-conditions for its exit from the "ghetto" in which it had been enclosed.[3] But this is only one of the factors that allowed the party to present itself as one of the protagonists in the transition phase which culminated in the March 1994 parliamentary elections. Without taking into consideration the other positive long-term forces,[4] other factors contributing to the rise of the MSI can be identified in the role played by Francesco Cossiga during the last phase of his presidency, in the effects of the referendum campaign brought forward by Mario Segni and last, but not least, the political initiative undertaken by Silvio Berlusconi to create a new political formation on the right-wing of the political spectrum. In order to better understand the unexpected political outcome of 1994, it is useful to look at what happened before the elections.

From Cossiga to Berlusconi through Segni

The "externalizations" which sprinkled the last year and a half of Cossiga's term in office represented the moment for the re-launch of the MSI.[5] With his daily polemical attacks against the establishment - stimulated by the Gladio affair -[6] the president gave voice to widespread dissatisfaction with the mix of inefficiency and patronage that had been characteristic of the Italian civil service. But he also expressed views close to the MSI's traditional political platform: from presidentialism to the criticism of the "residual aspects of state socialism" present in the ex-communist left. And, what was more important, he pushed the point that it was necessary to relegitimize the ex-fascist party, to declare the Second World War over, and to move toward a transition to a Second Republic no longer conditioned by the predominance of party organizations. In criticizing the structural supports of the First Republic and his party's inability to respond positively to the end of the Cold War, Cossiga added his apologies to the right in being held responsible for the 1980 bombing of the Bologna train station - thereby tacitly admitting the role played by the state's secret service. Cossiga supplied the MSI with so much political support that the party secretary, Gianfranco Fini, attributed to Cossiga, (dubbed *il piccconatore*, the pick axe man), the role of mentor. Fini went as far as establishing a direct line with the president's office and promoting his re-election. The MSI's 1992 electoral campaign was formulated along the lines championed by the president, thereby allowing the MSI to reabsorb almost all of the loss in votes the party suffered during the previous regional and parliamentary elections.

In the protagonist role assumed by Cossiga, there emerged a connecting link with another of the elements that were a part of the political culture of the MSI and contributed to its rebirth: the personalization of politics, an increase in the importance of a leader's charismatic traits and a redefinition of the role of the party organization. The emergence of this trend in Italian politics has been evident since the beginning of Bettino Craxi's control of the PSI, but it reached its peak at the beginning of the 1990s through the rise of movements which in great part were identified by the public with their leaders: Bossi's Lega, Orlando's Rete and the referendum movement promoted by Mario Segni.[7] The MSI, which from the beginning had pointed to the individual qualities of its leaders (one of the building blocks of its anti-party approach), did not have any difficulty in inserting itself into this trend. The choice of attributing to Fini the exclusive role of representing the party, beginning with appearances on television, was an obvious reflection of this strategy and paralleled the positive results attributed to Michelini and Almirante's previous television appearances. Fini, avoiding the mistakes made during his first experience as party secretary, efficiently exploited the increased importance of mass communication: on one hand to promote a positive image of the party and, on the other, to strip away the language of the past, which had previously marked the MSI (Diamanti, 1995).

The success of the referendum initiative on the single preference vote and the approval of the law for the direct election of city mayors - fundamental stages in the process of personalizing the political process and political identification - were received by the MSI with a certain amount of satisfaction. However, the proposal in the second Segni referendum of April 1993 that the electoral law be changed in the direction of a more majoritarian system, produced a different reaction. The party's strong opposition to the proposal was based on the fear, in principle understandable, that jettisoning proportional representation carried with it a serious risk of the complete exclusion of forces on the extremes of the political spectrum. The simplification of electoral competition around a bi-polar scheme and the subsequent need to create wide-ranging alliances was not seen as a positive development by a party, which, during the previous forty years, was accepted as a partner only by the monarchists. But, against all expectations, the reform that was supposed to reduce the MSI to the role of pressure group operating outside parliament, or, at best, reduce its influence to specific geographic areas - i.e some provinces in the centre-south and in Trieste and Bolzano - became the springboard for its reaffirmation.

The base for this unexpected outcome was the coming together of new rules for the election of city mayors and the first effects of the *Tangentopoli* investigations. The collapse of their party organization under the pressure of the judiciary forced the DC, PSI, PRI, PSDI and PLI to propose local candidates with little stature or without political and/or administrative experience. Already in the June 1993 administrative elections, the weakness of the previous governing parties encouraged a number of moderate and conservative voters to shift their support to political parties in competition with the five-party government coalition: the Northern League in the northern regions and the MSI in the centre-south. The logic of the two-ballot system increased the size of the phenomenon to the point of electing MSI mayors in 14 towns with more than 15,000 inhabitants. It is evident that, presented with the alternative of voting either for a candidate from the left or one from the "extreme" right, many ex-supporters of the DC and other centrist parties preferred to vote for the latter. Proof of this attitude was provided by the results of the November 1993 administrative elections: the MSI, though presenting itself almost everywhere without partners, succeeded in winning 19 other cities, four of which were provincial capitals - Benevento, Caltanissetta, Chieti and Latina - and in many other cities its candidates appeared in the run-off on the second ballot. In Rome and Naples, where the MSI list had already gained more than 30 per cent of the vote during the first round, the MSI candidates (national secretary Gianfranco Fini in Rome and Alessandra Mussolini, the Duce's granddaughter, in Naples) received respectively 46.9 and 44.4 per cent of the vote on the second ballot. These results had already certified the party as an indispensable component in the creation of any future anti-left-wing front.

At this point, a significant number of the necessary conditions for the passage of the MSI from its traditional role as a right-wing protest party to a more constructive role had been established. In the first place, the political space available to the MSI had increased. The diffusion of a majoritarian political perspective, sustained by public opinion and the media, set the stage for the need to choose between left and right and Fini's party was in a position to occupy one of these political positions by itself. Since the end of the war, the notion of the right had been abandoned by all the other political parties (even by Giovanni Malagodi's PLI), becoming, as a result, the exclusive domain of the neo-fascists.[8] Secondly, some of the impediments which before had restricted the party's ability to attract voters disappeared. On the one hand, the fall of the Soviet Union reduced the fear of communism and, even more importantly, enticed some voters to abandon their atavistic support of the Christian Democrats, not because of that party's role as an impediment to the advances of the PCI, but because they were able to confine the PCI within an institutionalized parliamentary process requiring compromise and cooperation. On the other hand, the explosion of the corruption scandal reduced the DC's capacity to engage in patronage, thereby releasing a large part of its electorate into the electoral marketplace, especially in the southern regions. Millions of votes were once again potentially "available".

Finally, the gap of democratic legitimacy, which had kept the MSI outside the main political arena for a long time, was overcome. In fact, the search for new and credible parties to dominate the country during *Tangentopoli* turned the MSI's previous shortcomings into positive characteristics. Given that the party had been kept at the margins of the political system, it was not contaminated by corruption and public patronage in the eyes of the public. Its lack of organizational and programmematic renewal was not presented by the party as a refusal to become involved in jockeying for personal advantage which had been associated with the former governing parties, especially the PSI. The MSI's authority and nationalistic proclivities were now interpreted as guarantees of responsibility and respect for the national interest.

Having come out of the "freezer" with the November 1993 local elections, the

MSI remained isolated in the political arena after Cossiga abandoned his attempt to create his own "Gaullist" political movement. The possibility of carving up the country in agreement with the Lega, as had been proposed by Rauti in creating a populist alternative to the old parties' system, was not supported by Fini or Bossi. The Lega and the MSI seemed to be headed toward a clash for the control of moderate voters at the same time as the DC, reeling from its electoral defeats, started to move toward the left under the leadership of Mino Martinazzoli. In the meantime, the attempt to win other local government races pushed the left toward emphasis of its unitary strategy. It was at this point that the entry into politics of Silvio Berlusconi and his new political party became decisive factors for the MSI.

The unqualified support Berlusconi offered to Fini during his run-off with the leftist candidate, Rutelli, in Rome caught the neo-fascist candidate by surprise and seemed initially to embarrass him.[9] But Berlusconi's move recognized the party's coalition potential which in the past the party had never enjoyed. The signal sent by the owner of Fininvest to conservative voters was clear: in order to stop the left at a time when the DC seemed to have entered into its death throes, it was time to forget past prejudices against the MSI and create a centre-right confederation. Berlusconi had hoped for a time that Mario Segni, due to his considerable support, would assume this task, but the tendency on the part of many leaders of the referendum movement to establish working relationships with the progressives undermined the possibility of taking into consideration the new role of the MSI.

Before the solution proposed by Berlusconi saw the light of day, a number of problems had to be overcome. One of these was the open hostility manifested by Bossi's Lega toward the MSI. For the *leghisti*, the MSI was by far the most centralist party and guarantor of the privileges the southern regions enjoyed from state intervention. Another problem was that the alliance had to be joined by political groups credible to public opinion and with their own political status. It was not only necessary to create a new political formation tied to a liberal-democratic perspective, but also to reign in the Lega's secessionist ambitions and the MSI's nostalgic connotations. On this basis, new political actors - such as the Forza Italia clubs, the Pole of Liberty and the National Alliance - had to be created (Di Virgilio, 1994).

National Alliance: a political movement suspended between the past and the future

The attempt to create a political movement wider than the MSI - initially proposed by Fini after the elections in Rome and Naples - had behind it a long-term strategy and a few short-term considerations. To a certain extent, the proposal was oriented toward the acquisition of those votes which were ideologically oriented toward the right, but which historically had remained within the DC due to Cold War logic. It can be said that this objective had remained a constant in MSI strategy from its origins till the present. Michelini had incorporated it in the attempt to create a centre-right coalition led by the DC in the 1960s to keep the left out of government. Almirante tried to use it as the base for several initiatives: the anti-communist front which remained on paper; the National Right formed on the basis of unification with the remnants of the PDIUM, the monarchist party of Lauro and Covelli; and the Constituent Right and the Popular Union for Liberty led by ex-DC deputy Augostino Greggi aimed at competing with the DC, but also influencing it from the outside. Between 1976 and 1979 the secessionists of National Democracy tried hard to realize this goal when they split from the MSI. Therefore, it was not odd that the proposal resurfaced once the DC, which had monopolized conservative sentiments, started to crumble.

What was different this time were the surrounding political conditions. The crisis of the DC made possible the return of "the free floating right-wing voter", though the majoritarian electoral system threatened to restrict the significance of the change. The temptation of highly-principled isolation had already brought harm to the Lega, whose candidates were summarily defeated by the opposing electoral bloc in almost all of the cities of the North (with the sole exception of Milan) during the 1993 local elections. The defeats (even if narrow) of Fini and Mussolini in the mayoral elections represented another alarm bell. It was on this basis that the proposal made months before by political scientist Domenico Fisichella gathered momentum. Fisichella proposed the regeneration of the right through a renewal of its image and political programme in the form of a "National Alliance" to counterbalance the formation of a "Democratic Alliance" by the centre-left parties.

In order to become reality, the proposal needed to find valid interlocutors who could make the reorganization of the right-wing of the political spectrum credible. For a party which in the past had emphasized the importance of identity and belonging, such a change was not easy. When the idea was launched, very few independent personalities decide to join: Fisichella himself; the ex-head of the Guardia di Finanza, Ramponi; the ex-Christian Democrats Publio Fiori and Gustavo Selva; and very few others. The difficulty of giving the National Alliance a separate identity from that of the MSI was evident during its inaugural meeting. The 22 January 1994 did not witness the birth of a new political formation, or the embryo of a federation, but only a new label under which the diffused territorial organization of the MSI could operate.

What impeded Alleanza Nazionale from following the course of its predecessors was the unexpected appearance of Forza Italia. Based on its rhetoric and the context within which it placed itself, the entry of Berlusconi as an aspiring prime minister and head of a new party served to increase the crisis of the Italian political system and to attract the polemical attacks of the opposition. Covered by the presence of Berlusconi, Fini was allowed to concentrate on presenting a calm and balanced image which induced leaders of the progressive coalition, such as Occhetto and D'Alema, to recognize his democratic credentials in a manner as would have been unthinkable before. The change in attitude of the left reinforced the appearance of a transformation that, in reality, still had to take place. Despite the fact that Alleanza Nazionale was a political entity without an identity and autonomous structure (it continued to reiterate the MSI's traditional positions, focused on traditional morality, law and order, presidentialism and nationalism (Ignazi, 1994a)), the media referred to it as if the new party already existed. In news broadcasts and newspaper reports, Fini became "the coordinator of the National Alliance".

The agreement with Forza Italia, the Centre Union and the Christian Democratic Centre to present common candidates in a large part of the electoral constituencies of the centre-south under the banner of the "Good Government Pole", represented another step toward full legitimization for MSI/Alleanza Nazionale that would be fully rewarded by the electoral results. With 5,202,398 votes in the chamber of deputies election, or 13.5 per cent of the total, the party achieved an historical triumph. But the measure of its importance within the winning alliance cannot be measured only by this statistic. What was also important was the attractive power of its candidates,[10] the encouraging results achieved in many electoral districts of the North in competition with the Pole of Liberty lists (from which it was excluded due to opposition from the Lega) and the defeats sustained by the moderate alliance in areas such as Abruzzo in the South, where Alleanza Nazionale was not allowed to join the list due to internal conflicts.

From membership in government to the dissolution of the MSI

Despite the fact that the electoral victories in March and in the June European parliamentary elections (with 12.5 per cent) were organized exclusively by the MSI leadership and that the number of independents elected on the party lists in 1994 was less than the percentage elected in 1992 (Verzichelli, 1994), the entry of the party into government emphasized once again the need to transform the party.[11] The polemics on aspiring minister Mirko Tremaglia's "unacceptable" background as soldier of the Salò Republic, the suspicion expressed abroad by some socialist and Danish ministers, the Israeli government's refusal to comment on the Berlusconi government, the motion of reprimand passed by the European Parliament and the criticism coming from the foreign press (most notably the New York Times) were all clear examples of the obstacles that Alleanza Nazionale still had to overcome. Neither Fini's gesture prior to the March election of paying homage to those buried in the Fosse Ardeatine, nor the balancing of the Alleanza Nazionale ministers (two independents, one woman, and two moderate members of the party), nor the condemnation in parliament of totalitarianism were sufficient to overcome them. Alleanza Nazionale's opponents and its allies/competitors in the Lega were ready to highlight any sign of continuity with the past, and the Alleanza Nazionale leadership and cadre obliged them with a number of statements, from Fini, who stated that Mussolini was "the greatest statesman of the 20th century", to the continuous gaffes committed by the party press in using neo-fascist slogans and images. Also embarrassing was the background of a number of parliamentarians and leaders in local government who had their roots in the street violence that characterized the party in the past.

Trying to modify the image and substance of the party in order to make it comply with the new exigencies and at the same time providing Alleanza Nazionale with some substance were among the neo-fascist leadership's problems after the elections. Entering a government whose programme differed significantly, in parts, from Alleanza Nazionale's political culture - the MSI had always criticized liberal society and consumerism - the MSI felt the need to differentiate itself in order to maintain its own identity. It did this by projecting itself as the "social conscience" of the coalition.[12] This was possible because it had at its disposal a party organization that derived its inspiration from neo-fascist roots and ideals. Moving the emphasis toward new members who had been attracted to the party by the March electoral victory did not resolve the contradiction, though the fact that the new members were driven more by "career" than by pure idealistic motivations (Panebianco, 1982) certainly provided the basis for a gradual de-ideologicization of politics within an organization that had conserved a strong emotional and "sacred" conception of its identity.

During its eight months in government, the problem of the party's dual nature re-emerged in various forms. The leadership clearly wanted to reassure that conspicuous part of Alleanza Nazionale's electorate (approximately half of its total) were oriented toward the centre and that the party no longer looked back to fascism for its inspiration. At other times though, the party reverted to positions which were more in line with its old political orientations. This was the case when Alleanza Nazionale ministers, under secretaries and parliamentarians attacked "the entrenched elites" in the form of Mediobanca, Fiat, Bank of Italy, Constitutional Court, and the President of the Republic, Luigi Scalfaro. Also, the old behavioral patterns rose to the surface, unleashing a wild melée in the chamber of deputies, when the Green deputy, Paissan, accused Alleanza Nazionale of adopting the same corrupt practices of the old five-party coalition. The mix of old and new in Alleanza Nazionale was notable in the party's continued denunciation of the political methods of the First Republic while distributing among its friends and followers all of the favours of patronage that were available to it.

Despite these problems and the growing instability of the government due to Bossi's increased dissatisfaction with government policies and the social tensions generated by the financial bill, participation in the government produced a conspicuous return for the MSI. The resources gained by the MSI were varied in nature. It saw increases in its power to make nominations, its ability to establish previously unthinkable relationships and its public image was reinforced. MSI leaders were among the most interviewed politicians in newspapers and on radio and television. The reinforcement of the relationship with Forza Italia, encouraged by the need to reign in the Lega, was an integral part of the party's strategy of presenting itself as a responsible political force firmly anchored on the right, but not at all subversive of the democratic system. This effort succeeded in that one of Berlusconi's major opponents, Eugenio Scalfari, the editor of La Repubblica, admitted that Alleanza Nazionale had succeeded in bringing the last remains of fascism into the democratic process and Vittorio Foa, one of the most prestigious representatives of the resistance, recognised that Fini had undertaken a transformation of the MSI similar to the one that changed the PCI into the PDS.

But if the party succeeded in surrounding itself in a halo of respectability through the efforts of its leaders, such as the former deputy-Prime Minister Tatarella who personified the "petit bourgeois soul" of the party (Diamanti, 1995: 78), its history and cultural baggage continued to create problems. Under this perspective, the signs of revisionism undertaken by the leadership (Tartarella in an interview with an Israeli newspaper went so far as to condemn not only fascism, but also the extreme right!) appeared to be sporadic, not completely convincing and tied to tactical considerations. There was no confirmation that the leadership's pronouncements had substantially changed the fundamental orientation of the party's immediate cadres and base. The conditions for a reconsideration of its positions were lacking because of the fortuitous circumstances linked to Cossiga and *Tangentopoli*. The party realized its dream of entering government without having to undertake a fundamental rethinking of its positions and the moment of its greatest triumph was not the time for engaging in such a re-evaluation (Ignazi, 1994c).

At the time of the need to expand the coalition to include Buttiglione's Popular Party and avoid Alleanza Nazionale's relegation to a subordinate position in the coalition, Fini was able to impose the decision that did away with the symbol of the MSI and transferred its membership to Alleanza Nazionale. The ratification of this move was to be carried out by convening the last congress of the MSI and, following a procedure already adopted for the change of the PCI into the PDS, holding the first congress of the "new" political formation.

The Fiuggi Theses and "Post-Fascism"

In preparing the change in political formations, the MSI secretary made use of his increased credibility and the highly centralized structure of the party organization. Fini presented the theses of the upcoming congress without a preliminary internal debate and used them as a test of the party's unquestioned support of the leader. The purpose of the theses was to represent a radical break with the past. The theses contain a number of radical departures. The references made to Croce and Gramsci as representing part of the National Alliance's cultural heritage and the statement that the right is not "a by-product of fascism" and has as part of its legacy "those political values negated by fascism" (Theses, 1994: 8) are surprising. Even if they were not new[13] and were inserted in a rather confused programmematic context - even the choice of presidentialism is vague and lacking any specification of whether it refers to the president of the republic or the prime minister - the changes immediately attracted the attention of the media, stimulated debate among the opposition parties and divided informed commentators. The theses re-launched the party at a moment when its greatest achievement, becoming a member of the Berlusconi government, started to wane.

On a wave of euphoria that was not diminished by the fall of the Berlusconi government, the 17th congress of the MSI was celebrated on 25-27 January 1995. The theses were approved by ovation. Among the traditional leaders, only Rauti sought to keep the old MSI alive. But in doing so he helped Fini by drawing a clear line between Alleanza Nazionale supporters and diehard fascists.

Having put out the "flame" (symbol of the MSI), Fini placed a much reduced version in Alleanza Nazionale's symbol. The change appeared to be more cosmetic than real, but it nevertheless represented a new phenomenon in the history of the right. For the first time since 1945, the right enjoyed a central role in the Italian political system.

Two of the major problems in the transition from the MSI to Alleanza Nazionale were: the effective difference between the two political formations and the way the new party was seen by outside observers. On the first point, the doubts were understandable. During Alleanza Nazionale's first congress, voting rights were given to 850 regional delegates elected on the basis of fixed lists and approximately 1,500 delegates who attended the last MSI congress. The "new" party did not have a statute. The congress only approved the first four articles, which gave all powers to the president, a position to which Fini was elected by acclamation. Its organizational structure was unclear. The number of groups representing Alleanza Nazionale at the local level was, according to official figures, 1,650 with over 33,000 members. This certainly represented an over-estimation of the actual numbers composing Alleanza Nazionale and it was not clear how the "new" Alleanza Nazionale local structure corresponded to the "old" MSI structure consisting of 8,412 sections and 250,000 members.[14] In addition, Alleanza Nazionale's national assembly, which substituted the MSI's central committee, was elected through a procedure that could only with difficulty be defined as democratic. The members of the national assembly were appointed/elected following a number of procedures: 200 members were appointed by the national leadership, another 200 were designated through a ballot in which voters were not allowed to express their preferences, a further 50 were elected in a ballot that allowed members to indicate their preferences and the final 50 were selected directly by the president. The result of the selection process was that an overwhelming majority of the members of the national assembly were Fini supporters; the roles within the national leadership were distributed to ex-missini. The result was that by the end of January 1995 the new party did not have an autonomous structure that could differentiate it from its origins as the MSI.

In other ways, the triumphs of the two years of 1993-94 have left a traceable mark on the MSI in its transformation into Alleanza Nazionale. The pretext of embarking on the road of post-fascism still had to be verified. It should be remembered that 22 years ago Jacques Nobercourt, at the time Le Monde's Italian correspondent, observed that the new course initiated by Giorgio Almirante at the 10th Congress of the MSI-DN was the prelude to the transformation of the party from a "neo-fascist movement to a respectable right-wing movement". Unfortunately, subsequent events did not follow the course of his prediction. But, with the introduction of a majority system and entry into government, the "external" image of the party undoubtedly underwent a transformation. Its leaders were well aware of the costs of regression. There remains the unknown question of the response within Alleanza Nazionale in terms of the organizational structure and programme in case the conditions which recently characterized the party were to change. A return to the opposition and a more accentuated level of competition within the centre-right might feed attempts to align the party along the lines of the post-industrial extreme-right parties (Ignazi, 1994b) that have emerged in other European countries, but which have been temporarily abandoned by Fini in terms of the party's alignment at an international level. Only the future will answer this question and tell us if the history of neo-fascism has definitely been relegated to folklore, or whether it still has a definite role to play in Italian politics.

Notes

1. Giorgio Almirante, who led the party from 1969, was forced to resign in 1987 because of ill health. He died five months later. Upon his retirement, the party's leadership group fragmented, moving from division over the candidacy of Gianfranco Fini for the secretaryship, to support the leader of the internal opposition, Pino Rauti, (who was elected party secretary at the party's 16th congress in January 1990) and finally to Rauti's resignation in July 1991 after a series of spectacular electoral defeats. In May 1988, a few hours after Almirante, Pino Romualdi died. The latter had always played a leading role in the party as a founding member and as spokesman for the party's right.

2. We prefer to refer to anti-politician rather than anti-party sentiments because the latter were extensively diffused among the public even prior to the explosion of the mani pulite scandal which brought these sentiments to bear against other institutions, such as the civil service.

3. We are referring to the 1980s which saw, especially due to the efforts of Bettino Craxi's PSI, a relaxation of the conventio ad excludendum in relation to the MSI. A significant indicator of the MSI's immobilisation during this period was the inability to take advantage of the crisis affecting the traditional parties. This crisis, instead, led to the growth of the Greens, the autonomous lists - above all the Leagues in the northern part of the country - and numerous single-issue political organizations, such as the Pensioners Party, the Party of Hunters and Fishermen, etc.

4. Among these Ignazi (1994c) points to the de-radicalization of political conflict after the 1970s and the historicization of fascism promoted by Renzo De Felice and his students.

5. "Externalizations" refers to the off-the-cuff remarks made by Cossiga during interviews with journalists during his regularly scheduled and, more often, unscheduled news conferences.

6. The clandestine structure created by NATO at the beginning of the 1950s through a "stay behind" programme in case of a leftist victory. Cossiga publicly defended the objectives of the organization to the point of bragging about covering its existence in the past.

7. It should be remembered that the use of referenda is tied to the popularity of another charismatic figure of Italian politics, such as Marco Pannella.

8. In the MSI there was always a strong "nationalist left" tendency which harked back to the socialist fascism of Salò and was wary of becoming involved in a conservative alliance. On this point, see Ignazi (1989) and Tarchi (1989).

9. The two leaders had previously not been on good terms. Two years before publication of *Presidential Republic*, the future vice-president of the council of ministers, Pinuccio Tatarella, had strongly attacked Berlusconi for constructing his media empire "on the basis of political and party support". His friendship with Bettino Craxi was embarrassing for Fini even in the aftermath of his support, inducing Fini to remain aloof during the electoral campaign.

10. Research carried out by Bartolini and D'Alimonte (1994) shows that in single-member districts Alleanza Nazionale candidates running under the banner of the Good Government Pole attracted more votes than did the separate party lists Alleanza Nazionale had joined for the proportional vote: the average was 37.8 to 34.5 per cent.

11. Despite this, as Ignazi (1994c) has already indicated, the 12 Alleanza Nazionale under-secretaries "were selected on the usual basis of any traditionally-structured party: the resources are distributed according to criteria of fidelity to the leader, or the importance of the post held within the party organization", so that "those who enter the government have had long and faithful careers within the MSI party organization".

12. This pretense can be questioned given that in the survey carried out by SWG for RAI's Giornale Radio during the trade union mobilization campaign against the finance bill, the MSI voting base was the only one which judged the use of strikes in labour negotiations in a negative manner.

13. Almirante, in a televised debate in the spring of 1973, had stated that democracy and liberty represented "primary and unrenounceable values" and hailing the objectives of the resistance with which they were associated. Fini, during an interview with Le Monde on 17 June 1994, declared "I accept defining myself as an anti-fascist if this means love of liberty and democracy".

14. Even in this case, the statistics have been manipulated. In 1972-73, at the time of its maximum expansion, the party declared at the most 2,843 sections and 239,075 members. From unofficial sources, it is possible to hypothesize that in the fall of 1994 the number of members was around 100,000.

References

Bartolini, S. and D'Alimonte, R. (1994) "La competizione maggioritaria: le origini elettorali del parlamento diviso", *Rivista Italiana di Scienza Politica,* Vol. 24, No. 3, pp. 631-686.

Chiarini, R. (1991) "La Destra italiana: Il paradosso di un'identità illegittima", *Italia Contemporanea,* 185, pp. 582-600.

Diamanti, I. (1995) "Partiti, modelli", *Almanacco 1995 di Politica ed Economia.*

Di Virgilio, A. (1994) "Dai partiti ai poli: La politica delle alleanze", *Rivista Italiana di Scienza Politica,* Vol. 24, No. 3, pp. 493-547.

Ignazi, P. (1989) *Il polo escluso: Profilo del Movimento Sociale Italiano,* Bologna: Il Mulino.

Ignazi, P. (1994) "Alleanza Nazionale" in Diamanti, I. and Mannheimer, R. (eds.) *Milano a Roma: Guida all'Italia elettorale del 1994,* Rome: Donzelli.

Ignazi, P. (1994b) *L'estrema destra in Europa,* Bologna: Il Mulino.

Ignazi, P. (1994c) *Postfascisti?,* Bologna: Il Mulino.

Panebianco, A. (1982) *Modelli di partito,* Bologna: Il Mulino.

Sartori, G. (1982) *Teoria dei partiti e caso italiano,* Milan: SugarCo.

Tarchi, M. (1989) "L'impossibile identità : Il neofascismo tra destra e sinistra", *Trasgressioni,* Vol. IV, No. 2, pp. 3-26.

Tarchi, M. (1993) "'Esuli in patria': I fascisti nella Repubblica italiana" in Pozzi, E. (ed.) *Lo straniero interno,* Florence: Ponte alle Grazie, pp. 185-209.

Tesi politiche per il XVII Congresso Nazionale del MSI-DN (1994), "Pensiamo l'Italia, il domani c'è già. Valori, idee e progetti per l'Alleanza Nazionale", supplement to Secolo d'Italia, 7.12.1994.

Verzichelli, L. (1994) "Gli eletti", *Rivista Italiana di Scienza Politica,* Vol. 24, No. 3, pp. 715-739.

III. policies

nine

The success of 'mani pulite': luck or skill?[1]

Vittorio Bufacchi

Corruption has been at the centre of the political scene in Italy since the first results of the Mani Pulite ('Clean Hands') inquiry by the pool of magistrates in Milan became public in February 1992.[2] There is now conclusive evidence to suggest that by the early 1990s corruption, even by Italy's unflattering standards, had reached levels previously unknown. In the Italian context, corruption did not refer to cases of isolated petty swindles, but to an inescapable reality founded on an extensive network of relations present in all sections of civil society. In the city of Milan, appropriately dubbed Italy's immoral capital, (Della Porta, 1993) a pervasive corruption market dictated virtually all decisions taken by public officials, with perverse consequences: while state laws and regulations were constantly violated with impunity, those politicians and entrepreneurs who refused to respect the illicit rules and conventions of the corruption market saw their careers end early and their *de facto* exclusion from public contract tenders.[3]

It was only in 1992 that Milan's extensive system of corruption was exposed, with unprecedented consequences. The success of the investigation by the pool of magistrates in Milan was so extensive that it shook Italy's stagnant political system to its very foundations. By February 1994, two years after the first *Tangentopoli* arrest was made, 100 senators (out of 325) and 338 deputies (out of 630) were under investigation for corruption.[4]

It is not surprising to find, therefore, that over the last few years corruption scandals have been the subject of many studies, and both major and minor cases of corruption have been extensively documented.[5] However, for the most part, these accounts have chronicled only the wide extent of corruption in Italy and there have been only a few attempts to understand its nature and development.[6] In attempting to understand the factors that brought the system of corruption into the open, most commentators (echoing a popular view) have pointed to the enterprising heroics of the pool of investigating magistrates in Milan.[7] As we shall see, this view is also held by the magistrates themselves, as well as by many influential politicians who believe that the success of the investigations on corruption, for better or worse, cannot be separated from the individuals who conducted the inquests.

While acknowledging their well-deserved place in Italy's recent history, in this chapter I will try to set the foundation for an alternative form of explanation. The basic argument which I will try to defend is the following: the success of the Milanese magistrates between 1992 and 1994 is as much due to luck as it is to skill, therefore a full explanation of recent events concerning corruption in Italy must say something about the fortuitous circumstances that assisted the magistrates in their investigations.

The analytical framework of the approach favoured in this chapter follows closely in the footsteps of Brian Barry's analysis of power, whose analogous approach deserves to be quoted at some length:

> There are two ways of getting outcomes that you want. One is to bring them about yourself by exercising power. The other is to have them occur (often as a result of the exercise of power by others) without exercising any power yourself. Someone who is commonly in a position to obtain wanted outcomes by exercising power is powerful; someone who commonly obtains wanted outcomes without exercising any power is lucky. (Barry, 1989)

For the purposes of this chapter it is not necessary to examine the complexity of the relation between power and luck. The point is that desired outcomes can be the result of either power, or luck, or a mix of the two. The same analysis can be applied to the case of corruption in Italy. The collapse of the market of corruption in Italy can be explained as the result of either the skill of the magistrates (power), or to fortuitous circumstances such as the spontaneous disintegration of this highly fragile market (luck), or to a combination of these two factors. In this chapter I want to challenge the widely-held view that the skill of the magistrates was the predominant cause behind the collapse of the system of corruption. Instead I will be arguing that the magistrates were at least as lucky as they were powerful.

What does it mean for the magistrates to be lucky? The brief answer to this question is that the magistrates' good fortune is determined by the fact that their investigation into corruption took place at a time when the system of corruption was already on the verge of collapse. In order to substantiate this claim, it will be necessary to take a closer examination of some crucial mechanisms of the market of corruption. The starting point of this analysis is the view that the causes of the success of the Milanese magistrates are in part endogenous to the system of corruption, not exogenous to it. In particular, the structure of the entrepreneurs' pay-off in the corruption market had changed for the worse by 1992. The expansion of the market of corruption was such that in 1992 it had reached an unsustainable equilibrium point. An equilibrium is a state in which people's plans are consistent with each other.[8] The fact that the equilibrium point in the corruption market could no longer be sustained means that many entrepreneurs, who for many years took advantage of the system of corruption, for the first time found themselves in a losing position.

The fact that many protagonists of the corruption market found themselves in a losing position is perhaps the best explanation of a curious and unprecedented phenomenon that characterized the Mani Pulite investigation, namely, the fact that the accused were willing to testify to their culpability, so much so that large numbers of them spontaneously went to the authorities to confess their involvement in illicit transactions. The aim of this chapter is to suggest that in 1992 the corruption market in Italy could no longer sustain an equilibrium point and that as a result this market was undermined by the same actors who operated within it. If I am correct in my hypothesis (and at this point it is still only an hypothesis), then the magistrates in Milan cannot be fully credited for the success of the Mani Pulite investigation. The fact that in 1992 the corruption market was on the verge of collapse indicates that the magistrates were at least as lucky as they were powerful.

The investigation 'Mani Pulite'

Although investigations into corruption in Milan started as early as 1988,[9] the first major breakthrough was triggered by a singular incident, the implications of which no-one predicted. On the 17 February 1992, Mario Chiesa, a Socialist Party-appointed director of an old people's home in Milan (Pio Albergo Trivulzo) was accused of corruption by a small businessman, Luca

Magni, holder of a cleaning contract with the institution. It appears that after paying kick-backs to Chiesa for a number of years, Magni decided to turn himself in and cooperate with the magistrates in order to provide evidence against Chiesa. With the full backing of the police, Magni entered Chiesa's office with a tape-recorder hidden in his brief-case and recorded the conversation leading to the payment of a seven million lire kick-back.

What few people could have predicted is that following this incident a snow-ball effect set in, whereby a number of people who were, or had been involved in, illegal activities linked to corruption decided voluntarily to confess their crimes. Neppi Modona has aptly summarized this phenomenon:

> Not only those who were formally notified of being investigated both recognized their own responsibility and exposed those of others, but dozens of potential offenders, *especially entrepreneurs,* turned themselves in spontaneously in order to confess the payment of kick-backs (Neppi Modona, 1994:527-528).

Neppi Modona adds that the main cause of the "geometrical" increase of investigation lay most probably in the willingness of the accused themselves to testify. As legal experts pointed out, the illegal transfer of money does not leave behind paper traces and can be established only on the basis of confessions by those involved. Even the payment of a bribe to a Swiss bank account can be verified only after the accused has supplied magistrates with the name of the bank and the account number.[10]

The chain of confessions on the part of the entrepreneurs that followed from Magni's decision to co-operate with the authorities was so extensive that one of the Milanese prosecutors said of people who went spontaneously to the bench in order to confess their crimes: "It's like the Iraqi Army at the end of Operation Desert Storm. Now many are coming to us with their hands up before we even chase after them".[11] According to an official document produced by the Milan investigative magistrates (25 October 1994), two years and eight months of investigative "achievements" produced the staggering results reported in Tables 1 & 2:

Table 1

Number of cases passed on to the public prosecutor's office in other districts:	574
Number of cases still open:	729
Number of cases already dealt with by the investigative magistrates:	847
Sentenced	221
Acquitted	24
On remand	592
Barred by limitation	6
Deaths	2
Returned to the Public Prosecutor's Office	2
Total number of individuals under investigation:	2150

Table 2[12]

Illicit funds returned:	30 Billion It.L.
Illicit funds confiscated in Italy:	42 Billion It.L.
Illicit funds confiscated abroad:	25 Billion It.L.

Not surprisingly, it has been argued that the Mani Pulite investigation was the final blow that crumbled Italy's First Republic, a view shared amongst others by Antonio Di Pietro himself: "The investigations have crushed the so-called First Republic, I have not left my work unfinished" (La Repubblica, 7 December 1994).

Explaining the incentive structure that led to the chain of confessions is a prerequisite for a comprehensive understanding of Mani Pulite. As we shall see, the standard interpretation so far is that the magistrates were instrumental in securing confessions. Our intention is to swim against this current and argue that the confessions were, in part, triggered by the worsening structure of the entrepreneurs' pay-off. As the equilibrium point in the market of corruption faded away, a number of individuals found themselves worse-off, and this may have been the incentive they needed to confess their sins.

Confessions and the magistrates' role

There is no doubt that the investigations into corruption in Milan were an unquestionable success. Between 1992 and 1994, as the traditional political parties were increasingly crushed under the weight of the evidence of corruption accumulating in Milan's public prosecutor's offices, the magistrates increased in popularity. In particular Antonio Di Pietro, in part due to the extensive media coverage of Sergio Cusani's trial,[13] was seen as the redeemer of Italy's mischiefs, as the man who single-handedly brought down the pervasive system of corruption. This view soon became popular wisdom, so much so that the investigative magistrates at the centre of the investigations on Mani Pulite began to see themselves as political (albeit un-elected) actors. Thus we find that in September 1994 Antonio Di Pietro drafted a proposal for a legislative solution to the problem of corruption, which included stiffer penalties for guilty parties.[14]

While the success of the investigation by the magistrates in Milan has been as surprising as it has been spectacular, a number of the accused raised doubts about the legitimacy of the un-orthodox methods used by the Milan magistrates during their inquiries, claiming that the legal guarantees accorded to the accused had been infringed. Most notably, Sergio Cusani compared the court in Milan to an "Arab souk", where confessions and indulgences are traded. Among other apprehensions, he voiced the concern that pre-trial imprisonment was used as a means for extorting confessions from the accused (La Repubblica, 26 December 1994).[15]

Although Cusani's accusations have subsequently been thrown out, his crusade against the magistrates in Milan attracted some sympathy. Similar criticisms were raised by a number of public figures, including many prominent politicians, who became concerned by the increasingly politicised role of the Milanese magistrates.[16] The complex relationship between Berlusconi's government and the pool of Milanese magistrates needs to be analyzed in some detail.

Following the March 1994 elections, soon after Berlusconi was nominated as head of government, one of his first political decisions was to offer key posts within his government to Antonio Di Pietro, undoubtedly the best-known and most popular magistrate in the Mani Pulite investigations. Perhaps surprisingly,

Di Pietro declined the offer to become either minister for home affairs or Minister of Justice, declaring that his work as part of the pool working on the *Tangentopoli* affair was only half done and he wanted to finish it. Soon after this incident, the relationship between Berlusconi and the magistrates in Milan deteriorated and Berlusconi's friendly face gave way to direct confrontation between these two centres of power.

Thus, in the latter part of 1994, the government in general and Italy's prime minister, Silvio Berlusconi, in particular endorsed Cusani's concerns. On 13 July 1994, conveniently timed to coincide with the national hype resulting from Italy's success in the semi-final of the soccer World Cup, a government decree that addressed the touchy issue of pre-trial detention was passed. The decree re-qualified the gravity of the charges for those accused of corruption, thereby abolishing pre-trial detention for bribery and corruption suspects. Furthermore, the decree banned the media from reporting suspects' names during criminal inquiries.

Immediately after the government issued the decree, the four Milan magistrates applied for a 'transfer' on the grounds that the new legislation would not allow them to continue their work effectively. Their decision was dramatically announced by Di Pietro, regarded by the general public as a national hero and arguably more popular than Berlusconi himself, on television. A public outcry ensued, fuelled by the release of 2,137 remand prisoners, 189 of whom were held under bribery or corruption charges. Berlusconi's coalition allies, the Northern League and Alleanza Nazionale, opposed the new legislation, which was eventually rescinded by the government on 18 July and formally blocked by the Chamber of Deputies three days later.

The tension between Berlusconi and the magistrates was not defused by the above incident: the minister of justice, Alfredo Biondi, ordered a ministerial investigation into the Milan magistrates' activities. The investigation, to be carried out by Ministry inspectors, was greatly resented by the Milan magistrates and the judiciary generally. Elena Paciotti, spokeswoman for the Italian Magistrates Association claimed that certain aspects of the inspection "are disquieting and worrying", the first symptoms of "an unprecedented, serious interference"(La Repubblica, 28 June 1994).

The open confrontation between the judiciary and the executive took yet another turn on 22 November. While hosting the UN conference on international organised crime in Naples, Berlusconi received a formal warning from the pool of magistrates in Milan that he was under investigation (*avviso di garanzia*), together with a request to appear for interrogation (*ordine di comparizione*). Berlusconi was wanted for questioning in connection with allegations of bribery and corruption relating to an investigation into bribes paid to Italy's tax police by three companies which are part of Berlusconi's business empire in return for a favourable tax audit.[17]

Berlusconi's response took the form of an eight-minute televised message, in which he categorically rejected all claims that he was about to step down: "We are not prepared to allow a disgraceful abuse of criminal justice to massacre the first rule of democracy, which says that he who has the votes to govern shall govern"(Financial Times, 23 November 1994). In the following few days both Berlusconi and his close associates in the government severely admonished the magistrates for undermining his legitimate power, restating the need to curb the powers of the judiciary.

Shortly after this incident, on 6 December, in a surprising move, Di Pietro decided to abandon his post with the pool of magistrates coordinating the Mani Pulite investigations. In a letter to his superior, Borrelli, Di Pietro justified his resignation on the grounds that his work as magistrate was being unfairly employed for ends other than that of justice, although Borrelli has pointed out that the only reason Di Pietro resigned was because of the interference with his work caused by the Ministry of Justice inspectors.

On 13 December, Berlusconi was interrogated for seven hours by a trio of magistrates from the pool of Mani Pulite, Borrelli-Davigo-Colombo. Coming at the end of seven difficult months at the helm of the Italian state, this incident signalled the beginning of the end of Berlusconi's political reign. In fact, less than two weeks later, on 22 December, at the height of a tense debate in parliament, Berlusconi delivered his resignation speech, bringing to a close the 52nd government in Italy's post-war history.

Looking back at the prolonged arm-wrestling between the magistrates in Milan and Berlusconi, it cannot be denied that the 'objectionable' methods used by the Milanese magistrates in the conduct of their investigations became an important issue and perhaps even one of the key factors behind the success of Mani Pulite. For example, Alberto Vannucci(1994) pointed out that all the actors involved in the corruption market hold considerable bargaining power, based on access to threatening information. It follows that after the first corrupt player is arrested, this individual finds him-or-herself in a real-life prisoner's dilemma. According to Vannucci, the objectionable, but efficient skill of the magistrates conducting the Mani Pulite investigations was to create conditions whereby those under investigation had a strong incentive to confess and this was done by reproducing the incentive structure of the prisoner's dilemma.[18] Vannucci argues that the ability to recreate the conditions of the prisoner's dilemma helps us to understand the success of the magistrates in the early stages of the Mani Pulite investigation. In fact, Vannucci concludes that the magistrates in Milan were the crucial factor that triggered the confessions.

Such a view raises several questions. First of all, every competent investigative magistrate is supposed to reproduce prisoner's dilemma situations in order to extract a confession from the accused; therefore, there are no reasons to believe that the Milan magistrates were doing anything special. From this point of view, the *Tangentopoli* affair does not yield any novelty.[19] After all, the very same magistrates who were the protagonists of Mani Pulite had been around for a number of years, though it was only in 1992 that they were able to break the wall of *'omertà'* 'that had until then obstructed all major investigations into corruption. Moreover, as pointed out by Neppi Modona, it would have been very difficult for the excluded entrepreneurs to supply definitive proof of wrong-doing in the allocation of contracts.

Contrary to Vannucci's view, it can be argued that something crucial had changed by 1992, namely the structure of the entrepreneurs' pay-off in the corruption market. It follows that the causes of the success of the Milanese magistrates are endogenous to the system of corruption, not exogenous to it. In order to vindicate the above claim, it is necessary to closely analyze the nature of the market of corruption in Italy: as this market grew more and more extensive, it also became more and more inflexible towards the needs of individual actors, who saw the structure of their pay-off take a negative turn.

The market of corruption

In what follows, a model will be introduced which attempts to explain the nature of the corruption market. This model is necessary in order to understand the concept of an equilibrium point in the market, as well as the frailty of the system of corruption itself. When applied to the Italian case, and to Milan in particular, this model will clearly show the pivotal role of political parties in fostering corruption.

Let us start from a simple hypothetical situation, that of a public official who oversees a tender for a public contract (*gara di appalto*) and a number of firms who wish to obtain such a contract.[20] Let's assume that the official wishes to *sell* the tender to one of the firms for the price of a kick-back. To the extent that the expected costs of entering into the corrupt transaction (hereafter CT) are less than the expected gains, the firm will be willing to secure the tender by paying the kick-back.

Even assuming that there is a potentially corrupt official (hereafter CO) and a potentially corrupt entrepreneur and that both would gain from the CT, a communication problem ensues: how are they going to tell each other of their willingness to enter into such exchange? The realm in which they operate is illegal and, therefore, they cannot openly advertise their intentions. Moreover, their actions are stigmatized by social norms. Therefore, they have to be careful not to give away their intentions, yet they do not want to be secretive to the extent of ending up with no interaction. The communication problem would be easily overcome in a situation where corruption were already organized and widespread. In such a scenario, the public official could run a parallel, unofficial tender, considered "normal" by enterprises. Only the ones who accept the new rules of the game would be still in the market. However, in a situation where corruption is still not the rule, but the exception, such a procedure would be extremely visible and the risk of being exposed very high. It follows that the less widespread corruption is, the higher the cost involved in searching for a partner.[21]

A solution to the conundrum is to send a *signal* which will be understood *only* by those who are willing to enter into the corrupt transaction. The signal is a device to ascertain the disposition to enter into the CT, without testing it in the open. A signal is supposed to reveal a disposition without incurring the costs of probing. Such costs, in an illegal realm, are evident. Mistakes can be severely punished by authorities. The signal is the trigger that sets the wheels of corruption in motion.[22]

In real life situations, signals may be extremely diverse. Family connections, place of origin, club membership or exclusive educational establishments may provide the basis for a relevant signal, since they all pass the crucial *costly-to-fake* test.[23] In fact, in order to be credible, signals must be difficult to fake, which explains why it is not possible to successfully utilize a signal for a long time *without acquiring the identity which goes with it*. For example it is very hard to pretend to be a member of a family without actually being a member of it, or to be a member of an ethnic group without actually showing - at least at some crucial moments (such as festivities) - the correct signals which testify membership.

Notwithstanding their virtues, signals associated with family relations, or place of origin may not prove to be very effective since they fail the extension test, that is to say, these signals do not extend very far. This is not to say that these signals, at some time or another, were not used in Italy. Place of origin was especially a bonding element among actors in the corruption market. Although all these various signals were to some extent used in Italy, an alternative, more efficient solution to the communication problem was found, namely, party affiliation. Using party affiliation as a signal has a number of advantages. First, party affiliation stands the scrutiny of the *costly-to-fake* test. Though people may be shy on the way they vote, once they decide to join a party, they perform a public act. They commit themselves to a number of public activities that will make their membership known rather quickly. The party itself will exercise a scrutiny on the fake members, that is to say, on those who pretend to be members, but in fact are not.

Secondly, the party will also pass the extension test. A party is an organization that will reach a far greater number of people than a family and of a far wider social and professional background than a club. Also, more generations will be represented than those who have a common school experience.

Such an institution would also provide *social invisibility* for contacts as well as the physical and conceptual space where the public official could address his "demand for corruption" to the entrepreneur. To belong to the same party facilitates communication, as explained by Maurizio Prada, the treasurer of the Lombardy DC, who acted as a collector of kick-backs for his party: "To address such a touchy issue (*tema scabroso*) (i.e. handing over of a bribe) was eased by the fact that the interlocutor was a member of the party. I mean that it was easier to accept the situation"(Carlucci, 1992:22).

An ideological justification, whether sincere or not, for handing over or accepting a bribe could have been supplied behind the closed doors of the party headquarters. For example, since the Second World War, fighting or supporting communism were justifications for what, in a different context, would have been dismissed as bribery. In such a context, the moral cost of corruption reaches a negative value. Moral value is attached to pursing ends set by organizations other than the state and the rule of law.

The signal of party affiliation was the crucial resource in the first stages of the corruption market in Italy. A crucial by-product of using such a form of signalling should be analyzed. The party has property rights over the signal, monitoring membership and utilization of its label. When faced with a CO from its own ranks, the party has two choices: either to throw the CO out, or to claim part of the income that will accrue to the actors involved in the CT. In case the party follows the second course of action, it will scrutinize the performance of the CO as a collector of illicit funds. To the extent that the performance is considered to be positive, COs will receive party support throughout their career. Careers are important for COs because the further they rise up the career ladder, the greater their opportunities for raising illegal funds. Such a vicious circle will bring the party to grant its label only to the most obedient and 'efficient' COs.

This will in turn increase the party's income. These newly acquired financial resources from the illegal market may be invested in further augmenting the number of loyal party members it can place in crucial public offices. This has been the case in Italy, in the form of what has come to be called *lottizzazione*, or "allotment", whereby all aspects of the public sphere, from senior jobs in state-owned banks to the political control of RAI, the state broadcasting organisation, are parcelled out among the parties.[24]

Permeability of state institutions to party influence is the crucial factor for understanding the nature of Italian corruption. It is also crucial in accounting for the diffusion of corruption *Italian-style*. The more the political parties control state institutions and influence their decisions, the greater will be the role of the parties. Holding the opportunities for corruption constant, corruption will infiltrate a given social system depending on its institutional framework. The weaker state institutions are, as opposed to parties and lobbies, the greater the chances are that corruption will spread.

The equilibrium point

So far I have tried to explain how the market of corruption is born and why it grows. In what follows, the frailty of this market will be exposed. The key to our analysis is the following point: *corruption spreads as long as the population converges to a new equilibrium point which yields a superior pay-off.*

A process of learning enables the "honest" population - which was once blind to signals - to realize that a certain correlation holds (signal + success in the tender), hence more members will try to recognize and respond to the signal. This model holds for Italy, where dishonesty proved to be a more efficient strategy for a number of reasons. Bribes were only apparently paid by the entrepreneur, where, in fact, the collective paid for it. The cost of public works would rise enormously once they began. Thus the entrepreneur was able to discharge the kick-back paid to the party on the state's finances, by claiming that costs had increased in the meantime. On the other hand, state bodies would deliver as long as the entrepreneur had duly paid the kick-back. It follows that kick-backs were in effect paid by all tax payers - who saw their taxes rise - and by public service users - who experienced inefficiencies and delays. L. Ricolfi vividly makes the point:

> All too often one forgets that the *kill* was made by the entrepreneurs rather than the politicians. While the latter only retained a percentage of between one and 10 per cent on the value of production orders, the former were either selling their products at prices well above the market rate or were allowed to claim higher production costs (Ricolfi, 1993:136-7).

Ricolfi continues by showing that the cost of contracts awarded after 1993 (when presumably no kick-backs were paid) was roughly *half* that of in the past. This means that before 1993 it was *double* the market price. Who was pocketing the difference? The entrepreneur, of course, who paid only a small fraction back to the parties. The deal was very tempting: 'I get 10 and pay (to the parties) one'. It was an offer nobody could refuse.

The more corruption spreads, the less the need for the *invisibility* offered by the party. Gradually, the need for invisibility becomes superfluous, because it is common knowledge among all those taking part in the tender that an illegal, alternative system is operating. As bargaining becomes explicit and openly carried out in public officials' offices, party affiliation will no longer be a *secret* signal among a few corrupted entrepreneurs and COs in a generally honest society. Instead, entrepreneurs will openly pay parties by paying a single CO. The CO will in turn split their illegal incomes with the party.

A major increase in the level of corruption increases the number of people who collect kick-backs.[25] There are two aspects of this phenomenon worth considering. First, it is important to emphasize that contrary to the basic laws of economics, an increase in supply of COs does not bring about a reduction in the price of the kick-back. In other words, the cost of each kick-back will not be reduced under a more extensive level of corruption, as one would expect, instead the opposite is, in fact, the case. The cost of each kick-back will not decrease because there is no competition among the suppliers. The market for bribes is characterized by the fact that a public official has a monopoly over the resources he controls. There are no substitutes for his services. The citizen or the entrepreneur cannot "shop around" until they find somebody offering a "competitive" price for the service. He is then forced to buy always from the same supplier. The increase in the number of COs does not increase the supply of people who offer the same service. A CO in a competitive market for bribes would be a price-taker. On the contrary, the monopolist CO sets the price.[26]

Secondly, the expansion in the number of people who collect kick-backs will produce an enforcement and a co-ordination problem within each party. Given that the party ceases to act as provider of invisibility, how is it going to make sure that corrupt officials will not by-pass the party and pocket the kick-back? The more corruption spreads, the greater will be the CO's independence from the party structure. He, or she, may still split the illegal income with the party, but at this point the money may be used as resources in internal party-faction struggles, rather than simply to enrich party coffers. For example there is conclusive evidence to suggest that this was a realistic concern for the Socialist party.[27] The leader of the PSI, Bettino Craxi, was 'terrified' that kick-backs would end up in the wrong pockets. Craxi himself has made this point absolutely clear in a revealing book, *Il Caso C.* (The C. Affair), where he explains how different groups and centres of power within the PSI were increasingly able to escape the checks set up by the party's central headquarters to monitor both their means of self-finance and the political line being taken on key issues (Craxi, 1994:27&38)

Following his *decisionist* style of leadership, Craxi did everything within his powers to bring the party in line. Valerio Bitetto, a Socialist Party-appointed member of the board of ENEL, the state electricity company, was a privileged witness of these efforts:

> I was designated to this post by the PSI, and on that occasion I met personally with Craxi, whose actual words were the following 'don't be idle in your new post'. In other words, he told me that my job was to obtain votes for the PSI and funds for the party (Panorama, 14 February 1993).

Bitetto was heavily controlled by the centre and often reminded that his job was constantly on the line:

> I was being supervised by Bartolomeo De Toma, an engineer who had Craxi's utmost faith. Yet it was Craxi himself who had the final word. On the grounds of my achievements, it was Craxi who would eventually decide if I had successfully passed the exam and was therefore fit to be re-elected to my post. *I ought to stress that the way my actions were being monitored was extremely rigid. Craxi, like all the other political leaders, was*

obsessed that the money raised through corruption would end up in the wrong wallets (Panorama, 14 February 1993).

In order to avoid local party officials by-passing the centre, a process of centralization in the collection of kick-backs took place. This process took two forms. Major firms were invited to pay their kick-back directly to the national headquarters of certain political parties.[28] Alternatively, the process of centralization was enforced by tightening the control within the party structure between the centre and periphery. These changes are well documented for the PSI under Craxi. A number of people, loyal to Craxi, were assigned the role of collecting kick-backs and had to report directly to the chief. This has been documented by Vannucci for a case in Viareggio, where the collector, who was not even a party member, exercised the role of *de facto* administrative secretary for the party in Tuscany (Vannucci, 1992). The same applies for De Toma, the "supervisor" mentioned by Bitetto, who effectively acted as the shadow administrative secretary for the Socialist Party.[29]

In the last years of Craxi's reign, he made a rather successful effort in increasing the chances that money paid to the Party would in fact reach the party's coffers, rather than being lost in the pockets of party officials around the country. In order to do so, entrepreneurs were asked to pay a lump sum each year to the party. Such a sum would allow them to enter into tenders, rather than pay a kick-back on each contract they obtained (Ricolfi, 1993:136).

So far we have described some mechanisms that made it possible to reach an equilibrium where corruption was pervasive. What remains to be explained is how and why, at a certain point, the pay-offs of staying in the market of corruption changed for the entrepreneurs.

The incentive to be corrupt

Above, I asserted that the reason why people involved in exchanges of corruption testified cannot be explained simply in terms of the objectionable methods of the Milan magistrates in the conduct of their investigations. In what follows, the basic assumptions of an alternative explanation to the collapse of the corruption market in Italy will be provided, whereby the mechanisms that triggered the confessions can be found in the nuts and bolts of the market itself. In particular, the analysis will be grounded on the general frailty of the market of corruption, focusing on the nature of the good which was used to pay the kick-back, and its implication for the entrepreneurs in terms of their financial resources.

The evolution of the market amounted to a specialization process. Transaction mechanisms evolved so that actors could obtain (or steal) the greatest amount of resources in the most efficient way. The specialization process produced an 'optimal' adaptation to the environment. On the other hand, however, individual actors became more vulnerable to sudden outside shocks, such as delays in state payment of contracts. The bribe was efficiently collected but the delivery of state funds to overcome the cost of bribing became increasingly slow. An increase in specialization amounts to a reduction of flexibility as far as environmental changes are concerned. As argued by Zamagni, this is "the main cause of the spectacular fall of the system of corruption that we have witnessed nowadays in Italy"(Zamagni, 1994:104).

Who will be the first victims of the reduced flexibility of the system? The nature of the product sold by the enterprise will alter the ability to endure the costs of corruption. For example, a company selling infrastructure will be in a different position from one selling information. A company operating in the media sector, such as Berlusconi's Fininvest, sells a good that is demanded and highly prized by the political class as well. This enables the company to pay for the kick-back *in kind*, by charging reduced prices for political advertising, inviting politicians to talk-shows, or giving preferential treatment in 'serious' news programmes. The ability to pay for a kick-back *in kind* rather than in monetary form has the added advantage that it does not weigh negatively on the finances of the company. Furthermore, it is not legally punishable.

After all, a television channel must still produce television programmemes. In financial terms, the decision to give greater prominence to a certain politician rather than another has a marginal cost equal to (almost) zero. Having the opportunity to pay kick-backs in kind also has the advantage of not incurring penal risks, as Ricolfi rightly points out. By paying in kind, actual money transactions are reduced and so is the risk of being investigated by magistrates (Ricolfi, 1993:137). This should explain why Berlusconi's Fininvest empire has so far escaped investigations into the granting of air-wave rights. A widespread belief among Italians is that the faithful support given by Berlusconi to Craxi's PSI was paid back by Craxi's government through a number of favourable government decrees, such as the Legge Mammì.[30] Furthermore, it is not accidental that Berlusconi's troubles are with the Guardia di Finanza (Italy's special tax-inspectorate police force), since the latter could not be paid in kind (i.e. with granting TV time), but only in cash.

On the contrary, a seller of goods such as hospital needles or cleaning services cannot pay in kind; the kick-back has to be paid in cash. This increases the financial risks of the entrepreneur, who becomes exposed to the schedule of payment by the public authorities administering the public contract. In fact, it is only after the public contract is fully paid that the entrepreneur will be in a position to recover the previous investment made in the form of a kick-back. The schedule of payment for public contracts vis-à-vis liquidity becomes crucial. The private entrepreneur has to advance great sums of money. The less he, or she can count on a sound liquidity situation, the more exposed he, or she is towards the banking system. For the entrepreneur, the fact that the payment of his work by the public authorities is not delayed becomes of crucial importance. The entrepreneur in Italy faced "a public administration which is often in the red, thus forced to pursue its ends without the allocation of the required sums of money and following increasingly complex and atomized procedures" (Vannucci, 1992:146).

The increasing slowness of the state to pay public works hit the smallest and more vulnerable companies more severely than larger companies. Not all companies were able to sustain paying for the increasing cost of kick-backs, when there was a delay in the payment for the work already accomplished. The companies that had a sound financial base, and therefore faced fewer liquidity problems, were in a better position to weather the storm when payments were delayed. De Mico, who was involved in one of the first scandals of corruption in Milan, has pointed out that his company could endure delays since in terms of liquidity it was financially very sound. He added the following, enlightening remark:

> The same does not apply for those firms who are constantly struggling, who are willing to accept requests of up to seven or 10 per cent in kick-backs, since they are not able to withstand the slowing down and interruption of work that goes with a demand for unreasonably priced kick-backs (Vannucci, 1992:55).

These entrepreneurs would have been marginal to the system and started to lose out considerably. The system was becoming increasingly predatory, rather than "fair". It should then not come as a surprise that the first defectors were in fact liquidity-stricken small businesses, such as Luca Magni's, the man who incriminated Chiesa, and Alessandro Marzocco, chairman of a company that supplied buses to the city of Milan. Apart from the fact that both companies went bankrupt shortly afterward, they shared an important characteristic, namely, they were companies that could not successfully exit from the local market (the market of corruption) and compete internationally. They were highly dependent on public contracts and, at the same time, were not in a position to pay the kick-back in kind. To Magni and Marzocco, dishonesty as a strategy was no longer superior to honesty. It is here that the frailty of the corruption market is most apparent, which may explain why its internal contradictions eventually undermined the extensive, pervasive and deep-rooted system of corruption.

A further question worth mentioning is why confessions occurred first and foremost in Milan rather than in other parts of Italy, such as Sicily or Campania, where corruption was just as widespread. Though I do not have the space to discuss this point at length, the answer lies in the presence of organized crime. In the *mezzogiorno*, the mafia, the camorra and the 'ndrangheta actively participated in organizing the corruption market (Della Porta, 1994; Gambetta, 1993:214-220). In these contexts, organized crime would supply a crucial resource that was not so readily available in the North: credible violent threat to people (politicians and entrepreneurs alike) who wanted to defect from the system. It is well documented that the mafia had supported illicit business cartels through threatened or actual violence, with a resulting increase in the cost of testifying. As Calderone puts it: "people are afraid of being physically attacked and no one wants to run even a minimal risk of being killed. The mafioso, instead, is not afraid to take risks and so he puts the lives of others at risk" (Della-Porta-Vannucci, 1994: 200). In Palermo alone, 34 entrepreneurs and 78 shop-keepers were assassinated by the mafia between 1978 and 1987 (Santino and La Fiura, 1990: 400).

Conclusion

The aim of this chapter was to question the widely held belief that the success of the Mani Pulite investigation can be attributed exclusively to the work of the Milanese magistrates. Instead, this chapter suggests that an adequate framework for understanding the success of the Mani Pulite investigation ought to start from an analysis of the internal logic of the corruption market. In particular, the spectacular success of the Mani Pulite investigations may have something to do with the fragility of the market itself. The more the market of corruption grew, the more fragile it became, until eventually the equilibrium point could no longer be secured. As a result, the pay-offs for many individuals changed for the worse. It was this change in pay-offs that induced many individuals to exit the market of corruption altogether; exiting took the form of spontaneous confessions to the investigative magistrates.

While the analysis of the collapse of the corruption market is presented here as an alternative to the one which centred upon the role of the magistrates, in fact, we are not suggesting that these two forms of explanation are mutually exclusive. The point is not to deny that the magistrates played an important role in what is, undoubtedly, one of the most distinguished chapters in Italy's recent history. Instead, this chapter has argued that the pool of magistrates were fortunate to be conducting their investigations at a time when their efforts coincided with the changing pay-offs of the individuals they were investigating.

Notes

1. This chapter is part of a research project I started one year ago with Federico Varese. I am indebted to Mr Varese for innumerable instructive discussions on this theme, and for his many insights and valuable suggestions throughout all the stages of the writing process, especially Parts III, IV and V; this chapter could not have been written without his generous support. While I remain solely responsible for any errors in the chapter, I must share all its merits with Mr Varese. I am also grateful to Giacinto della Cananea, Mark Donovan, Shari Garmise, Robert Leonardi, Rosa Mulè, Cesare Onestini and Cheryl Thomas for their comments on an earlier version of this paper.

2. Between 1992 and 1994 the Milan pool included the investigative magistrates (*sostituti procuratori della Repubblica*) G. Colombo, G. D'ambrosio (co-ordinator), P. Davigo, P. Ielo and A. Di Pietro. Their immediate superior was S. Borrelli (*Procuratore della Repubblica*). By Mani Pulite we refer to the investigations on corruption in Milan that were carried out by the pool of magistrates in Milan since 1988, while by *Tangentopoli* we refer to the substance of such investigations, that is, the widespread corruption that was uncovered in Milan.

3. For a wide range of instances, see Alberto Vannucci (1994).

4. Il Corriere della Sera, 16 February 1994. Quoted in Mark Donovan (1995).

5. A. Pamparana (1994) and Andreoli, M (1993). There are also a number of publications valuable for reproducing extracts from court files: in particular see A. Carlucci (1992); 'Tangentopoli. Le Carte Che Scottano', supplement to Panorama, February 1993; 'Di Pietro. Le Sue Inchieste', supplement to *Avvenimenti*, No.48.

6. Among these few exceptions, D. della Porta (1992) and A. Pizzorno (1992).

7. A. Pamparana - E. Nascimbeni (1992); A.Vannucci (1994); Sarah Waters (1994).

8. In the words of Jon Elster (1984:118) "an equilibrium point is a set of individual strategies each of which is optimal against the other". See also Jon Elster(1989: Ch.11).

9. Such a date has been supplied by Di Pietro himself. See Pamparana and Nascimbeni (1992:16).

10. See P. Davigo (1994). We are grateful to Renato Finocchi for bringing this paper to our attention.

11. Quoted in F. Sidoti (1993:346).

12. Table 1 and 2 are taken from La Repubblica, 26 October 1994. The number of people under investigation increased to more than 2500 by the end of the year; see Il Corriere della Sera, 17 December 1994.

13. Sergio Cusani acted as the intermediate link between his boss Raul Gardini, the tycoon of Italy's chemical empire, and the Italian political class. Gardini paid a kickback valued at

approximately 153 billion lire to all major political parties in order to buy their support for a government decree that would have secured him a tax-break worth approximately 1000 billion lire. For a full account of Cusani's trial, see Pamparana (1994).

14. Di Pietro made his proposal public at a conference in Cernobbio. Aware of the criticisms he was likely to attract, he claimed to be speaking as a citizen rather than as a magistrate; see Il Corriere della Sera, 4 September 1994. For an account of the institutional and political set-up of the Italian judiciary, and of the impact of judicial actions on the Italian political system, see C. Guarnieri (1995).

15. G. Cagliari, involved in the Enimont scandal and former president of the ENI, committed suicide on 20 July 1993. He left a letter explaining his suicide as an "act of rebellion" against a legal system which sought to "annihilate and destroy people, not to do justice".

16. See L'Espresso, 28 June 1992.

17. The companies in question are Mondadori, Mediolanum and Videotime.

18. As one of the magistrates in the pool of Mani Pulite, Piercamillo Davigo, has explicitly claimed that it was necessary to create a non-metaphoric prisoner's dilemma. Quoted in Vannucci (1994:106).

19. I am grateful to Cheryl Thomas for bringing this point to my attention.

20. Mani Pulite is mainly about entrepreneurs and public officials, though some investigations have been conducted into more trivial issues, such as the illegal issuing of driving-licenses. We limit ourselves - for reasons of space - to discuss only these two actors.

21. See S. Zamagni (1994).

22. Path-breaking work in the economics of signalling has been done by A.M. Spence (1974). Recently, more sophisticated work on signalling for inscrutable commodities has been done by D. Gambetta (1994).

23. Using toads as example, R. Frank (1994:204) has analyzed the costly-to-fake property of credible signals. See also J. Krebs - R. Dawkins (1984).

24. In the case of RAI, what this meant is that the main television channel (RAI 1) was controlled by the Christian Democrats, the second channel (RAI 2) by the socialists and the third, smaller channel (RAI 3) by the then communists. The three channels had their own news programmeme, where the different political orientations were clear.

25. See J.C. Andvig - K.O. Moene (1990).

26. The moral costs for each agent on both the demand and the supply side will decrease as the incidence of corruption increases. As corruption becomes widespread, there is no more shame in addressing the tema scabroso of corruption, hence there is no longer any need to justify ideologically the "demand" for corruption. The entrepreneur that did not accept the system of corruption could opt for the exit option. Exit implies either closing down the business altogether, or operating in markets outside the reach of COs (such as the international market for the same products, or by changing sector of specialization, moving as far as possible from sectors where public officials can ask for bribes). Exit is of course a strategy that not all can follow. It seems to be the case that Olivetti followed this strategy (See De Benedetti in La Repubblica, 18 March 1993, quoted in Vannucci (1994:154). However, this option is not open to everybody: only very efficient firms could compete in the international markets, and to change sector would imply investing a lot of capital in changing the process of production.

27. While in this chapter the PSI figures as the only example, the same analysis probably applies to

the Christian Democrats as well as to the other major parties involved in corrupt transactions.

28. This was admitted by Vincenzo Lodigiani during his trial. See 'Di Pietro: le sue inchieste', *Avvenimenti*, No.48, 1994, p.53.

29. Craxi refers to these collectors of kick-backs in his book, *Il Caso C.*, p.30.

30. Although Berlusconi's Fininvest controlled 45 per cent of the market and 85 per cent of commercial television, thanks to the Legge Mammì passed in 1990 this was not judged to be an infringement of the anti-monopoly legislation. This law was challenged by a number of small television operators, and it was only at the beginning of December 1994 that the Constitutional Court ruled Berlusconi's Fininvest media empire unconstitutional.

References

Andreoli, M. (1993) *Andavano in Piazza Duomo,* Milan: Sperling & Kupfer.

Andvig, J.C. and Moene, K.O. (1990) 'How Corruption May Corrupt', *Jounal of Economic Behaviour and Organization,* Vol. 13.

Barry, B. (1989) 'Is It Better to Be Powerful or Lucky?' in Barry, B (ed.) *Democracy, Power and Justice: Essays in Political Theory,* Oxford: Clarendon Press.

Carlucci, A. (1992) *Tangentopoli,* Milan: Baldini & Castoldi.

Craxi, B. (1994) *Il Caso C,* Milan: Critica Sociale.

Davigo, P. (1994) 'I Limiti e Cotrollo Penale sulla Corruzione e i Necessari Rimedi Preventivi' in Alberti, D and Finocchi, R (eds.), *Corruzione e Sistema Istituzionale,* Bologna: Il Mulino.

della Porta, D. (1992) *Lo Scambio Occulto,* Bologna: Il Mulino.

della Porta, D. (1993) 'Milan: Immoral Capital', in Hellman, S and Pasquino, G (eds.), *Italian Politics: A Review,* London: Pinter.

della Porta, D and Vannucci, A (1994) 'Politics, the Mafia and the Market for Corrupt Exchange', in Mershon, C and Pasquino, G (eds.), *Italian Politics. Ending the First Republic,* Boulder: Westview Press.

Donovan, M. (1995) 'Corruption in Italy: A Dominant Reality', Working Paper, Centre for Mediterranean Studies, University of Bristol.

Elster, J. (1984) *Ulysses and the Sirens,* Cambridge: Cambridge University Press.

Elster, J. (1989) *Nuts and Bolts for the Social Sciences,* Cambridge: Cambridge University Press.

Frank, R. (1994) *Microeconomics and Behaviour*

Gambetta, D. (1993) *The Sicilian Mafia,* Cambridge Massachussets: Harvard University Press.

Gambetta, D. (1994) 'Inscrutable Markets' *Rationality and Society,* Vol. 6, No. 3, July.

Guarnieri, C. (1995 forthcoming) 'The Political Role of the Italian Judiciary' in *Deconstructing Italy,* Berkelely: Berkely University Press.

Krebs, J. and Dawkins, N. (1984) 'Animal Signals: Mind Reading and Manipulation', in Krebs, J and Davies, N (eds.) *Behavioural Ecology: An Evolutionary Approach,* Sunerland, M.A: Sinauer Associates.

Neppi Modona, G. (1994) 'Tangentopoli e Mani Pulite: Dopo le Indagini i Processi' in Ginsborg,

P, (ed.) *Stato dell'Italia,* Milan: Mondadori.

Pamparana, A. and Nascimbeni, E. (1992) *Le Mani Pulite,* Milan: Mondadori.

Pamparana, A. (1994) *Il Processo Cusani,* Milan: Mondadori.

Pizzorno, A (1992) 'La corruzione nel sistema politico', in della Porta, D. (ed.) *Lo Scambio Occulto,* Bologna: Il Mulino.

Sidoti, F. (1993) 'The Italian Political Class', *Government and Opposition,* Vol. 28 (Summer), No. 3.

Riciolfi, L. (1993) *L'Ultimo Parlamento,* Rome: La Nuova Italia.

Santino, U. and La Fiura, G (1990) *L'Impresa Mafiosa,* Milan: Franco Angeli.

Spence, A.M. (1974) *Market Signalling,* Cambridge Massachussets: Harvard University Press.

Vannucci, A. (1992) 'La Realta' Economica della Corruzione Politica. Un Analisi di un Caso', *Stato e Mercato,* No. 34.

Vannucci, A. (1994) *Il Mercato della Corruzione,* Unpublished PhD Thesis, Pisa: Scuola Superiore S. Anna.

Zamagni, S. (1994) 'Sul Processo di Generazione della Corruzione Sistematica' in Barca, L. and Trento, S. (eds.), *L'Economia della Corruzione,* Rome: Laterza.

Waters, S. (1994) 'Tagentopoli (sic) and the Emergence of a New Political Order in Italy' *West European Politics,* Vol. 17, No. 1, pp 169 - 182.

The Fourth Man: the dismantling of terrorism in Italy

Loretta Napoleoni

At the beginning of 1994, Mario Moretti, one of the founders of the Red Brigades, wrote in his memoirs (Moretti, 1994) that he had been the sole executioner - though in the presence of all the other jailers - of Aldo Moro. His confession came at the end of a period in which former terrorists and criminals had made important revelations regarding the assassination of the then president of the DC. In the fall of 1993, a new ballistic report on the killing of Aldo Moro's bodyguards had triggered a new round of investigation. According to the report, seven weapons were fired in the via Fani ambush, not six as previously thought. The new evidence not only invalidated the reconstruction of events given by Valerio Morucci, a key collaborator in the Moro trials, it also implied that a member of the Red Brigades commando which carried out the tragic assault on 16 March 1978 was still unidentified. The ballistic report reopened a painful wound in the history of post-war Italy and fuelled a fresh round of revelations. Saverio Morabito, boss of 'ndrangheta, alleged that the man in via Fani was Antonio Nirta, a mafioso infiltrated into the Red Brigades by the Italian secret service. Antonio Savasta and Alessio Casimirri, repentant ex-members of the Red Brigades, claimed soon after that the unidentified man in via Fani was Germano Maccari, a Roman craftsman jailed for two years after the violent attacks carried out by the armed group, Formazioni Armate Combattenti. Adriana Faranda, an important figure in the reconstruction of Moro's kidnapping, went even further. In a dramatic and emotional confession she stated that Maccari was the mysterious Ingegnere Altobelli, Moro's fourth jailer and his material killer. To thicken the plot further, Prospero Gallinari, the man regarded for fifteen years as Moro's assassin, refused to confirm or deny the new evidence from his cell in the Roman prison of Rebibbia.

So who killed Moro? Chances are that the full truth will never be known. However, one has to ask how important it is to know the exact number of bullets fired in via Fani, or how many men fired them. The assassination of a public figure of Moro's stature transcends the technicalities and the dynamics of a common murder. Its symbolism is far too apparent to let investigative uncertainties cripple the search for a dignified end to the cycle of violence ignited and fuelled by terrorism. Nevertheless, the new ballistic evidence released at the end of 1993 blocked the proposal of *indulto* - the reduction of sentences which had been inflated by anti-terrorist emergency legislation to pre-emergency levels. This proposal was considered to be a dignified way to conclude the tragedy of terrorism by the 300 left and right-wing terrorists still imprisoned.

The events of 1993-94 suggest a few considerations. The strategy of investigative magistrates involved in pending terrorist trials still focused on the technicalities of politically motivated crimes and inevitably undermined their symbolism. This attitude, coupled with the sensational tone which accompanies press reports on investigations, not only represents a serious obstacle to the formulation of a final solution to terrorism, but, more importantly, continues to project an obsolete image of the phenomenon. The danger is that by postponing the closure of a chapter of political violence beyond its natural history, the spirit of the armed struggle will be kept alive (Bradford University, 1995) and used by common criminals and mythomaniacal individuals to justify their crimes,[1] or by supporters of '*dietrologia*' to describe the illegal nature and functioning of what is known as the 'hidden government' of the First Republic.[2] It will be argued in this chapter that at the origins of indifference towards the symbolism of politically motivated crimes are the serious difficulties that the Italian state still has in addressing the dramatic phenomenon of terrorism; difficulties which determine its unwillingness to become - even if only to close the final chapter of a tragic conflict - the primary interlocutor of terrorists. Such reluctance is the direct consequence of the dilemma that terrorism poses to the modern state, presenting itself as a crime with war aims (Gilbert, 1994). This chapter will address three sets of issues. The first traces the nature of the relation between left-wing terrorism and post-war Italy through the armed struggle of the Red Brigades; the second will highlight the limits of the instrument of the law, which, in the ultimate analysis, can only partially deal with the complexity of the phenomenon of terrorism; the third will look at the *battaglia di libertà*, started in 1987 by Piero Bertolazzi, Renato Curcio, Maurizio Iannelli and Mario Moretti, as the search for new legal routes to freedom away from the schemes proposed by the legal category of *pentiti* and *dissociati*, an initiative which led to the first proposal for *indulto* in 1989. It will be argued that, because of its war aims, to end the conflict terrorism requires an official agreement, a treaty, between the winner and the loser. In this context the pardon of *indulto* symbolises the peace treaty between the Italian state and its old enemies - left and right-wing terrorists.

The dychotomous nature of terrorism

Terrorism has become a characteristic mode of conflict in our time. As a socio-political phenomenon it came into its own during the second half of this century. In Europe, its origins lie in the rising tide of student and radical unrest of the second half of the 1960s - mainly as a result of the defeat of rural guerrillas in Latin America, but also following the emergence (or in some cases the reactivation) of urban terrorist groups in Europe, North America and Japan (Laqueur, 1977). The emergence of terrorism is, therefore, linked to the birth of its target : the post-war liberal and democratic state. Indeed, what distinguishes modern terrorism from 19th century revolutionary movements is the very nature of the targets chosen.

To the modern democratic state, terrorism poses a serious dilemma: how to deal with the phenomenon - as war or as crime? The double nature of the phenomenon springs from the double responsibility of the modern state: to preserve national security and to maintain civil order. Terrorists, convinced that they are engaged in a violent conflict sufficiently similar to war, commit crimes such as murder or kidnapping, which, they claim, should be judged within the context of war.[3] The state, on the other hand, in its role of guardian of civil order, insists on prosecuting them as common criminals (Gilbert, 1994).

The common criminality label attached to terrorists expresses the state's fear of letting them challenge its own legitimacy. By admitting that terrorists are a threat to its stability, the state would allow the question of its own legitimacy to be opened. One of the primary goals of terrorists is to undermine the representative nature of the democratic state and of its government (Gilbert, 1994). Such was the aim of the Red Brigades when they claimed to be the forces completing the revolutionary process started during the fascist regime and aborted by the First Republic (Franceschini, 1988).[4]

Dismissing terrorists as criminals also reinforces the state's claim to be the proper and only power to enforce the law against anyone who threatens civil order (Gilbert, 1994). The paradox of terrorism is that it can actually strengthen political coalitions and governments by forcing the opposition to form a compact front with the ruling elites. The DC's skilful exploitation of the climate of violence of the 1970s to stress its centrality and to introduce authoritarian legislation and later the 1978 *Governo di Solidarietà Nazionale* headed by Andreotti and fully supported by the PCI, represents an important example of this phenomenon.

The criminality of terrorism finds its philosophical justification in what can be defined as the "democratic syllogism". Representative democracies offer many legal channels through which the community can voice its dissent towards the rule of the political elites; therefore, there is no need for political violence. Anyone who uses it, breaches the proper procedures, does not play according to the rules of the game and, therefore, is a criminal. In essence, what the syllogism means is that in a representative democracy there cannot be a revolution, there can only be crime. However, the wide-spread emergence of terrorism in post-war Europe challenges this principle and requires an empirical analysis to identify the limits of its validity.

The political system established in post-war Italy represented a major departure from the pure model of representative democracy; more specifically, it lacked the democratic valve of alternate government. Of the two major parties representing two-thirds of the population, one, the DC, was always in power and the other, the PCI, was always the opposition. For many intellectuals, terrorism was indeed the price that Italy had to pay for having established a form of 'imperfect bipartitism' (Galli, 1986). However, there is no evidence of interdependency between this type of political model and terrorism; in Sweden from 1932 to 1976 a single party continually won electoral pluralities and dominated the executive branch of government without producing any significant outburst of political violence. More likely, the uninterrupted hegemony of the Christian Democrats contributed, in the 1960s and 1970s, to the polarization and embittering of conflicts between elites in power (including all parliamentary parties) and extra-parliamentary groups (Tarrow, 1990). The roots of a complex phenomenon such as Italian terrorism lie more deeply; they are interlinked with the emergence of the Italian political system and sprang from the same factors (historical, political, structural and international) which have made possible the departure from the pure model of representative democracy. Thus, terrorism and the 'anomaly' of the Italian system are the product of the same phenomenon: the implementation of the liberal and democratic model in a country inserted into the polarization of the Cold War; conditioned, therefore, internationally, possibly more than any other, because it was perceived as a strategic 'frontier' country.

Empirical evidence shows that the limits of the validity of the democratic syllogism rest upon the application of the fundamental principles of democracy. In Italy, the failure to guarantee the opposition access to channels of communications and transformation increased the vulnerability of the state and its institutions. In this context, terrorism ceased to be an unlikely eventuality and became a serious threat, resembling at times an all-out war, as suggested by the large size of the Italian armed community, the high number of people (over 4,000) jailed for crimes connected with terrorism, the number of people killed by terrorists, and the number of terrorists killed by the authorities. (See Tables 1 & 2).

Table 1

Yearly distribution of new defendants from left-wing terrorist groups

Year	number of new defendants	%
1971	21	0.5
1972	103	2.5
1973	5	0.1
1974	85	2.1
1975	74	1.8
1976	45	1.1
1977	90	2.2
1978	170	4.2
1979	393	9.6
1980	1021	25.0
1981	433	10.6
1982	965	23.6
1983	305	7.5
1984	86	2.1
1985	55	1.3
1986	36	0.9
1987	71	1.7
1988	28	0.7
1989	11	0.3
Missing data	90	2.2
Total	4087	100.0

Source : *La Mappa Perduta*, Cooperativa Sensibili alle Foglie, Roma, 1994.

Table 2

Yearly distribution of victims of left-wing terrorism and terrorist deaths

Year	Victims of left-wing terrorism	%	Deceased terrorists	%
1971	1	0.8	1	1.5
1972				
1973				
1974	4	3.1	3	4.4
1975	3	2.3	4	5.9
1976	8	6.2	3	4.4
1977	5	3.9	5	7.4
1978	28	21.9	3	4.4
1979	21	16.4	13	19.1
1980	24	18.7	12	17.7
1981	13	10.2	3	4.4
1982	13	10.2	6	8.8
1983	1	0.8	2	2.9
1984	1	0.8	2	2.9
1985	1	0.8	2	2.9
1986	1	0.8	1	1.5
1987	3	2.3		
1988	1	0.8	2	2.9
1989			1	1.5
1992			2	2.9
1993			2	2.9
Total	128	100.0	68	98.4

Source : *La Mappa Perduta*, Cooperativa Sensibili alle Foglie, Roma, 1994.

The emergence of terrorism inevitably unveils the weaknesses in modern democracies' defence against the phenomenon of armed struggle; weaknesses deriving from the failure of systems to provide the state with specific powers and instruments to fight back. Ironically, by accepting the democratic syllogism, Italian democracy avoided addressing an important issue: the interdependence between terrorists and the modern state.[5] As a result, terrorism as a socio-political phenomenon is often underestimated and, when it strikes, the sole defence at the disposal of the democratic state is criminal law.

The inadequacy of the instrument of the law is outlined by the fact that, in spite of its insistence that terrorists are common criminals, the state very rarely treats them as such. In one way or another, their crime is regarded as special because of its political and unselfish motivations (Gilbert, 1994, Moss, 1989, Ferrajoli, 1990). Terrorism, therefore, is a crime, but a very special one which, to be defeated, requires special treatment which existing criminal law (as well as the judiciary) cannot provide. Moreover, the uniqueness of the crime committed by terrorists is used by the state to justify its use of emergency legislation - special powers granted to the government allowing it to bypass the law and parliament in reputedly exceptional circumstances. In reality it is the double nature of terrorism which makes the existing criminal code and the judiciary inadequate to fight back.

The judiciary at war

An exceptional legal tool,[6] emergency legislation, is therefore the primary instrument at the disposal of the modern state for fighting terrorists. However, regardless of the 'exceptional' nature and task, its use is limited by well-defined legal boundaries. Unlike in authoritarian regimes, the possibility of bypassing the law and parliament in a democracy is permitted only within the 'perimeter' of the constitution. In Italy's case, the 1947 constitution, drafted and approved in the aftermath of fascism, had stripped the executive of all emergency powers, including the State of War, in order to prevent the rise of authoritarian regimes (Mortati, 1969). The only tool left at the disposal of the government was the *decreto-legge*, an emergency bill with a 60 day life span requiring, within that period, the ratification and full conversion into law by both chambers of parliament.

Within these constraints, the Italian anti-terrorist strategy had two specific aims: to avoid granting the armed community the status of enemies and to fight back using emergency legislation without openly going against the limits imposed by the constitution. These goals were achieved with a clever tactical manoeuvre, i.e. by shifting the focus of the armed struggle away from the state towards one of its institutions - the judiciary - to which the ruling elites delegated the difficult task of tackling the phenomenon of terrorism. This move produced several positive effects: it stressed the criminality of terrorists, it denied that the state was under threat and it simultaneously reinforced the role of the Italian Republic as the sole guarantor of law and order. In addition, recourse to the *decreto-legge* to empower the judiciary, instead of the executive, with exceptional powers, broadened the government's margin of manoeuvre in the use of emergency legislation, without running the risk of being the object of 'authoritarian' criticism.

The remilitarization of the police

With regard to the implementation of this policy, initially, the response of the Italian state to the challenge of terrorism was purposely ambiguous. Until 1978, after Moro's seizure, 'terrorism' had not appeared as a legal category and even then it was mentioned only in relation to the specific crime of kidnapping (article 289b of the penal code) for which penalties were double those for the non-political version. On a more general level, 'terrorism' was left undefined in the laws themselves and its interpretation was deliberately left to the local judiciary - officially to play down its significance and strategically to exploit the beneficial effect of the 'paradox of terrorism', i.e. the progressive weakening of parliamentary opposition vis-à-vis the authoritarian reforms introduced by the DC.

From 1974 to 1978, the use of emergency legislation centred on the re-introduction of authoritarian legislation. A series of special laws were aimed at re-militarizing the police. In 1974 the *Legge Bartolomei* reintroduced questioning by the police and extended their powers during informal investigations; in 1978, *decreto-legge* n.59 suppressed the presence of defence lawyers during the questioning; in 1975 the *Legge Reale* increased the terms of preventative custody by the police and widened the spectrum in which the use of arms was allowed for the prevention of crimes. Over the same period, the government's juridical policy reflected a clear willingness to reintroduce restrictive measures. Improved living conditions in prisons, brought about by the liberal reforms of the 1960s, were offset by a series of measures. In 1975 the prison reform law permitted the suspension of all rights for individual prisoners or sections of jails (article 90). Prison guards were granted the right to fire at prisoners attempting to escape or at anybody who tried to subvert order (law n. 374 of 28 June 1977); In 1977 the principle of isolation was extended to the prison system by the initial creation of 11 maximum security jails by ministerial decree.[7]

After 1978, these restrictive reforms, though not specifically directed to fight terrorism, proved to be important instruments in anti-terrorist policy. The differentiation between maximum security and other prisons, for example, was easily converted into a general means of separating members of the armed community from prospective recruits among ordinary criminals, while between 1981 and 1984, widespread recourse to article 90 resulted in the virtual isolation of 800 maximum-security prisoners from the outside world (Moss, 1989).

The magistrates'[8] management of political violence

From 1974 to 1978, the Italian ruling elite succeeded in maintaining common criminality as the boundary between the state and terrorists by simply reinforcing the powers of the police and introducing restrictive measures. Such a strategy, though not openly directed against terrorists, provided the groundwork for what, after Moro's killing, was regarded as a proper anti-terrorist policy. For the first time, the state openly showed its commitment to fight back against terrorism. Chronologically, the boundaries of this second round of emergency legislation went from the *decreto-legge Cossiga*, the blue-print for Italian anti-terrorist strategy (converted into law on 15 December 1979), to the *"legge sui pentiti"* (repentants' law) of 29 May 1982, the first major victory of the state over the armed community.

The seizure of Moro was followed by a serious escalation of political violence. From the beginning of 1978 to the end of the 1980s, the largest number of assassinations carried out by terrorists occurred. Of a total of 128 victims of left-wing terrorism from 1971 to 1988, 28 were killed in 1978, 21 in 1979 and 24 in 1980. The casualties inflicted by the state on the armed community were also heavy, of a total of 68 people, 19 died in 1979 and 12 in 1980, respectively 19.1 per cent and 17.7 per cent. As a result the country was on a virtual war footing. Road blocks and police and army patrols became a feature of everyday life for Italians. The size of the armed community had also increased dramatically. At the beginning of 1976 there were only three active armed groups - the NAR (*Nuclei Armati Proletari*), the Red Brigades and the FAC (*Formazioni Armate Comuniste*) - by 1979 there were 12. During this period the defence of the state was no longer in the hands of the carabinieri, but was progressively being transferred to the judiciary. A new scenario began taking shape whereby magistrates, in charge of pre-trial investigations, assumed the role of defenders of the Republic against the violent attack of terrorists. Moreover, from 1979 to 1982, the aim of the emergency legislation was two-fold: to facilitate the management of violence and the creation and diffusion of knowledge about it via the *giudici istruttori* and (*sostituti*) *procuratori del*La Repubblica (Moss, 1989), and to weaken their political motivation. To fulfil the first objective, magistrates' investigative powers were expanded in two ways. First, in 1978 they were empowered to ignore ordinary rules of secrecy covering enquiries in progress and to communicate their documents and findings to one-another as they were made (law 191 article 4). The new legislation was conceived to improve the coordination of magistrates' work within the constraints of the constitution, which, by prohibiting the reintroduction of special tribunals (article 102), blocked the formation of a central juridical body. The legality given to what, until 1978, had been informal oral exchanges proved to be especially valuable after 1980 by permitting the wide circulation of the transcripts of extended confessions from *pentiti*.

The second way magistrates' powers were expanded referred to the transfer to them of powers traditionally belonging to the police. Magistrates were increasingly compelled by law to order the arrest and preventative detention, and to refuse the release on bail, of persons for whom they felt sufficient evidence existed of involvement in politically-motivated crime. To complement the new legislation, arrest was made mandatory in 1979 for all acts covered by the 'terrorism and subversion' label and was accompanied by the removal of magistrates' discretionary powers to order an offender's provisional release. Again, in 1979, the maximum period between arrest and definitive sentencing was increased, for acts of terrorism, to ten years and eight months. As a result, defendants could spend years in prison before coming to trial, as happened to the central defendants in the *Processo 7 Aprile* who were imprisoned for three to four years before the case was finally brought to court.

Undermining the political motivations of terrorists proved to be a much more difficult task. The exhuming of '*reati associativi politici*' (crimes of political association), introduced by the fascist regime and never removed from the legal code, was the first strategic weapon offered to the judiciary for this task. It proved to be particularly versatile because such crimes lacked a formal description and the conditions of their application had not been much elaborated in the jurisprudence of the Republic.[9] Therefore, their definition could be left entirely up to the discretion of magistrates. 'Armed insurrection against the state' (article 284 of the penal code), 'armed band' and '*concorso morale*' (conspiracy) became empty boxes to be filled by magistrates who could use them as leverage with terrorists. Indeed, in the 1980s these crimes were used as legal multipliers of penalties imposed by the courts on the '*irriducibili*' (unrepentant). A striking example was the decision of the Roman magistrate Francesco Amato in February 1982 to extend the accusation of armed insurrection to everyone already convicted or awaiting trial for membership in the Red Brigades. The charge carried a maximum sentence of life imprisonment.

However, initially the *reati associativi* did not weaken the armed community, which showed an incredible degree of ideological commitment, especially when dealing with the judiciary. The defendants in the Red Brigades' first trial in 1976 even managed to extend their struggle into the court with the so-called, '*processo guerriglia*'[10], which became an embarrassment for the state and the judiciary. Instead, the breach in the Red Brigades' ideological stronghold came from the army - the special anti-terrorist unit of General Dalla Chiesa's carabinieri. At the end of 1979, Patrizio Peci, a disillusioned member of the Red Brigades' *colonna torinese* (Turin column) was singled out by Dalla Chiesa who moulded the figure of 'full collaborator' around him [11]. This move started a chain reaction. Within months Roberto Sandalo, Roberto Garigliano, Gianluigi Cristiani and Marco Barbone had followed Peci's example. Dalla Chiesa's achievement was to allow terrorists to establish the practice of opening a dialogue, accepting communication with their former enemies. Once a terrorist had taken that difficult step, magistrates were able to negotiate the price for a final way out of terrorism.

For magistrates and the state, full collaborators represented the first major victory over the enemy. Strategically, their confessions facilitated the difficult task of identifying the armed community and therefore needed to be encouraged. However, Italy's penal code, reminiscent of the Napoleonic legal code, lacked the presumption of innocence,[12] prevented the granting of immunity and also disallowed the common law process of plea bargaining (Von Tangen, 1994). This meant that to give full collaborators substantive cuts in their sentences, new laws had to be introduced. Law 15 of 1980 offered a reduction of up to one-half in all sentences and the conversion of a life sentence into no more than 20 years, in return for full dissociation from fellow-conspirators and demonstrably effective collaboration with the police and the judiciary. Law 304 of 29 May 1982 (better known as the *legge sui pentiti*) offered strong incentives to include an exhaustive list of contacts, putting full collaborators under a great deal of pressure to extend their revelations as widely as possible. Full collaborators also offered magistrates a splendid opportunity to strike a serious blow at the ideological commitment of terrorists. To this task former terrorists were transformed into '*pentiti*'[13] by their public repudiation in court of the armed struggle and of their former selves. To maximise the exposure of the phenomenon of repentance, *pentiti* were encouraged to became the principal interpreters of terrorism, replacing the intelligentsia as the key mediators of meanings. Both magistrates and the press concentrated on the significance of the admission of having embraced the wrong cause, shifting the emphasis of the justice mechanism away from the crime and towards the single individual; in this way the political symbolism of public confessions ended up transcending the criminality of the terrorist actions committed by the *pentiti*.

A personal justice?

The instrumental role that the legal category of *pentiti* played in the judiciary's anti-terrorist strategy became apparent during the third phase of emergency legislation, from 1983 to 1987, when terrorists were brought to trial. The yearly distribution of new defendants from the armed community illustrated in Table 1 confirms this phenomenon. It shows two peaks: the first in 1980 when 1021 people were arrested for crimes related to terrorism (25 per cent of a total of 4087) and the second in 1982 when 965 people were arrested for similar crimes. However, in 1983 there were only 305 new defendants and in 1984, only 86. These data confirm that by 1983 the core of the radical left-wing community had been arrested and was either on trial, or was about to be and that the effort to defeat terrorism was no longer concentrated on hunting terrorists so much as on punishing them.

The full collaboration of repentants was used to construct law 304 in 1982 around the figure of the *pentito*, aiming to encourage confessions by reducing penalties. To justify the special treatment promised to former terrorists, magistrates regarded the political motivation of the crime committed as a mitigating circumstance. Overall, the law was well received, though the bargaining spirit upon which *pentiti* made their confessions made it possible for former terrorists who had committed murder to receive penalties much milder than their non-political equivalents. A striking example was the penalty received by the *pentito* Marco Barbone who spent only three years in jail for killing Walter Tobagi. For the state and the judiciary however, the importance of the law went well beyond the punishment of single individuals and rested upon the introduction of a discriminatory element in the judgment of politically-motivated crimes. This principle exhumed from the liberal juridical tradition of the 19th century bourgeois state, was born in sharp opposition to the repressive nature of the ancien regime,[14] which discriminated in favor of political crime[15]. During the season of the great terrorist trials, the extenuating circumstances of political motivation granted to pentiti found ideal terrain for implementation. At the same time law 304 offered a unique opportunity for judges and the courts to use the discriminatory principle as a lever to create a new category of defendants - that of '*dissociati*'.

From 1983 to 1987 - a period characterised by '*maxi-processi*' against terrorist organizations such as the Red Brigades and Prima Linea - the core of state anti-terrorist policy shifted to the courts of law, where a large number of terrorists were brought to trial. The strategy pursued during the previous period had mortally wounded the armed community so that emergency legislation could now be primarily used to facilitate the task reserved for judges, i.e. that of interpreters and evaluators of the phenomenon of terrorism. Paying specific attention to the meaning of armed struggle - in sharp contrast with their role of *intra-partes* observers - judges opened a breach in the dichotomy of *pentiti/irriducibili* to insert a group of former terrorists who were in the legally anomalous position of wishing to abandon armed struggle without acknowledging unconditional allegiance to the state and to its demand for retrospective information.

As magistrates had moulded the category of *pentiti*, judges became the primary interlocutors for *dissociati* (Moss, 1989). This task was facilitated by the much-weakened role of lawyers, who had watched the boundary between their clients and the state became clouded with ambiguities. The facilitation of police interrogation, for example, and acceptability of some procedural violations permitted by emergency legislation had drastically reduced the powers of defence lawyers. Even more serious was the danger of stepping into illegality that stemmed from uncertainty about the dividing line between offering legitimate assistance to clients and participating in their activities; from 1977 to 1981 as many as seven lawyers were indicted for belonging to armed bands.

Although the ruling elite had always strongly opposed the reintroduction of special tribunals, the modifications produced in the judiciary and in the law by the emergency legislation had had, by 1983, a great impact upon criminal procedures and the functioning of the courts. Both the traditional mediatory role of lawyers towards magistrates and the solidarity within their own category had been disrupted. The refusal of those who considered themselves "political prisoners" to respond, either to the investigating magistrates or in court, reduced the defence role to a mere technical performance, while lawyers of *pentiti* saw their legal functions eliminated by their client's confessions. Paradoxically, a magistrate, the *pubblico ministero*[16], replaced the defence lawyer as mediator for the *pentiti* in court (Ferrajoli, 1990). Because of the special treatment granted by the law on repentants, lawyers were inclined to suggest to clients that they confess, thus projecting a false image of cooperation between the category of pentiti and the state. On the other hand, lawyers for the *irriducibili* were publicly identified with the armed community. Nomination of lawyers and acceptance to defend repentants were perceived as political statements. This atmosphere sometimes succeeded in eliminating informal reciprocal assistance such as the circulation of interrogation transcripts, weakening further the capacity of the lawyers to respond to the reduction in their role and power.

The most striking consequence of the abrogation of the lawyers' traditional function of translating their client's understandings, actions and descriptions into legal terms was the disruption of the principle of cross-examination (Ferrajoli, 1990), which completely threw the structure of the trials off balance. In such exceptional circumstances, judges were able to shift the object of the trials away from the crime committed and towards the criminals. More and more trials centred upon the confessions of *pentiti* and the reconstructions of *dissociati*, which were given a status similar to that of 'evidence'. The bargaining nature of the confessions and reconstructions reflected heavily in the punishment of *pentiti* (law 304 of 29 May 1982) and of the *dissociati* (law 34 of 18 February 1987). Penalties were clearly related to the position of the defendant vis-à-vis the political motivation of the crime committed and not the crime itself.

In sharp contrast with the so called '*leggi premiali*', political motivation acted as an aggravating circumstance in the punishment of *irriducibili*. Law 110 of 18 April 1975 increased the penalty for possession of arms to a maximum of 15 years for terrorist purposes versus eight for the non-political equivalent. *Decreto-legge* 15 December 1979, subsequently converted into law 15 on 6 February 1980, stated that for crimes demanding a penalty other than life imprisonment, the penalty was increased by half if the motivation for the crime was terrorism. The same law raised the maximum penalty for murder from 21 years to life imprisonment for terrorist aims. In 1983 the crime of *reati associativi*, which demanded a maximum penalty of life imprisonment, was extended to all defendants who had been members of the armed community. *Irriducibili* were also excluded from the benefits of amnesties and reduction of penalties because they had been members of an armed band. Legitimation of the harsh form of justice used to punish *irriducibili* came from the fascist criminal code which demanded higher penalties for politically-motivated crimes than for their non-political equivalents.

A peace treaty to end the war

The empirical analysis of the juridical scheme upon which Italian magistrates and judges built their anti-terrorist strategy appears reminiscent of the logic of war. The inner message contained in the *leggi premiali* is that of the soldier who, by joining the enemy camp, becomes an ally (Università 'La Sapienza', 1988). Although with this instrument the judiciary succeeded in bringing to trial the bulk of the armed community and reduced terrorism to a sporadic phenomenon, it had not defeated terrorism. The 'silence' of the *irriducibili* was emblematic of the presence of a high degree of conflict. The transition from one camp to another was unacceptable, because it represented a humiliating solution to what, by 1987, resembled more and more a defeated army.

The first attempt to negotiate the surrender to the state came in December 1986 in an open letter signed by Bertolazzi, Curcio, Iannelli and Morucci. The document recognised that the international, social and political conditions under which the armed struggle had taken shape had disappeared. The war was over. Though the initial reaction of the *irriducibili* was hostile, within a few months support for what had become known as the *battaglia della libertà* increased considerably. In 1989, the Antigone association began drafting legislation aimed at levelling out the discrepancies in penalties between *pentiti* and *dissociati* on one hand and *irriducibili* on the other. The aim was to offset the aggravating circumstances that political motivation had played in punishing the *irriducibili*. The initiative produced proposal 4395 of 6 January 1989 for a law of *indulto* whereby life imprisonment was converted to the maximum temporal penalty of 21 years and all other penalties were reduced by half. The proposal was unsuccessfully presented for approval in the previous three legislatures. The beneficiaries of a law of pardon would be no more than 300 people. At the end of 1994 a total of 224 former left-wing terrorists were still in prison, of which 147 were *irriducibili*, 62 *dissociati,* and 13 *pentiti.* Only 77 had life sentences.

Technically, the proposal maintains a fundamental difference between those who had chosen to use the *legge premiali* and the *irriducibili*. While for *pentiti* and *dissociati* political motivation resulted in a reduction of penalties, in the proposed law of *indulto*, it does not play any role. The penalties for the crimes committed by terrorists are identical to their non-political equivalents. In a conciliatory gesture, former terrorists demand to be judged by the law exclusively on the basis of their crime. Paradoxically, their acceptance of the legal responsibilities of the crime committed is reminiscent of the initial reaction of the state to the phenomenon - that terrorism is a crime and should be judged within the context of its criminality.

Why then, has the state been so reluctant to approve the proposal for *indulto*? Realistically, there are no major legal obstacles to the shortening of the terms of imprisonment of former terrorists; their public renunciation of violence, their good behaviour in prison and the success of the *legge Gozzini*[17] all confirm that the likelihood they will commit crime once released is very slim. More likely it is the symbolism attached to a gesture as political as the concession of *indulto* which, until 1994, represented the greatest impediment. The parliamentary parties of the First Republic were not ready to grant the 224 former terrorists listed in Table 3 the status of political enemies. Possibly because in the history of united Italy there are many examples of this type of leniency - the Indulto of 1989 and the pardon of crimes committed by the *Fasci Siciliani* ordering the insurrection of Lunigiana - and all clearly symbolise the end of a conflict and the beginning of a new era.[18]

Table 3

Former left-wing terrorists who would benefit from pardon

	Non-Repentant		Dissassociated		Repentant		TOTAL
	ERG	PT	ERG	PT	ERG	PT	
TOTAL	77	70	17	45	1	12	226
In Prison	61	42	-	6	1	6	
Article 21	13	8	4	7	-	-	
Suspension							
of Sentence	2	-	-	-	-	-	
On partial release	1	20	13	32	-	6	

ERG - Life Imprisonment
PT - Penalty different from life imprisonmet
Articele 21 - Legge Gozzini, permission to work outside prison

source : Data Bank of 'Sensibili alle Foglie', data to November 1994.

However, since 1994 the profound consequences generated by the transition from the First to the Second Republic have significantly modified the political landscape. A new Republic is taking shape and new political forces are involved in its development; a gesture of leniency towards the tragic years of political violence of the First Republic could not be more appropriate. A tentative interpretation of the motives behind the failure of *indulto* to become law during the present system seems connected to the low priority of the problem in comparison with other pressing juridical matters.

In the changing political climate in which the new republic is emerging, the pardon of 300 former left and right-wing terrorists is not high on the political agenda. If the proposed law does not encounter any firm opposition, it also does not attract great support. The positive reaction of PDS, Rifondazione, Alleanza Nazionale, the approval of Giuliano Ferrara of Forza Italia and the positive attitude towards it expressed by Tiziana Maiolo, president of the *commissione giustizia* in the lower chamber of parliament, have so far not progressed beyond verbal recognition of the validity of the proposal.

To complete this analysis, an additional factor should be mentioned - an element which though it does not openly act against the acceptability of *indulto*, impinges upon its implementation. This factor is the belief among certain groups that keeping the chapter of political violence open is instrumental in unmasking the illegal actions committed by the political elites of the First Republic. In a reconstruction of the past which resembles a Machiavellian political thriller, a connection is believed to exist between the national and international secret services, left and right-wing terrorist groups, the 'hidden government' and the ruling political elites. Confessions of former criminals, such as Antonio Nirta at the end of 1993, have been used to substantiate this theory. In this light, the revelations about Moro's fourth jailer by Adriana Faranda, a *dissociata* turned *pentita*, are not only aimed at lifting the heavy burden of responsibility from Gallinari, a sick man in need of heart surgery who has been refused permission to be released for medical treatment more than once. More importantly, they are a desperate attempt to make all the truth of those tragic years, even the not-so-relevant details, known in order to clear away unsubstantiated and demeaning accusations.

Conclusions

From this brief analysis it emerges that the compelling problem terrorism poses to the modern state is how to conclude the tragic chapter of political violence. From the *battaglia di libertà* of the former Italian terrorists to the peace process of Northern Ireland, the new challenge of terrorism is no longer war, but peace. The successful destruction of the dichotomy between the two divergent political-philosophic approaches of state and terrorist, achieved by the Italian judiciary with the legal categories of *pentiti* and *dissociati*, offers only a partial solution to this problem. Though the majority of former terrorists rejected the terrorist ideology and embraced the state vision of terrorism as a crime by submitting to its justice, the refusal of *irriducibili* to submit to this logic on the basis that it was too humiliating, prevented the official closure of the conflict according to the parameters of criminality.

It is apparent that through this new challenge terrorism poses the same dilemma for the state: should former terrorists be treated as criminals or soldiers? In this context the *battaglia di libertà* which declared the end of the conflict and the total surrender implicit in the proposal for a law of pardon, the *legge sull'indulto* of 1989, embody a peace treaty between the *irriducibili* and the Italian state. In exchange for the symbolic recognition of the political motivation of their crimes, former terrorists agreed to accept full responsibility for their actions, demanding that the penalties they suffered be levelled to those for the non-political equivalent. This proposal, while confirming the criminality of the phenomenon, also stresses its war aim and is, therefore, coherent with the double nature of terrorism.

Although today there are no major obstacles to the pardon of former terrorists, the proposal for *indulto* has a very low priority in the political agenda of the new Republic. There is, however, a certain danger in delaying a final solution of the conflict - the manipulation that forces not fully committed to the new era of Italian politics may exercise over the dark and tragic heritage of terrorism. The revelations of former terrorists regarding technical details of their crimes - at the high price of contributing to the imprisonment of former members of the armed community - should be regarded as their attempt to avoid such manipulation; a gesture which stresses once again the exhaustion of the conflict and the need for a peace treaty. The war is undoubtedly over; it is time to let history judge its meaning and the leniency of men, its defeated soldiers.

Notes

1. A striking example is the attack on the military base of Aviano on September 1993, revendicated with a leaflet bearing the symbol of the Red Brigades by Paolo Dorigo, husband of Alberta Bilia, brigatista jailed for life for the killing of Tagliercio.

2. It is sufficient here to remember that the revelations of Nirta were used to support the theory that members of organised crime ('ndrangheta, mafia and camorra) had been infiltrated by the secret service. A carabinieri general, Francesco Delfino, was even suspected to have been the link between organised crime and the secret services. To date there is no evidence that the Red Brigades were infiltrated and used as an armed group of the extreme right by the 'hidden government'.

3. According to Paul Gilbert, the type of conflict terrorists are engaged in differs from the one depicted by the 'just war' theory, lacking its 'punitive' or 'defensive' characteristics. As a form of warfare, terrorism is often regarded as 'unjust war', a violent confrontation sufficiently similar to war to be judged in accordance with its rules. This concept is not unknown in modern European culture. During the Weimar Republic, terrorists were granted the status of war prisoners. See Karin Bellingkrodt, La Festungshaft, Teoria e Prassi del "Carcere d'Onore", per il Delitto Politico nella Repubblica di Weimar, in *Il Delitto Politico*, Roma, Sapere 2000, 1984.

4. There are three socio-political components to the Red Brigades - the '*operaista*' of Mario Moretti, the marxist-leninist of Renato Curcio and Margherita Cagol and the '*comunista-partigiana*' of Alberto Franceschini which specifically rejected the view that the WWII resistance represented a period of national collaboration and political violence which successfully overturned fascism in favor of democracy. According to Franceschini and the '*gruppo dell'appartamento*', the resistance was an aborted revolution. This view was shared by the extra-parliamentary left as well as the armed community.

5. During the formulation of the constitution, a proposal to proclaim a state of siege for reasons of public order was presented by Crispo and subsequently rejected.

6. Article 77 of the constitution specifically mentioned the fact that the government exercises an authority *extra ordinem*.

7. The first maximum security jails - Favignana, Asinara, Cuneo, Fossombrone and Trani - were ready by July 1977; specially renovated sections were also added to various existing prisons.

8. In this chapter the definition of magistrates provided by Moss has been applied and related to the functions of some members of the judiciary in the old criminal code. According to Moss, magistrates refers to *giudice istruttore* and *(sostituto) procuratore del*La Repubblica. Though each had different functions and powers, in the case of political violence, the investigations and accounts were largely collaborative exercises and they can, therefore, be treated as belonging to a single category.

9. "Before 1979, the use of armed insurrection in Italy had been rare. Apart from cases involving revolts against Italian colonial rule in Africa, four trials were known to have taken place between 1889 and 1945, with a further four cases after 1948. With the exception of the then most recent instance - the alleged Borghese coup d'état of 1970 for which the charge was dismissed by the Assise Court in Rome in 1978 - all previous episodes had concerned either isolated individuals or municipal jacqueries of very limited duration and involvement". Moss, 1989 pg. 201.

10. Defined as such for its parallels with the Red Brigades' guerrilla attacks in the cities of the North, the *processo guerrilla* established the terrorist practice of remaining silent during trial and to refuse any form of defence. The essence of the processo guerrilla was the disruption of the courts by discharging defence lawyers, symbolising the refusal to recognise the juridical authority of the state.

11. 'Full collaborator' refers to the exchange of useful information about the armed struggle to the police or magistrates. It does not necessarily imply the public denunciation of the armed struggle which the *pentito* declared in the courts. Thus full collaborator is the first stage towards the creation of the category of *pentiti*.

12. Article 27 of the constitution states that the defendant is not considered guilty until proven guilty. Though it would be wrong to say that in Italian criminal law the defendant is guilty until proven innocent, his position is somehow in-between the presumption of innocence of the common law codes and the presumption of guilt of the Napoleonic code.

13. According to law 304 of 1982, *pentiti* fully cooperate with magistrates and police in giving the

names of members of the armed community, identifying hiding places and reconstructing terrorist attacks. *Dissociati*, as envisaged by law 34 of 1987 admit their crime and agree to reconstruct terrorist attacks, but refuse to mention names and to identify hiding places. Both *pentiti* and *dissociati* publicly denounce their affiliation with the armed community and their role as fighters. *Irriducibili* are former member of the armed community who rejected the authority of the courts of law and remained silent during their trials. After 1987 they agreed to discuss the political motivations behind their actions.

14. We refer in particular to the crime of *lesae maiestatis*.

15. Introduced as a juridical category by the July Revolution of 1830, the concept of political crime is the product of the juridico-political culture of the 19th century bourgeois, which introduced the distinction between common and political crime.

16. In the old criminal code the *pubblico ministero* was the *(sostituto) procuratore della* Repubblica of pre-trial investigations.

17. Law 663 of 10 October 1986, known as the *legge Gozzini*, allows prisoners to work outside jails and to obtain special permissions to visit their families.

18. Perhaps the example that most stressed the political nature of *indulto* is the pardon of all political crimes at the end of World War II. In a remarkable gesture of peace, Palmiro Togliatti offered his former enemies, the fascists, two pieces of legislation: the *indulto* of 1953 and of 1959. The aim was to end the cycle of violence, erasing the residues of civil war, and start a new era of national solidarity.

References

Ferrajoli, L. (1990) *Diritto e Ragione*, Bari: Laterza.

Franceschini, A. (1988) *Mara, Renato ed io*, Milan: Mondadori.

Galli, G. (1986) *Storia del Partito Armato*, Milan: Rizzoli.

Gilbert, P. (1994) *Terrorism, Security and Nationality*, London: Routledge.

Laqueur, W. (1977) *Terrorism*, London: Macmillan.

Moretti, M. (1994) *Brigate Rosse*, una Storia Italiana, Milan: Anabasi.

Mortati, C. (1969) *Istituzioni di Diritto Pubblico*, Padua: Cedam.

Moss, D. (1989) *The Politics of Left-Wing Violence in Italy*, London: Routledge.

Tarrow, S. (1990) 'Minority Hegemony in Italy: the Softer They Rise the Slower they Fall' in Pempel, T.J (ed.) *Uncommon Democracies: the one Party Dominant Regime*, Cornell: Cornell University Press.

University of Rome, ' La Sapienza' (1988), *Delitto Politico ed Amnistia*, transcript of the conference held in Rome, Faculty of Law, 19 January.

University of Rome, ' La Sapienza' (1988) *Confliti Politici, Emergenza, Quale Soluzione?*, transcript of the conference held in Rome, Faculty of Literature, 24 February.

von Tangen, M. (1995) *Peace Study Briefing Number 45*, Bradford: University of Bradford.

eleven

International market reaction to the 1994 parliamentary elections and the Berlusconi government

Mark Donovan[1]

In the opening months of 1994 the international financial markets expected the left to come to power in Italy. The prospect did not dismay them. Indeed, whilst there was a widespread expectation that the year ahead was going to be a difficult one for investors world-wide, Italy was specifically identified as a good prospect (e.g. The Times, 6 January 1994). Whilst the right's unexpected victory at the end of March was, nevertheless, greeted with warmth, the honeymoon period enjoyed by Silvio Berlusconi was extremely brief, bordering on the non-existent. Why did the markets react the way they did?

Several reasons have been given for the markets' failure to welcome the left's defeat. On the one hand, government critics pointed to foreign concerns about the presence of "fascists" in the coalition and about the coalition's instability, its alleged lack of economic determination and the incompetence of its ministers. Taking attack to be the best form of defence and maintaining Italy's tradition of highly-polarised political rhetoric, several figures from the new majority, some very senior, accused the markets of being host to speculators and effectively sabotaging Italy's economy. Conspiracy theories raged, with perhaps the most distasteful blaming Italy's poor performance in the markets on American-Jewish finance which failed to understand the nature of the National Alliance and the significance of Gianfranco Fini's leadership of it.

Beside the more partisan views lay more technical and mundane arguments such as that international markets were concerned by what would happen to Italy's debt management if Umberto Bossi's federal ambitions were realized, and that markets reacted to international, not merely Italian, stimuli. Thus, the coincidence of deteriorating market conditions with Italian political developments was largely just that - coincidence. Worsening indicators reflected changing global conditions such as the rise of the US dollar and the appearance of signs indicating the reversal of the long trend of falling world interest rates. Nevertheless, in so far as markets react to national developments including political events, what markets were mostly presented with in Italy were signs of political and, from a financial perspective, economic weakness.

Italy's political difficulties were to a significant extent rooted in the quarter-century long failure of Italian governments to control the national budget. The demand that something be done about this in order to enable Italy to comply with the convergence terms for European monetary union (EMU) as stipulated by the Maastricht Treaty (Daniels, 1993), was one factor behind Italy's political earthquake. This upheaval had, as one analysis of the 1994 election put it, brought "Milan to Rome" (Diamanti and Mannheimer, 1994) i.e. put representatives of the country's business elites in political power. Any sign of government weakness was therefore troubling to investors - and to this extent did indeed present an opportunity to speculators.

The signs of governmental weakness were many. One of the most significant was the highly conflictual relationship between Umberto Bossi and Silvio Berlusconi. A further major contribution to raising doubts in market-makers' minds about the ability of the political system to produce a government able to at least begin to put the country's financial situation on a sound footing was provided by the fact that Berlusconi spent the entire year with a legal "sword of Damocles" hanging over his head. Already the judiciary, backed by the electorate, had swept away one well-entrenched political elite. Judicial investigation into Berlusconi's business empire might also sweep away a political figure and movement with the shallowest of roots. The general expectation was that Forza Italia, the quasi-party backing Berlusconi, would disintegrate if Berlusconi resigned as a result of judicial action. Were that to happen, Italy's political and economic situation would be very uncertain indeed, and markets could be expected to nose-dive.

The primary interest of foreign markets before and after the 1994 election was in the political system's ability, or lack of it, to bring the budget deficit under control, thus laying a basis to reduce the accumulated debt. This would require both stability and political will on the part of the government. The question was whether the right that had come to power possessed these qualities.

Political Economy and Left/Right Polarization

After a decade or more in which the relevance of talking in terms of left and right in Italian elections had been questioned, and a half-century in which the ruling bloc had claimed to be based on the centre, the context of the 1994 election campaign was one of profound bipolarization and intense speculation about which camp, left or right, would win. Commentators largely wrote off the centre. The identification of left and right was clear cut in terms of the parties presenting themselves. The Progressives, centreed on the Democratic Left Party (PDS) formed the left, the Berlusconi alliance of Forza Italia, the National Alliance and the Northern League constituted the right. However, in terms of economic programmes there was some confusion, even, it has been argued, an 'inversion' of left and right content (Diamanti & Mannheimer, 1994: xvii).

On the one (left) hand the Progressives, continuing the PCI's decades-long obsessive search for legitimacy, courted the national and international financial markets assiduously. Whilst Communist Refoundation carried out a more radical and effectively independent electoral campaign from within the Progressive coalition, its strident counter-point to the left's dominant theme of responsible (and painful) reform carried little or no weight as an indicator of a putative left government's economic programme. It was clear that a PDS-backed government's economic policy would be ultra-responsible. Indeed, austerity rather than spending seemed to be the likely order of the day. On the other (right) hand, the Berlusconi-led coalition, whilst generally presenting itself, at least as regards its northern components, as a neo-liberal coalition favouring the strengthening of market competition, stressed something quite different in its electoral campaign. Here, the creation of jobs (a million of them) and the maintenance of established standards of welfare were very much to the fore.

These apparent reversals of association - the left with financial probity and rigour, the right with jobs and welfare - to a large extent reflect the strategy decisions of the leading elites on left and right. But they also reflect the ambiguity of liberalism and especially of market reform. They do not indicate the transformation, or reversal, of the meaning of left and right. Moreover, what Dahrendorf called the sociological bias differentiating left and right continued and indeed may even have been reinforced (Diamanti and Mannheimer, 1994, xv). Thus, whilst, as many commentators have pointed out, the crucial economic task facing any contemporary Italian government, whether of left or right, is essentially the same: taming the continuing annual deficit and bringing the accumulated debt under control, there are different ways of effecting such a programme. The left's orientation towards using the market not only matched political interests such as challenging Silvio Berlusconi's near monopoly of national private television; it was also embedded in a strategy of ensuring that dependent workers' relative economic positions were not worsened and of ensuring that the pain, and gain, of adjusting Italy to a more efficient and competitive international economic position was spread across Italy's social classes, primarily by improving tax collection. On the other hand, the new Italian right, whilst containing committed liberals in prominent positions, was dominated by conservative social forces with a clear vested interest in continuing state largesse and avoiding rigorous anti-monopoly legislation. Thus, for its critics, the right comprised a political amalgam united not by any ideological sensitivity, but by the objective of maintaining a series of oligopolistic and/or privileged positions which contradicted both market logic and the national interest. Thus the northern and allegedly liberal parties Forza Italia and the Northern League did have a common economic interest with the southern and statist Alleanza Nazionale after all - blocking market reforms aimed at undercutting their different privileges. Critics of the 1994 budget, as proposed by the government, judged it to reflect this conservative and socially unjust orientation, rather than a reformist, social liberal one.

In the winter of 1993-94, then, international market analysts saw in the reformed Italian left the prospect for the judiciary's attack on systemic political corruption and the consequential freeing of economic actors from the need to follow non-market logics, to be built upon politically. This would further strengthen the country's real economy which had already been boosted both by the substantial devaluation which followed the country's abandonment of the Exchange Rate Mechanism (ERM) in September 1992 and by tripartite agreements between the social partners and the government in 1992 and 1993. Market logic, operating in a political context designed to foster a collective national interest, would, for the first time in decades, become the dominant determinant of resource allocation. The economy would boom. As one observer put it, political reconstruction would allow Italy to "become one of the healthiest economies in Europe" (The Times, 6 January 1994).

The markets' positive view of the left was not abandoned when Berlusconi entered politics, brokering the tripartite Liberty Pole. The right's governing credentials were questionable and the left continued to be looked on with favor (John Pitt, 1994). This suggests that the markets viewed the prospect of a left victory favorably for the serious reasons indicated. It was not a counsel of despair. Far from it. Indeed, as the new right-wing coalition made head-way and the left's victory became less assured, the international market climate began to change (Market Report, Financial Times, 8 March 1994) and as the election approached the new political uncertainty caused the markets to exhibit signs of anxiety. The preferred result, according to a Corriere della Sera survey of institutional investors, fund managers and brokers carried out in early March was a victory for the centrist alliance (Financial Times, 25 March and 6 August 1994). This forlorn hope probably indicated the desire for political stability above all.

Brief Honeymoon, Bitter Divorce

Initial market reaction, including anticipated reaction, to the right's electoral victory was positive (Market Report, Financial Times, 29 March 1994). Whilst this may, in part, have reflected a somewhat atavistic response by market-makers to the victory of a right-wing government it probably reflected relief, above all, at an apparently decisive outcome. International election coverage focused, as is normal, on the chamber of deputies results where Berlusconi's electoral alliance gained a large majority. Such a result had been far from certain. Not only had voters exhibited spectacular volatility over the previous two years, but the electoral system was completely new and had generally been lambasted. Allegedly, it combined the worst features of different systems and was quite incapable, in particular, of guaranteeing a majority for any potential government. Finally, the political contenders themselves had been new and, in many respects, unknown.

In no time at all, it became clear that the result was not clear cut. The right lacked a majority in the senate and there were severe doubts about the compatibility of the different forces comprising Berlusconi's alliance, as well as about the intentions of that strange grouping. Most observers doubted that the electoral alliance could be turned into a governing coalition. That such a government was eventually formed reflected two things. First, the new mass expectations generated by the coincidence of left-right polarization in 1993/94 with electoral reform and the way the March vote outcome was received - as victory for the right and defeat for the left. These perceptions created the overwhelming sensation that for the first time Italian voters had been able to express their view as to what government should be formed. Secondly, all three parties in Berlusconi's alliance had so much to gain by sticking together. And so much to lose by falling apart. The shotgun engagement of January was thus followed by a shotgun wedding. That foreign markets reacted uncertainly was hardly surprising.

Justification for market concern soon arrived when Umberto Bossi's vitriolic attacks on Berlusconi caused the latter briefly to suspend coalition negotiations threatening an immediate return to the ballot box (Financial Times, 6 April 1994). The following five weeks of negotiations provided plenty of time for international speculation as to the significance of the election outcome to mount. James Baker, the former US Secretary of State, for example, put the election result in a continental context speaking of the "danger of a European involution towards the extreme right" (Corriere della Sera, 13 October 1994), whilst in early May, Euro-Socialists exploited the platform presented by the European Parliament to engage in an act of symbolic politics - threatening to boycott council of ministers' and other meetings attended by Italian "fascists", and voting to remind Italy to remain faithful to the fundamental values which underlay the foundation of the European Community (Financial Times, 6 May 1994).

Such political fireworks and hyperbole did not greatly impress hard-nosed market analysts, but Bossi's hard bargaining to obtain the Interior Ministry and his deeply polemical position vis-à-vis Berlusconi were disconcerting enough. Equally indicative of the fragility of the coalition was Berlusconi's last minute shuffle to put Cesare Previti in charge of Defence rather than Justice. The latter portfolio was too sensitive for the man who, as Berlusconi's lawyer, advised him not only in regard of the judicial investigations into corrupt tax dealings by one of the Berlusconi companies, but also, ironically, about the whole issue of conflict of interest resulting from a financial and industrial magnate becoming head of government.

If markets were sensitive to signs of instability and lack of firmness of purpose, they were also sensitive to the new governing parties' general lack of economic expertise. This was not reflected in the government since the treasury and finance ministers (Lamberto Dini and Giulio Tremonti respectively) were highly respected technocrats, but other cabinet ministers repeatedly evidenced their failure to appreciate market psychology. In June, in the wake of a particularly budget-sensitive decision by the Constitutional Court (on pension rights) an official government spokesman, Giuliano Ferrara, was appointed to soothe foreign exchange reactions to incoherent and foolish ministerial statements (The Guardian, 18 June 1994; La Repubblica, 24 June 1994). The Sunday Times also reported memories of a clash of interest between markets and the new government's leading economic figure. Thus, in June 1992 it had been Lamberto Dini who, as deputy governor of the Bank of Italy, "had taken bitter public issue with... Goldman's economist David Wilton" (The Sunday Times, 8 May 1994). Goldman Sachs's "sin" had been to predict Italy's devaluation and exit from the ERM. Albeit not just in Italy, market analysts had increasingly found themselves with different interests to government and central bank officials. Concern about the evolution of Italy's political economy was also seen in debate over the course of Italy's privatization programme and in the highly sensitive area of national bank autonomy.

Whilst privatization in broad terms went ahead there was much dissatisfaction with its course. Reporting on this in mid-May The Economist argued that Mediobanca, Italy's leading and hegemonic merchant bank, was successfully undermining the government's policy goals, above all that of creating a competitive capital market. What was good for Mediobanca, was bad for Italy (The Economist, 14 May 1994). It was also bad for the coalition since it increased the Northern League's distrust of Silvio Berlusconi. Enrico Cuccia, Mediobanca's president, was particularly disliked by Giancarlo Pagliarini, the Northern League budget minister, since he personified the dominant role played in Italy's economy by a narrow, oligopolistic elite (Corriere della Sera, 8 April 1994). In seeking to maintain his bank's pole position, and against the spirit of its privatization, Cuccia acquired indirect control of the two major state banks, Credito Italiano and Banca Commerciale, over the summer. These banks held much of Fininvest's debt (see The Guardian, 22 October 1994) and the indebtedness of Fininvest, and the consequent vulnerability of Berlusconi's media empire to anti-monopoly legislation, was allegedly one of the more personal motives behind Berlusconi's entry into politics.

Cause for concern over Bank of Italy autonomy was given by the patent inability of the three coalition parties to agree on a nomination to replace Lamberto Dini, now a cabinet member, as Director General of the Bank. The general perception that intra-coalition struggling for party influence continued to pre-empt decision-making in the national interest was bad enough, but the National Alliance, with some backing from within Forza Italia, appeared to take a strident nationalist and party political line towards the Bank, accusing its elites of belonging to a "clerico-marxist" or "clerico-progressive" culture (Corriere della Sera, 20 August 1994). President Scalfaro himself intervened to admonish the National Alliance. The result of government delay and political speculation as to what would happen at the Bank, avidly reported by the press, became a dominant item on the informal agenda of the Madrid IMF summit. The possibility that political instability might be carried into the Bank of Italy, hitherto a stable anchor point in Italy's political economy, so alarmed international financial circles that the Bundesbank itself intervened, albeit subtly, in the debate (Corriere della Sera, 3 October 1994).

By the time the Bank of Italy affair first blew up in July, however, the government was well on the way to losing the markets' confidence. The Constitutional Court decision of June had visibly caught the government on the hop and, despite suggestions to the contrary, it was clear that the markets were preoccupied by less fundamentally political concerns than the National Alliance's "neo-" or "post-fascist" identity. Their concern was that the government appeared preoccupied with an exquisitely political matter - power. And that at the expense of economic action.

July was a bad month for the government. On July 13 the Justice Minister, Alfredo Biondi, moved to limit the judiciary's powers of preventive arrest. Coming just two days after the Milan 'pool', famous for initiating *Tangentopoli,* had announced that corruption charges would be brought against Silvio Berlusconi's brother, Biondi's move looked like a self-interested attack on the judiciary. The entire Milan team of public prosecutors announced its resignation, later withdrawn when the government backed down. This confrontation with the judiciary not only lost Forza Italia support domestically, it also had a profound impact on the markets. On the one hand it confirmed nervousness about the government's stability - twice in July rumours swept the London markets that ministerial resignations were imminent. On the other it consolidated the market perception that party political interests, not governmental policy-making and the national interest, were to the fore. This view was increased by the government's failure to act on the budget front, contrary to early promises, and by its apparent preoccupation with the judiciary and also state television - RAI. Market doubts, the declining lira, the consequent inability to further cut interest rates and, in turn, to reduce the impact of the government's debts formed a vicious circle that undermined Italy's attractiveness to investors. A series of market-making reports by major investment institutions confirmed that the new government had lost the support of the markets (The Times, 31 July 1994; Corriere della Sera, 10 August 1994).

One measure of the international financial community's weak development of positive attitudes to the new government's financial credibility, and the way this evaporated over the summer, can be seen in the evolution of the differential between interest rates on ten-year government bonds sold in Italy and those sold in the form of Eurolira by the European Investment Bank (see Table 1). Both are expressed in lira, the difference is in the source of their supplier - the government (the Treasury) or the European Investment Bank. Where the difference (column 3) is positive it indicates that a greater return is required to persuade investors to buy the government bond.

Table 1

Average daily interest rates on Lira Bonds

	10 year BTP benchmark	BEI 2003 in Eurolire	DIFFERENCE (BTP - BEI)
Jan	8.66	8.33	+0.33
Feb	8.78	8.52	+0.26
Mar	9.45	9.13	+0.32
Apr	9.06	9.14	-0.08
May	9.39	9.53	-0.14
Jun	10.51	10.52	-0.01
Jul	10.77	10.79	-0.02
Aug	11.56	11.50	+0.06
Sep	12.04	11.66	+0.38
Oct	12.07	11.09	+0.98
Nov	12.04	11.44	+0.60

Notes: BTP - Treasury bond; BEI - European Investment Bank
Source: Data supplied by Banca Credito Italiano
Methodology: G. Adami, La Repubblica, 7 November 1994

Data from early 1995 confirmed that foreign investment in Italy shifted dramatically from a positive inflow, amounting to 127,000 billion lire in 1993 (circa 50,000 million sterling), to a net outflow from March 1994. This outflow continued through into October 1994, thus all but coinciding with

Berlusconi's government. The return to positive foreign investment flows in November resulted in an annual net inflow of just 17,000 billion lire. Sharply increased exports, up 10 per cent in 1994 compared to 1993, nevertheless kept Italy's balance of payments positive (Corriere della Sera, 3 January 1995; La Repubblica, 26 and 28 January 1995).

Another measure of the government's poor standing was the lira exchange rate. In the year following the lira's exit from the ERM (September 1992) the lira depreciated by some thirty per cent against the deutschmark, several times coming come close to the psychologically important 1,000:1 rate in 1993. In July 1994 the lira plunged through this 'barrier' and, thereafter, moved erratically towards 1,050 as the year - and the government - unwound. Commentators were, however, unanimous in arguing that this trend did not in any way reflect the 'real' economy of inflation rates, pay claims, industrial costs and output etc.

Naturally, the left was not slow to exploit international concerns and Italy's weakening performance in the markets. The opposition's job is to criticise, but the markets' lack of confidence provided 'neutral' and authoritative external criticism. Moreover, the right could be cast as the betrayer, whether through incompetence or self-interest, of the national interest. The opposition's use of the government's poor standing in the markets was self-serving of course, but it was effective. Indeed, it caused the government parties particular pain because domestic critics had all along cast doubt on the idea that Berlusconi and co. either intended, or were able, to fundamentally reform Italy's political economy. Those critics claimed that objective foreign forces now confirmed their judgment. It is, perhaps, for this reason that whilst foreign markets, Confindustria and eventually, even the President of the Republic among a host of other elite figures, agreed that lack of effective government action and a superfluity of ministerial verbiage were the cause of Italy's poor financial image, early August saw an upsurge of conspiracy theory attacking market speculators.

This regurgitation of a dominant theme of the inter-war period when fascism and communism alike saw financial speculation as personifying all that was evil about capitalism, now saw Umberto Bossi condemned for deliberately destabilising the government economically as well as politically. Amongst the 'explanations' for Bossi's alleged behaviour were that he was seeking to damage Berlusconi who, whilst he was his coalition ally, was his electoral rival, and even that he was simply seeking to make money to support his party - even to finance his own television channel! In the same period a sustained attack by Giuseppe Tatarella, the National Alliance's deputy prime minister and minister of post and telecommunications, focused more generally on "strong and invisible powers" undermining the government and the national interest. The powers to which Tatarella referred included the country's most prestigious institutions - the Bank of Italy and the Constitutional Court. It was in this super-heated atmosphere that Clemente Mastella, the labour minister from the Christian Democratic Centre, attacked the "New York Jewish lobby" for its failure to understand the direction in which Gianfranco Fini was leading the National Alliance. (Corriere della Sera, 11 and 12 August 1994).

Not surprisingly, these attacks not only provoked alarm but also brought ridicule upon the government, exposing as they did its lack of in-depth experience and expertise. They also did much to affirm the curious harmony existing between the centre-left and the national financial establishment (Corriere della Sera, 12 August 1994). This was, perhaps, an indirect confirmation of the view expressed by international market-makers at the start of the year: that a stable centre-left government was what Italy needed. At the same time, however, those same markets were increasingly aware that the political crisis in Italy was far more profound than they had at first thought (The Economist, 13 August 1994).

When the government finally presented its budget in early October there was much favourable comment in international markets. However, there was a lot of damage to be undone, and whilst the budget may have seemed, to conservatives, a model for other countries to follow, it remained no more than a set of proposals until it completed its passage through parliament - precisely where Italian budgets had always floundered of course. That the budget was likely to disintegrate as it journeyed through the two chambers was made more likely by the larger political picture which was one of growing instability. A full-blown confrontation between the executive and the judiciary had developed by now, and this was seen not merely to be destabilising in itself, but, worse still, it was correctly interpreted as a symptom of a deeper politico-institutional malaise (Corriere della Sera, 6 October 1994).

From the Budget to the Government Crisis

Within days of the government presenting its budget a senate amendment made it appear that taxes would have to be raised, contrary to the election promise that they would be both simplified and cut. Government statements that this option was not being considered put the government's entire economic strategy in doubt (Corriere della Sera, 8 October 1994). Rumours of Silvio Berlusconi's imminent arrest on October 11 then brought accusations of 'financial terrorism', repeated on Berlusconi's private television networks, and even allegations that Italy's own representatives overseas were acting as fifth columnists, undermining Italian interests. The government's delicate political situation was further demonstrated the same day by the report of the "three wise men" who had been appointed to examine the fundamental conflict of interest involved in Berlusconi's becoming prime minister.

At a much more basic level, the broad-based popular perception that the budget was fundamentally an attack on the welfare state and on pension rights in particular, brought three million people out on to the streets of the major cities as part of a general strike on Friday 14 October. The attention of foreign commentators began to focus on Berlusconi himself, with the technical aspects of the budget proposals and the cabinet's technical ministers being praised, but the prime minister personally being lambasted for having squandered the political capital that he had acquired by the election (see e.g. the comments of Rudiger Dornbusch cited in Corriere della Sera, 25 October 1994).

By the end of October, in the run-up to the local elections, Bossi had begun the operation of detaching himself from the government. At the same time the near-absence of Forza Italia as an organization was continuing to cause problems inside Berlusconi's own party, which did rather badly in the local elections, and further demonstrations against the budget brought a million people on to the streets of Rome in mid-November. Another general strike was also scheduled for 1 December. The right threatened mass counter-demonstrations in favor of the government, but there was little effective follow-up and only derisory numbers turned out in a small number of pro-government demonstrations. The strike was avoided, but at the cost of postponing pension reform until 1995. The budget was unravelling.

In a final, convoluted interpenetration of politics and economics, the oppositions withdrew most of their proposed amendments to the budget in early December to allow it to complete its passage and leave sufficient time before the close of parliament for a vote of no-confidence to take place. The government, nevertheless, had to continue making its own amendments, with Lamberto Dini, the Treasury Minister, finally being forced to admit that taxes would have to be raised, election promises notwithstanding. But of far more concern to the markets was the reversal of the entire nature of the budget. From being about

decisive reform it became a series of stop-gap measures. Thus, the International Monetary Fund, in a letter to the government, described the budget as "perplexing because it is based on temporary measures of an uncertain outcome".

The political crisis came to a head in the week before Christmas. Goaded by the resignation of the Lega Nord ministers, Berlusconi himself resigned rather than face parliamentary defeat in a vote of no-confidence. Whilst the lira continued to oscillate, nearing 1,050 to the deutschmark, the somewhat perverse reaction of the Milan stock exchange was to rally. This effect, rather contrary to the usual behaviour of markets faced with government collapse, was ascribed by one commentator to the belief that the coalition's fall would end the year's protracted instability and to the judgment that "Mr. Berlusconi's coalition has been so disastrous that any prospect of change is being viewed as positive". (Lex, Financial Times, 22 December 1994).

Conclusions

Any idea that political stability would result from the fall of Berlusconi's government was misconceived given the extreme difficulty that subsequent coalition negotiations faced, with early, but possibly again indecisive, elections likely. Yet it is undoubtedly true that under the comparatively short-lived (even by Italian standards) Berlusconi government a particularly large gap opened up between the country's 'real economy' and its financial status. Whilst hot-heads denounced speculators, wiser and more prudent voices recognised that steady foreign investment withdrawals reacting to government instability were the main financial issue, although negative international market attitudes towards Italy's political crisis were part of a vicious circle in which currency speculation was encouraged. Nevertheless, the prime cause of 'speculation' and disinvestment was the state of Italy's political economy. Markets were essentially reactive.

Global trends, too, were important. Generally, after Italy's (and the UK's) withdrawal from the ERM in late 1992 and the August 1993 change to wide fluctuation bands in the ERM, conditions for investors got much more difficult. Attention turned away from Europe to the triad (dollar/yen/deutschmark) currencies. What attention remained in Europe focused on Italy and Sweden - the latter moving fast to become a high-deficit country like Italy. Both these countries raised their interest rates in the summer, in both cases provoking negative market reactions because of the

interaction of their debt situation and changing international circumstances (Survey of World Economy and Finance, Financial Times, 30 September 1994; Leader, Financial Times, 13 August 1994). Nevertheless, Italy's stock market finished the year up, in marked contrast to the rest of the European exchanges, all suffering from rising interest rates. Italy's unique position, however, rested on gains made in the first months of the year and a general trend of decline from May all but wiped out these earlier gains (Corriere della Sera, 31 December 1994).

Whatever weight one places on mitigating international and inherited circumstances, the Berlusconi government failed in its political economy. It not only made many policy mistakes, it also adopted the wrong policy style. In economic matters as in political, the Berlusconi government acted as though it had a secure and stable majority when it had not. The consequence was to heighten its instability and the interaction of domestic and international reactions to this produced a vicious circle. An early indication of the government's determination to act 'decisively', was seen in the successful nomination of both chamber presidents (speakers) from the majority, reversing 18 years in which the president of the lower house came from the opposition. Its moves against the judiciary and public broadcasting were equally decisive, though in the former case at least the government more than met its match thanks to overwhelming public support focused on Antonio Di Pietro. Similarly, in airing its draft budget before the summer recess the government received warnings from the health, labour and industry committees in the senate that its proposals were unacceptable. Those warnings were ignored. So too was much of the friendly advice of the governor of the Bank of Italy (The Financial Times, 4 August 1994). The government's policies and policy twists progressively alienated nearly all of Italy's organised groups domestically, failed to convince foreign investors and caused even the IMF to express its 'perplexity'.

Yet one question remains - could anyone have done better? Putting aside the faults of the Berlusconi government, what Italy needed to satisfy the demands of foreign investors was structural political change. The creation of strong, legitimate government required the completion of the process of political restructuring and probably further institutional reform. On the one hand, government had to be based on a solid coalition with clear electoral backing, giving it a majority in both chambers of parliament. On the other, the opposition needed to feel 'guaranteed' - able to prevent the abuse of parliament by a strong government majority and convinced that it could, in principle, win

the next election. This meant, respectively, a strong parliament to match strong government (see the argument of the PDS leader and President of the Chamber of Deputies 1992-94, Giorgio Napolitano - Corriere della Sera, 16 December 1994); and an agreement regulating the role of the media, especially television, in the country's political life.

The need to create a fair regime of media coverage for the country's political forces was one of the four key issues identified by the new prime minister, Lamberto Dini (Berlusconi's Treasury Minister), in January 1995. The other priorities identified were reform of the regional electoral system (which remained proportional); pension reform (left outstanding by Berlusconi's December agreement with the unions); and an emergency mini-budget.

Dini's cabinet was, as the markets had widely hoped, a technocratic one. More so, in fact, than Ciampi's 1993-94 government, in that all its ministers and even its under-secretaries were formally 'non-political'. Market reaction to Dini's government was, nevertheless, cautious. The complete avoidance of political nominations reflected an extremely tense situation in which fundamental political problems remained unresolved. Thus, whilst the process of the creation of two distinct political blocs continued apace, reinforced by Romano Prodi's emergence as prime ministerial candidate for the centre-left, party system restructuring provided a highly unstable context for Dini to operate in, whilst the timing and outcome of further elections remained uncertain. Equally, the markets waited to judge the outcome of the projected tripartite accord on pension reform. The 'interregnum' nature of Dini's government was confirmed in February. Left and right were unable to agree to back the emergency budget, Berlusconi preferring to re-open the demand for immediate elections, and Dini was forced to resort to decree law to get his budget measures adopted. The accompanying exchange rate crisis saw the lira hit 1,100 against the deutschmark and the Bank of Italy was again forced to raise interest rates.

To regain credibility in the international financial markets Italy needed to move beyond the transition period between the so-called First and Second Republics which the Ciampi and Dini governments so clearly represented. Establishing the Second Republic meant much more was required than just early elections. It also meant the completion of the process of party system restructuring, accompanied by adequate constitutional guarantees, so as to recast government/opposition relations and hence provide strong government and a strong parliamentary framework able to guarantee the continuing operation

of such government on a consensual basis.

Note

1. I should like to thank the Banco Comerciale Italiano International for supplying me with data, and Jennifer Innes of the European Investment Bank and Leonardo Simonelli of Etrufin for their helpful discussion of the background to this paper for which I alone am responsible.

References

Philip, D. (1993), 'Italy and the Maastricht Treaty' in Hellman S. and Pasquino G. (eds), *Italian Politics A Review,* Vol. 8, London: Pinter Publishers.

Diamanti, I. and Mannheimer, R. (1994). *Milano a Roma. Guida all'Italia elettorale del 1994,* Rome: Donzelli.

index